A HISTORY OF
CRANLEIGH SCHOOL

A HISTORY OF
CRANLEIGH SCHOOL

ALAN J MEGAHEY

COLLINS
8 Grafton Street, London W1
1983

William Collins Sons and Co. Ltd
London · Glasgow · Sydney · Auckland
Toronto · Johannesburg

British Library Cataloguing in Publication Data

Megahey, Alan
  A study of Cranleigh School
  1. Cranleigh School—History
  I. Title
  373.422'165   LF795.C/

ISBN 0 00 217159 7

First published 1983
© Cranleigh School 1983

Photoset in Baskerville by
Rowlands Phototypesetting Ltd
Bury St Edmunds, Suffolk
Made and Printed in Great Britain by
William Collins Sons and Co. Ltd, Glasgow

TO
MY PARENTS

Contents

Illustrations

between pages

Maps and Charts

Abbreviations

CM	Council Minutes
Cr	The school magazine
CSA	Cranleigh School Archives
FMC	Finance (& Management) Committee Minutes
GBM	Governing Body Minutes
HMC	Headmasters' Conference
HMR	Headmaster's Reports to the Governing Body
OC	Old Cranleighan
SR	School Register

No history of Cranleigh School has appeared in print before except for occasional articles in the school magazine. An attempt is made here to tell the story, setting it where possible in the context of what was happening at other schools and in the nation at large. I hope some future historian may write an up-to-date history of the school for its bicentennial in 2065.

'Middle class education' was an issue in Victorian England, as it is an issue today. My feeling is that Cranleigh represents a more significant attempt to answer the question than do many greater independent schools, the histories of which are often regarded as normative. Cranleigh is in fact much more 'typical' of public schools in general over the past century, and as such its history tells us something about the middle classes, about educational practice, about boarding, and about Surrey.

I am grateful to the Headmaster and Governors for allowing me full access to all the documents. They have exercised no editorial control, and for mistakes of fact or interpretation I alone am responsible. The source material, it must be said, is limited. Consequently some questions – particularly about Victorian Cranleigh – are unanswerable. Other questions – such as the nature of the house system in Victorian schools, or the reasons for a probable faltering in public schools' confidence in the early part of this century – remain largely untackled by historians, and I have been able to offer only some tentative conclusions. J. R. Honey's book, *Tom Brown's Universe: The development of the Public School in the 19th century*, is one of the few historical works to tackle some of the more obscure corners in Victorian public school history and I have found it most helpful, especially as it is unique in dealing at length with Cranleigh and its place in the public school firmament.

Many people have helped me, in particular some one hundred Old Cranleighans who wrote giving me information or answering questions. I am grateful to them and to Tim Hastie-Smith, who did a great deal of work on the school archives when they were still in a raw state some five years ago. I owe a debt of gratitude, as does Cranleigh, to Pat Maguire, ex-second master, who first rescued and sorted the archive material and whose qualifications for writing this history are so much more impressive than my own. Thanks are due to the Master and Fellows of Magdalene College, Cambridge, who elected me to a schoolmaster fellow commonership, thereby enabling me to find time to write this book, and in such beautiful and hospitable surroundings.

My greatest debt is to my wife Elizabeth, and to my children Ann and Mark; they have not only lived in a busy housemaster's house at Cranleigh School; they have also had to live with Cranleigh's history for the past six years. Their help and encouragement have been invaluable.

Cambridge/Cranleigh A. J. MEGAHEY
1982

England and Education in the 1860s

IN FEBRUARY 1864, while some Surrey gentlemen were deciding on the curriculum for their new school at Cranleigh, J. A. Froude was lecturing the Royal Institution on 'The Science of History'. 'It often seems to me', he said,[1]

> 'as if History was like a child's box of letters, with which we can spell any word we please. We have only to pick out such letters as we want, arrange them as we like, and say nothing about those which do not suit our purpose.'

But as we look back on the 1860s those letters seem to spell out, in some very obvious ways, the story of a prosperous and powerful country. Indeed, arrange those letters how we will, England was at the height of her power as the world's mightiest nation, unchallenged on the high seas and in the market places of the world. The population of the United Kingdom was almost 29 million in 1861 – smaller than the populations of France, Russia, USA or the as yet still divided German states. But it was a rich and creative population. It was the most urbanized in the world, with over half the people living in towns. It was, to use George Kitson Clark's phrase, an 'expanding society':[2] expanding in terms of economic muscle and population; expanding in its creativity for England was still the workshop of the world; expanding in the sense that every year Britons travelled across the seas as emigrants or colonists or merchants, taking with them the English language, English culture and the entrepreneurial spirit. In that age of iron and steam the railways expanded each year, increasing the facilities for travel and business and helping to wear down the surviving elements of the old parochial, pre-industrial society.[3]

There was however a darker side to the picture. Charles Dickens and Lord Shaftesbury and Dr Barnardo exposed the seamier side of urban life. Richard Cobden feared that the march towards democracy had fatally faltered. Charles Darwin was the most prominent of those whose writings cast doubts upon the received truths of the Christian religion. John Stuart Mill worried about the grey and featureless society he saw evolving in England. And many of the leading lights in what Coleridge called the 'clerisy' – men like Mill and Froude, Matthew Arnold, F. D. Maurice, Charles Kingsley – were agreed that there were huge deficiencies in the England of their day in the field of education. More than at any time before or since, in the area of public debate, education was important. It was 'the nerve centre' of church-state relations.[4] It touched men's deepest beliefs for it encompassed 'moral training'.[5] It raised grave political questions, as when the educational reformer Robert Lowe proclaimed that 'a man must be the architect of his own fortune and rise by his own energy. All government can do is to remove obstacles from his path'.[6] It was a question of national importance. J. R. Seeley, much involved in 'the silent teaching revolution accumulated in Cambridge throughout the 1860s',[7] and a friend and walking companion of Cranleigh's first second master, asserted its import for the nation.[8]

> '. . . whether England has reached its highest point of greatness, and will now descend to a second place among the nations, or whether it has yet before it another era of brighter glory, depends on ourselves, and depends more than anything on the breeding which we give to our children'.

It was easier to assert the importance of education than to agree on what should be done. How far should the state intervene? How much should morality and religion be taught, and in what ways, and by whom? Should education be free? Should it be compulsory? Was the Established Church to be 'England's schoolmaster'? It is not surprising that the younger provincial radicals should wish to cut through the thickets of intellectual and religious debate and scruple: free, compulsory, universal, non-sectarian education would be their cry in the coming decades; their leader would be Joseph Chamberlain of Birmingham. Perhaps it is more surprising that the men of the Manchester School – men who believed in laissez faire and individual enterprise – were already looking to the state. Long before the radical initiative passed from Manchester to Birmingham, Richard Cobden was demanding 'a system of schools . . . paid for by all'. He told a Manchester audience in 1851:[9]

> 'I am for the education of the people. I believe the great mass of the people take less interest in this sectarian squabbling than many others of us are apt to imagine. The great mass of the people want education for their children; they are sick to death of these obstacles you throw in their way. I believe that when our extended franchise throws more power into the hands of the multitude, you will see that what I say is true – that there's a feeling for national education which will sweep away all these cobwebs with which you attempt to blind the great mass of the people . . .'

During the 1850s, 'the House of Commons became increasingly concerned with the question of popular education'[10] and, especially in the 1860s, it took action on a whole range of educational issues. Royal Commissions reported: Newcastle (1861) on elementary education, Clarendon (1864) on the 'great' public schools and Taunton (1868) on other public, endowed and proprietory schools. The Universities of Oxford and Cambridge were investigated and regulated by law. Acts of Parliament were passed dealing with endowed schools (1860, 1868, 1869), industrial schools (1860, 1861, 1866), poor law schools (1862), Sunday and ragged schools (1869), and public schools (1868, 1869). And the debate was to continue, as was the reforming activity. Indeed this was perhaps the only time that education became an electoral issue: 'the inadequacy of English educational institutions was second only to Irish disestablishment among the questions debated in the general election of 1868'.[11] The result was Forster's Education Act (1870) which, although it introduced neither free nor compulsory education, has been seen by one writer as producing 'a new type of society which radically altered the child's place in the community'.[13]

Revolutionary or otherwise, Forster's act only dealt with elementary education. It did not help the many parents who aspired to an education for their child which went on into the child's teens, and gave it some preparation for a career or for further education. While it was expected that working class children would naturally leave school at age ten or eleven (assuming they went at all) to go to work and increase the family income, what was to happen to middle class children? Archbishop Tait expressed a widely-held view when he wrote in 1865 that 'there has been somewhat of a standstill in the education of that most important class, which forms the very bone and sinew of the kingdom'.[13] Mid-Victorians were acutely aware of 'class', or at least of rank and gradation in society, even if they also believed – as one writer on middle class education put it rather extravagantly – that 'the classes of society in England interpenetrate one another, and make in their whole the most homogeneous people, with the exception of the Jewish nation, that the world has ever seen'.[14] The term 'middle-class education' was common in public debate and requires definition. One of the Taunton commissioners summed up widely held assumptions about middle class education:[15]

> 'Middle-class boys are boys whose general education ends between their 14th and their 19th years of age . . . It will be convenient to divide them into three grades . . . By the first grade is meant those boys who stay at school till they are in their 18-19th years of age. This grade is numerically small . . . By the second grade is meant those who stay at school till they are in their 16-17th years of age. This is in every respect the most genuinely 'middle' of any part of the class. By the third grade is meant those who stay at school only until they are in their 14–15th year of age. The boys of this grade approach nearest to and are often blended and confused with the scholars of the primary and lower schools.'

The Clarendon Commissioners had investigated schools catering for boys from the upper classes and those middle class boys who were, according to Fearon's definition, of grade one. The schools they dealt with were Eton, Winchester, Charterhouse, Harrow, Rugby, Shrewsbury, Merchant Taylor's and St Paul's. The commissioners also took note of some newer foundations which seemed to be of similar ilk: Cheltenham (founded in 1841), Marlborough (1843), Rossall (1844) and Wellington (1853). Others, such as Uppingham, Dulwich and Sherborne, might well have come within their purview, but were in fact left for investigation by the Taunton commissioners. They had the task of investigating a daunting thousand or so schools: most of these were 'endowed' schools or old grammar schools whose efficiency and scope were sadly limited. The ensuing act of parliament in 1869 merely sorted out the tangle and the abuses of educational endowments, but 'the results were disappointing and the opportunity of setting up an organized system of secondary education was postponed for over thirty years'.[16] In an age of voluntaryism it is not surprising that parliament was willing merely to curb the grosser abuses of the endowed schools, and leave it at that. But the commissioners had also investigated about 120 other schools: these were institutions which by and large modelled themselves on the Clarendon Schools and were part of, or were to become part of, the 'public school community' in the second half of the century. Parliament left these schools to their own devices.

In the thirty years from 1840 to 1869, no fewer than forty-one boarding schools were founded. The growth of the public school system was undoubtedly stimulated by the growing middle class demand for education, a demand not satisfied by the elementary schools or the old, decayed grammar schools, nor by the 'great schools'[17] because of their high fees and social exclusiveness. The system was stimulated too by the missionary activities of the devotees of Thomas Arnold of Rugby, and – on a more practical level – by the growth of the railway system. Most of these schools were Anglican and Christian belief inspired many of the founders. Nor were Anglican 'party' loyalties forgotten. Evangelicals (of various shades of opinion) were behind the founding of Cheltenham (1841), Trent (1866) and Monkton Combe (1868). Radley (1847) was a more high church foundation. But the most notably high church schools were the Woodard ones. It was to fight dissent, to educate the middle classes and to win them for the Church of England that Nathaniel Woodard began work in 1848. By 1870 there were schools for the upper middle class (Lancing), the middle class (Hurstpierpoint) and the lower middle class (Ardingly), with their fees graduated to suit the pockets of the different levels within the middle class. 'We must get possession of the Middle Classes',[19] wrote Woodard, and they were to be educated in schools imbued with that Anglo-Catholic spirit which he believed to be the essence of Christianity.[20]

The Revd J. L. Brereton was another visionary who planned to provide schools for the middle classes: unlike Woodard his fame has scarcely lived on after him:[2]

> 'I must say I feel very indignant at confessional Woodard receiving a magnificent recognition of his very minor services, and at your far greater ones being ignored. But I am not at all surprised ... Gladstone naturally turned away from a Protestant to a Romanizing person ...'

Brereton's schemes, while not necessarily 'greater' than Woodard's, were at many points very similar. The son of a Norfolk rector, Brereton had been at Rugby under Arnold, and at University College, Oxford, under Arnold's protege, A. P. Stanley, later Dean of Westminster.[22] Under these influences, he became a liberal or broad churchman, with a consuming interest in education. Rector of West Buckland in Devon from 1852, he became friendly with the local landowner, Hugh Ebrington, later 3rd Earl Fortescue. Together they conceived of a range of county schools which, like those planned by Woodard, would be of three grades to cater for the different ranks within middle class society. Like Woodard, Brereton planned a 'college' where boys from the schools could obtain teacher training or degrees. Unlike Woodard, he managed to get his 'county college' off the ground. It was founded in

Cambridge in 1873 and soon received the patronage of the Chancellor of the University, the Duke of Devonshire, who allowed his family name of Cavendish to be used for the new college. It survived only until 1891.[23] Cavendish came under attack from those Anglicans who disliked its non-sectarian emphasis and from Oscar Browning, who derided its social pretentions. Perhaps it was undermined, as J. R. Honey suggests, by the founding of the low-fee, strictly Anglican Selwyn College, by the decline in matriculations in the university, and by its distance from the centre of town.[24] But it also came under attack from the headmasters of some middle class schools, whose boys were the very ones for whom it was designed. In 1873 a group of five headmasters petitioned the Vice Chancellor of the University against the proposed college; one of the five was headmaster of the Dorset County School; another was Joseph Merriman, headmaster of the Surrey County School.[25]

Neither the Dorset nor the Surrey school was, in fact, a product of Brereton's county school movement in any direct sense. Brereton can be credited only with the founding of the Devon County School (now West Buckland), and indirectly the East Devon County School, the Bedford County School and Framlingham. Some of the principles upon which Brereton operated were to prove inimical to the clergy and laity of Surrey. They did not like the financial basis which he favoured – floating shares. Nor did they approve of his rather 'latitudinarian' approach to religion which Fortescue summed up:[26]

> 'We have laid down what we mean by County Education very clearly, and also what we do *not* mean, inter alia, *Diocesan or Exclusively Church of England Education . . .*'

But while Brereton and Woodard and the gentlemen of Surrey all might disagree about the precise religious nature or financial basis of their proposed schools, they were all eager to provide education for the middle classes, or the middle part of that 'garment without a seam, woven from the top throughout', which was the English class structure as pictured by Fortescue.[27] All these schools, and many others including numbers that have vanished almost without trace, were an important and growing element in what was coming to be called 'secondary' education. It was Matthew Arnold who had introduced the term from France in 1859,[28] and who five years later published an important work on the subject: *A French Eton: or Middle Class Education and the State*. Reviewing that book one writer, conscious of the deliberations of the Clarendon commissioners, drew attention to the importance of the new middle class foundations:[29]

> 'Probably the very best medicine which could be devised for the defects of Eton, Harrow and the other schools which the Royal Commissioners have been scrutinising would be the juxtaposition, and, to a certain extent, the competition of establishments of this kind. No wise man will desire to see root-and-branch work done with schools like Eton or Harrow . . . it is an addition of new that our secondary instruction wants not a demolition of old . . .'

CHAPTER ONE

Founding a Middle Class School (1862–1865)

THE COUNTY OF SURREY had a population of just over three quarters of a million in the eighteen sixties. The most densely populated area was in the north, along the southern bank of the Thames: Bermondsey, Camberwell, Lambeth, Newington and Rotherhithe. This 2% of the area of the county contained nearly half its population.[1] To the south of this working class area there were scarcely any suburbs, only the 'near-illiterate and ultra-conservative farmers of the Surrey clays'.[2] Rural Surrey would later provide a home for schools seeking refuge from the overcrowded conditions of London: Charterhouse and St John's (Leatherhead) in 1872, Christ's Hospital in 1902. As yet, in the 1860s, such 'middle-class private schools' as there were in Surrey were 'as bad as bad can be'.[3] It was as archdeacon of Surrey that Samuel Wilberforce had 'sensed the need for middle-class schools' and 'began to understand the magnitude of England's educational needs'.[4] Unfortunately the son of the liberator of the slaves did not stay in the area long enough to do much about it as he was made Bishop of Oxford in 1845. He retained however the interest in education that he had acquired in Surrey, and was able to make some contribution to the educational needs of the area when he returned as Bishop of Winchester in 1869.

The task was taken up by one of Wilberforce's first ordinands – John Henry Sapte. Sapte was the son of a Londonderry couple and was educated in Germany and Emmanuel College, Cambridge.[5] He served his first curacy at Cuddesdon, near

Oxford, where his rector was also the new diocesan bishop, Wilberforce. In 1846, no doubt at the bishop's instigation, he accepted the living of Cranley, where he was to spend the rest of his long life.[6] Sapte was one of those archetypal Victorian parish priests – long lived, strong willed, and a gentleman. He confirmed his status as a gentleman by marrying Caroline Gifford, daughter of the first Baron Gifford – whose fame is based on his role as prosecutor of the Cato Street conspirators, and who unfortunately died long before his daughter married the young rector whose fortunes he could no doubt have promoted had he lived. Sapte was to prove a tireless worker in his parish. It must have looked like a very unappealing living when he arrived at it: not quite the urban slum that young high church clergy were soon to be seeking out in an effort to evangelize the lower orders, but something of a slum nonetheless. It was a parish of about a thousand souls, mainly rough and illiterate labourers who were, at least nominally, members of the Church of England. 'Many of the marriages were not what is now considered 'respectable'. Bad language was the rule, the Cranleigh fighters were notorious'.[7] But such was the vigour of the new rector that within a few years he had managed to get the shopkeepers of the village to agree to no Sunday trading. He masterminded the building of a national school, opened in 1847. He helped to found the cottage hospital in 1859.[8] He remained as rector for sixty years, so that when he died in 1906 few people could remember there having been any other. Almost to the end of his life he was to be seen on horseback, visiting his parishioners in all weathers. It is hardly surprising that such an energetic parson, much influenced by Wilberforce, should turn his mind first to the education of village children and then to more adventurous schemes. He must have discussed his plans early in the 1860s with a local landowner, George Cubitt, who with Sapte must be regarded as the founder of Cranleigh School. *The Cranleighan* tends to regard Cubitt as the originator of the scheme,[9] but there is no evidence in *Hansard* that he spoke out on educational issues – or, indeed, on much else. But he was a good-hearted man; and he was wealthy. His father Thomas had, by 'a piece of hard-boiled speculation',[10] made his fortune in the 1820s and 30s building Belgravia. He was a supporter of the Great Exhibition, had rebuilt the frontage of Buckingham Palace, and was 'a liberal patron to churches, schools and charities'. When he died, he was a millionaire and his will was 'the longest on record'.[11] His son George had set himself up as a country gentleman with an estate at Dorking and was MP for West Surrey from 1860 to 1885 and, after the redivision of the county, for Epsom from 1885 until 1892 when he was raised to the peerage as Baron Ashcombe.[12] Sometime in 1862, he and Sapte began to lay plans for establishing 'a Middle Class School for the rural districts of the County'.[13]

Within the fine old Tudor walls of the Abbot's Hospital in Guildford, in November 1862, five laymen and eleven clergy met to discuss the project.[14] No doubt Cubitt had been hard at work using his contacts and these men, and other men recruited within the following months, were a prestigious band. Lovaine and Lyall were also MPs for Surrey; D. D. Heath (in due course a considerable benefactor of the school) had been a fellow of Trinity, Cambridge; so had E. W. Benson, Master of Wellington, who had been up at college with Cubitt. The Revd J. Chandler had been a fellow of Corpus Christi, Oxford, and the Revd H. Dupuis, a fellow of King's, Cambridge, and a master at Eton. Sir Walter Farquhar was MP for Hertford and a neighbour of Cubitt's; William Brodrick was a lawyer soon to become a Surrey MP, and later the first Viscount Midleton. The Headmaster of the local Grammar School also attended: the Revd Dr H. G. Merriman; he may have been a relative of Cranleigh's first headmaster but he played no further part in the scheme. At a second meeting in November 1862, two decisions were made: the name 'Surrey County School' was adopted, and a site was chosen – at Cranleigh. This was no doubt at the instigation of Cubbitt, who was prepared to purchase land there and hand it over for the new school.[15] By the end of the year, a prospectus had been drawn up, stating the purpose of the new foundation:

'The object of the promoters of the Surrey County School, is to provide a sound and thorough public school education, on the principles of the Church of England, for the sons of farmers and others throughout the agricultural districts of Surrey'.[16]

They went on to explain, in the familiar terms of mid-century educational polemic:

'While the upper classes are in full enjoyment of the foundations of the great public schools, and much has been done and still continues to be done to improve the education of the lower orders, the provision for the sons of farmers, and others engaged in commercial pursuits is so inadequate that the labourer's son often receives a better education than the son of his employer'.

Having stated their aims, money was the next priority. The committee had themselves promised over £800 in December 1862; by the summer of 1863 they had raised over £3,500 and felt confident enough to engage Henry Woodyer to draw up plans for an initial building to accommodate one hundred boys: at the same time 200,000 bricks were put on order.[17] By early September they had fixed on a date for the laying of the foundation stone and both the Archbishop of Canterbury (Longley) and the Bishop of Winchester (Sumner) had agreed to be present.[18] On 25 November 1863, a cold, wet day, the ceremony was performed and a luncheon held afterwards in Guildford. Meanwhile other possible benefactors were approached: among others the King of the Belgians, the Duke of Cambridge, the Earl of Onslow and the Duke of Buccleuch (successfully), and Jesus College, Cambridge (unsuccessfully). Local secretaries were appointed throughout the county to raise money and to make the scheme known; regular advertisements appeared in the five county newspapers. Also vital was the question of what should be taught in the school. A committee was appointed – six members of what was now being called the Council. E. W. Benson seems to have had most influence on it.[19] He had been a master at Rugby, and headmaster of Wellington since its foundation in 1859. It was he who answered for the as yet unopened school before the Schools Inquiry Commission. He explained there, as did the Committee in their printed report on the education to be provided at the new school, that there should be three main areas of study for all boys.[20] First: Latin. But within that Benson included Classics, English, Ancient or Modern History or Geography, and Scripture. He was no doubt thinking that in many public schools, all these subjects were taught by the classicists. Secondly, Mathematics. Within that Arithmetic, Drawing and perhaps Land Surveying would be included. Thirdly, a modern language would be taught – probably French, but not taught by a Frenchman: 'Foreigners in all schools have difficulties in discipline, which increase among a lower order of boys'.[21] When it came to publicizing the educational opportunities in the new school a more popular tone was adopted, and the subjects were listed:[22]

'Religious Knowledge; Writing and Dictation; the English Language and Literature, with English Composition; History and Geography; Arithmetic, including book keeping; Mensuration, and Mathematics; French and Latin. All boys will be instructed in Drawing and in Singing. A land surveying class will be formed for pupils who require it and who are sufficiently advanced; opportunity will be provided for extra lessons in Greek, and instrumental music, at the expense of the student'.

In fact, when the school opened several other subjects made an appearance in the time-table, notably science and shorthand.[23] It is perhaps surprising that some play was not made of the possibility of science being taught: it was a topic much discussed in the press in the 1860s, as a result of the Clarendon Commission's comments on the time-table at the great schools, and because of middle class pressure to make public school classrooms places where boys could be usefully prepared for business and industry. Perhaps this principle of utility did not operate in Surrey: the governors may have felt that for rural lads, 'mensuration' and 'land surveying' were appropriate and would make the right impression on prospective parents.[24]

Throughout 1864 and early 1865, the new buildings went up on the 'stiff, impracticable clay' of Cranleigh,[25] while the economic, educational and religious foundations of the Surrey

County School were defined and proclaimed. By the end of 1865, £10,000 had been received or promised. All this money came in the form of subscriptions. No endowment fund was established, presumably because it was reckoned that only enough could be raised to build and launch the school; thereafter it would have to develop and exist on its fee income. Indeed fee income, supplemented by occasional gifts or appeals, has remained the school's only significant financial resource ever since; no endowment exists. Nor did the governors seek to raise the money by creating a 'proprietory' school; this method was used at Marlborough, Haileybury, Rossall and at Cheltenham where the existence of 'share-holders' led to a considerable crisis early on in the school's history.[26] By setting up a school on the basis of donations the Cranleigh governors were saddling the new institution with the problem of paying off its debts and paying its way in the early years solely out of fee income, but at least the young school was free from the possible problems associated with shareholders or ex-officio governors. This need for the school to pay its way and run economically probably encouraged the development away from a purely 'county' school concept – by the time it opened the *Illustrated London News* declared: 'We are informed that the very natural inference which was drawn from the title – that this school is intended mainly, if not exclusively, for the county of Surrey – is, nevertheless, erroneous'.[27] It was wise for the school to emphasize this: while it had probably been tactically useful to appeal to the local gentry for the 'Surrey' school, it was only sensible for an institution so very near the Sussex border and not far from Hampshire and London to cast its net more widely when recruiting personnel. There was no retreat however from the religious tenor of the school, based on 'the principles of the Church of England' as the printed prospectus of January 1863 had declared. This was made clear, and indeed further defined, in a correspondence between Cubitt and a possible subscriber, a Mr R. Henderson of London, who objected to anything like 'sectarianism' and wanted assurance that pupils would not be forced into confirmation. Cubitt was able to disavow any such intention but made it clear that all pupils would be required to receive church teaching and to attend services.[28] Sapte also made clear, in a letter to another enquirer, that the school would be 'founded and conducted on the plain and simple principles of the Church of England'.[29] Neither Sapte nor any other of the governors seem to have been either Tractarians or very low churchmen; they were, to use Owen Chadwick's phrase 'stiff for the Church of England'. They resolved that they would see a headmaster who was 'a Clergyman of the Church of England or a Candidate for holy orders'.[30]

In fact when the post was advertised in February 1865, no mention was made of such a requirement. Nevertheless when the applications were received, seven of the nine were clergymen. Two – the Revd J. Merriman and the Revd J. W. Spurling – were interviewed in April. Merriman was appointed; he was aged 29. It was quite common for headmasters in the Victorian period to be appointed at such an early age: Butler of Shrewsbury was 24, Harper of Sherborne 29, Kennedy of Shrewsbury 31, Vaughan of Harrow 28, and Matchinson of King's, Canterbury 25.[31] The information on Merriman's first 29 years is sketchy.[32] He was born in the winter of 1835 at Shepshed in Leicestershire, the son of a small farmer. We know nothing of his own schooling but he went up to St John's College, Cambridge in 1856. It was a time when the college community was a lively one, and indeed a breeding ground for future public school masters.[33] Interestingly it was a college where one of the lecturers had recently built a chemistry laboratory and thus 'the first seed was sown towards the growth of a large chemical school' in Cambridge.[34] Merriman graduated fifth wrangler in 1860 and was elected to a fellowship. Between 1862 and 1865 he was ordained, spent some time at St Mark's College (for teacher training) in Chelsea, and taught at Bradfield.[35] When the Cranleigh headship was advertised it must have looked an attractive proposition to Merriman: the chance to become the founding headmaster at a school in the country and at an attractive salary. As a fellow of St John's he had a stipend of around £300 p.a.[36] The salary advertised for Cranleigh was

£250 p.a., plus £2 per boy. By the late 1870s, with the basic payment having been raised to £400, Merriman was to earn £1,000 p.a.[37] This compares favourably with the salary of the Warden of Radley which was a much more expensive school, and was at least double what he might have earned in a fairly good living. The living of Dorking, for instance, was worth only £300 p.a.[38] One statistician in the late 1860s reckoned that an income of £5,000 p.a. might be attributed to 'upper class' earners; an 'upper middle class' professional man might earn about £500 p.a., which would give him enough to employ three women servants, while a 'lower middle class' clerk might earn £99 p.a. An average doctor might earn £300–400 p.a.[39] So the headmaster of Cranleigh, with eventually a salary of some £1,000 p.a. and a free house, would be a wealthy man. There was another attraction in the job: Victorian headmasters were often, like Merriman, from humble origins, and they found in schoolmastering a 'career open to talents'.[40] The 'social escalator' effect is evident in Merriman's own case. His father had been a small farmer; his sons went to Cranleigh or to Cranleigh and then Charterhouse; his grandson went to Charterhouse; his great-grand-daughter married into the peerage. But men are not motivated solely by thoughts of financial and social rewards: a great attraction of public school headmastering must have been the opportunity – especially in a new school – to wield power and get things done, to be 'an autocrat of autocrats', as Cyril Norwood was still able to describe such men half a century later.[41]

Merriman was appointed in February; within a few months he and the education committee had drawn up a prospectus which gave not only educational details of the new school, but the usual necessary information: boys were normally to be admitted between the ages of 9 and 14; all articles of clothing were to be properly named, though only a school cap was a uniform item; there were to be only two holidays each year, Christmas and Midsummer; there would soon be third and two-thirds fees exhibitions obtainable on academic grounds; the fees were to be £30 p.a.[42] They were therefore much the same as the fees at Woodard's 'middle' school at Hurstpier-point, though twice those of his 'lower middle' schools at Ardingly and later Denstone.[43] Radley's fees were however more than double those at Cranleigh.[44] This enormous differential in the fees charged by different boarding schools would only even out in the mid-twentieth century. In 1979 the cheapest of these schools (Radley) charged £2,280, and the most expensive (Cranleigh) £2,373.[45] The school was to be advertised in the newspapers: in *The Times*, *Standard* and *Telegraph* twice a week, and in *Gardeners Chronicle*, *Surrey Standard* and *Surrey County Chronicle* once a week – further proof that the council were spreading their net more widely than the rural areas of Surrey. The other pressing need that spring was the recruiting of staff, which was left to Merriman – who first set out to find a second master, at a salary of £100 p.a. This was a common enough salary for a master at a smaller school in the 1860s, but again the differential is enormous. Were head-masters in modern times to retain their position relative to their second masters, they would have to earn in excess of £100,000 p.a.! Merriman was lucky to find the Revd R. H. Quick.[46] He was a few years older than Merriman and from a wealthier background. He had left Harrow after one term because of ill-health and had been tutored privately before going up to Trinity, Cambridge. He had been ordained, had served in several curacies and had taught at Lancaster Grammar School, the Royal Grammar School at Guildford and at Hurstpierpoint, whence he moved to Cranleigh. In later years he was to make a name for himself as an educationalist, campaigning for teacher training and a better curriculum.[47] He was something of a reformer, with strong views, though 'in his belief in magisterial responsibility for moral training, in his encouragement of friendly relations between master and boy, and in his emphasis on pleasure and interest as the basis of education, he was an orthodox Arnoldian liberal'.[48] He provided Merriman and the new school with some much-needed experience and ideas. Another vital appointment was made at the same time: Mrs Lane was engaged as matron/housekeeper at a salary of £40 p.a.[49] And another master was recruited in July: a Mr Poore, who was to live out and receive £75 p.a.[50]

In a widely circulated pamphlet of 1862 on middle class schools the Revd F. V. Thornton wrote: 'Do you ask now how we are to obtain such schools? The answer is plain. The middle classes themselves must take the matter in hand'.[51] The gentlemen and clergy of Surrey had done so; it remained to be seen whether their efforts would find support among the tradesmen, farmers and shopkeepers of the county. The founders had already, as an educational journal declared, made a 'contribution towards clearing up this great difficulty of the day'.[52]

CHAPTER TWO

The Merriman Years (1865–1892)

THE SCHOOL WAS TO OPEN its doors in the autumn of 1865. Merriman and Quick had much to occupy them during the long and exceptionally hot summer days as they prepared for the opening. The heat helped to dry out the new buildings – which as yet were incomplete, for only the east and south sides of the quad were finished, and there was no chapel or dining hall. The water supply was rudimentary; there was no piped water in the area so the school at first had to depend upon a deep hole dug near the entrance of Horseshoe Lane. No servants had as yet arrived, for there was nowhere for them to live, and as Quick remarked years later describing his own arrival: 'I naturally inquired for the masters' rooms. I was informed however that there *were* no masters' rooms'.[1] So headmaster and second master camped out, servantless, in the headmaster's house: it must have called for much the same qualities that some of their contemporaries were displaying on the mission field, or in the out-back. And there was another problem which was rather more than simply inconvenient: the problem of transport. The founders of Victorian schools often – as a modern writer has put it, 'as though by divination'[2] – chose a site near a future railway line or station. The Guildford-Horsham single-track line, with a stop at Cranleigh, had been in the planning stage since 1863; the opening date had been postponed again and again. The only alternative transport from Guildford – besides walking the seven miles, which some boys resorted to – was by fly at a cost of 16 shillings, more than £10 in modern values. Nor were the roads at all good: Horseshoe Lane, leading past the school entrance, was little more than a mud track. Up that track, in the summer of 1865, came H. A. Giffard, senior student (fellow) at Christ Church, Oxford, and one of the Schools Inquiry Commissioners. He offered Merriman and Quick further cause for gloom. Farmers, he said, were readier to donate money to a school than to send their sons to it. His visits to the schools at Guildford and Lewes had convinced him that even an offer of dayboy places would not attract much custom.[3] Nevertheless, preparations continued. 'Never did a great school begin with less promising auspices, and . . . it was only the extraordinary business capacity of its first head that prevented a fiasco'.[4] More staff were engaged; a school doctor was appointed; Mrs Lane organized the domestic side and hired a cook, a kitchen maid, a house maid, a linen maid and a manservant.

Michaelmas Day, 29 September, was the first day of term. Only eighteen boys turned up out of the twenty-five who had thus far enrolled, and to occupy buildings designed for 150. Three days later the railway finally opened and it carried large numbers of guests to the official opening of the school on 12 October. Charles Sumner, the Bishop of the diocese (Winchester, as Guildford had not yet been formed) arrived the night before and stayed with the High Sheriff of the county, Bradshaw, a member of the council who lived in fine state at Knowle. Next morning the venerable diocesan – he was 75 and a brother of Longley's predecessor at Canterbury – preached in the parish church, lauding the virtues of middle class education. Thereafter, the company moved up to the school where lunch was served in the classrooms which were acting as a temporary dining hall.[5] There were speeches 'of a very different class to those usual on such occasions', as the School Register recorded.[6] Perhaps this is a discreet reference to the disagreement which the religious newspaper, *The Guardian*, reported with some glee.[7] Earl Carnarvon, soon to be colonial secretary in the new Conservative government, praised the study of Latin and expressed the hope that although the school was to cater for

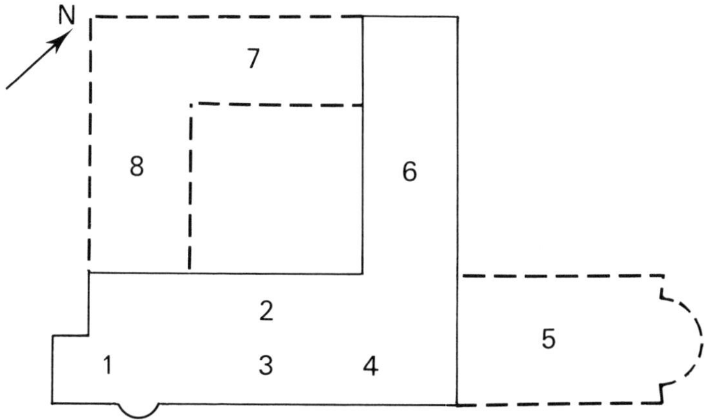

THE ORIGINAL SCHOOL BUILDINGS

The unbroken line represents the buildings completed by September 1865.
The broken line represents buildings completed by 1869.

1 The headmaster's house
2 On the first floor were the 'South' dormitories; on the ground floor were classrooms, two of which were at first set aside for use as a dining hall and as a chapel
3 Main entrance
4 The small corridor to the right of the entrance lobby, at first used as a gym; from 1869 it was the chapel corridor
5 The chapel, opened in 1869
6 On the first floor were the 'East' dormitories
7 On the first floor were the 'North' dormitories
8 On the ground floor the dining hall; on the first floor the 'West' dormitories

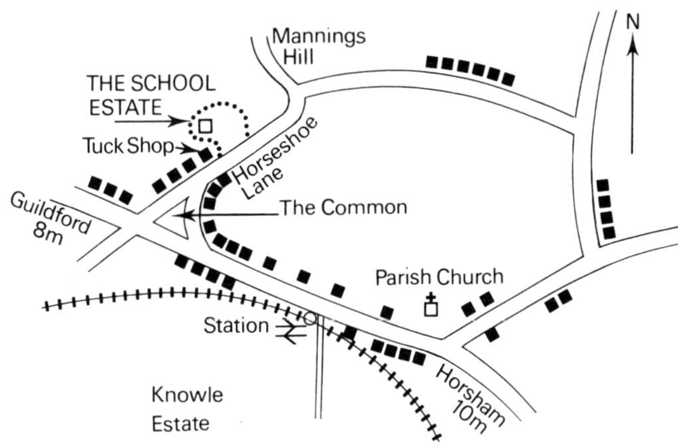

CRANLEIGH VILLAGE c. 1870

'the trading and commercial classes' the emphasis on the subject would nevertheless grow. Charles Buxton, who was Liberal MP for East Surrey, took a contrary view and praised the school authorities for not emphasizing Latin, and condemned 'the folly of grinding a child's mind at latin and grammar day after day'. It was Buxton's ideas which would hold sway at Cranleigh for some years to come.

But however the curriculum might develop the school was now officially open, even if numbers were small, the buildings incomplete and day-to-day existence interrupted by the work of the builders and contractors. The chapel was a classroom; the gym was a small corridor – soon to become the chapel corridor. There was almost no room on the eight acre site for playing fields. The first sports were held in a field by the rectory. Football was played during the first two terms, but in the rather desultory fashion of a small school in those days: the only available ground was the sloping field to the east of the entrance drive. Masters took part in the games. But boys continued to arrive and by the summer of 1866 there were 150 boys in the school; by the end of that year Cranleigh was as large as Charterhouse, Radley, Westminster, Lancing, Shrewsbury or St Paul's. The growth was steady and continued upward.[8] Facilities and activities expanded. The second master organized a library and dispensed hospitality to boys so liberally that, even though his stay was short, the impact he made was long-lasting: 'What good times we had! Was ever such jam and cake? Was ever a game like puff and dart? Was ever a host like ours?'[9] And a concert was held in the summer term, soon to become a regular fixture, featuring selections from Handel's *Messiah*, *Judas Maccabaeus* or *Acis and Galataea*, Mendelssohn's *Lebsgesang* and *Festgesang*, or Haydn's *The Seasons*. These were the favourites, featured each year at a summer or Christmas concert, and with visiting soloists. A choir was formed which greeted the diocesan bishop when he returned to confirm seventeen boys. By the time the chapel opened, in July 1869, the choir was singing a full service; Venite – Purcell; Psalms – Turle in D; Te Deum, Jubilate and Kyrie – Boyce in A.[10]

The young school faced problems as well, and not only those of unfinished buildings and 'frightfully ignorant' pupils.[11] At Whitsun 1866 – at a time of the year soon to be associated in the minds of old boys with their annual reunion – tragedy struck. Charles Garood became the first boy to die while at the school. He had been bathing illicitly with a friend in a stream near the old canal, a few miles from the school, when he got into difficulties and was drowned. He had been at the school since January, and was aged 14. The inquest was fully reported in *The Times*, the coroner concluding that 'no blame whatever was attachable to the authorities of the school'.[12] Nevertheless, it was hardly an auspicious piece of publicity for so young and unknown a school. It was followed a few weeks later by the death of another boy, Sidney Andrews, from an 'affection of the brain'.[13] Death was still common enough at schools but Cranleigh was small, with a reputation still to make; and in that respect even more worrying was the death from scarlatina of one of the boys – raising worries about infectious diseases which were to persist for another thirty years.[14] Far less serious, but disruptive enough in the somewhat Perrin and Traill atmosphere of a tiny masters' common room, was the crisis over masters' dinner. One young member of staff was displeased with its quality, and wrote to tell Merriman so in no uncertain terms. The headmaster, not one to prevaricate, saw the young man concerned and made peace with him, and at the same time saw that the quality of masters' dinner was improved.[15]

There was another problem for the young school which, even in the days before speedy communications and high-pressure salesmanship, had to be protective of its public image. For Merriman it seemed critical when the school's religious – or perhaps confessional – nature was publicly called in question. Lord Lyttleton, speaking early in 1867, contrasted Woodard's thoroughly Anglican schools with others like Trent and Cranleigh which were not 'theoretically Church of England'.[16] Lyttleton was chief Commissioner of Endowed Schools, a strong Anglican and a very influential figure; he was soon to become a 'reluctant secularist' in educational matters and come into open conflict with Woodard.[17] But for the moment, at the opening of Denstone, he had flung down a challenge to Cranleigh, as far as Merriman was concerned. It was hardly possible, trumpeted the headmaster, for any school to be more 'systematically connected with the Church' than Cranleigh with its publicly stated rules, principles and worship.[18] Certainly Benson had already testified before the Taunton Commissioners that Cranleigh was 'strictly a Church of England School',[19] as *The Guardian* had itself reported on the opening of the school.[20] Perhaps even the boys agreed! In February 1866 the debating society carried a motion 'that none but members of the Church of England ought to be admitted to Parliament' – and that nearly forty years after the emancipation of dissenters and Roman Catholics.[21] They picked up a more contemporary issue in the following month when they voted against the proposed abolition of church rate.[22] Just two years later, Gladstone carried abolition. In fact the campaign over church rate – the upkeep of part of the parish church being chargeable on the rates – was hardly a burning issue in the south east as it was in the west and east of England where dissent was much stronger. In the 1860s, most Cranleighans were probably Anglicans. But Merriman, while he was certainly strong on the Anglican ethos of the school, claimed in 1881 that 'Romanists, Nonconformists and Jews' had all sent their sons to Cranleigh. They did so in the knowledge that the school would not try to proselytize, but also on the understanding that their sons would attend Anglican worship in chapel.[23] This is a very clear echo of Sapte's stand on the nature of the school. The tradition persists to the present day. What has not persisted, as it has perhaps done in some of the Woodard foundations, is a certain 'churchiness' which did not survive much beyond the second world war at Cranleigh. By then, perhaps, the age of militant denominationalism was past, as it was not in 1893 when one of the founders boasted that the school

'was founded in connection with the Church of England, professing to teach the doctrine and to be guided by the discipline of the Church of England, and, looking back over the 28 years during which he remembered it, he did not think they had any right or necessity either to be ashamed of the principle upon which the school was founded, of the manner in which these principles had been carried out, or of the success which had attended their being carried out in their full and true sense'.[24]

Occasionally this 'churchiness' even led to exploration of such remoter areas of the Prayer Book as the commination service.[25] But perhaps true religion was better defined by a boy at the school in the 1880s who, on being taxed by a junior with the question as to what 'being religious' meant, gave a fine answer: 'it's waking up in the middle of the night and remembering that you belong to God, and turning over and going to sleep happy because of it'.[26]

It was all very well to claim that Cranleigh was a Church of England school; but something was missing.

> '"What is a college without a chapel?" Bishop Christopher Wordsworth once asked a friend, a canon of Winchester Cathedral. "An angel without wings" was the prompt reply. The Bishop went on his way rejoicing'.[27]

At the school's second speech day, in July 1867, Sir Stafford Northcote, arriving hot foot from the India Office, provided the needed stimulus. In a long speech he first applauded the aims of the new foundation, and noted that it answered an educational need of contemporary England. He noted, however, that 'in England there is no possibility of defining any class in society by saying where the middle class has its beginning and where its ending. English society is so shaded from one gradation to another that you cannot draw any line'.[28] This interestingly predates Disraeli's famous 'Manchester speech' when the party leader claimed that 'You have not merely a middle class, but a hierarchy of middle classes, in which every degree of wealth, refinement, industry, energy and enterprise is duly represented'.[29] But while Cranleigh existed to provide much-needed education, and was a fine achievement thus far, 'such an institution as this is not complete without a chapel', Northcote declared. During the summer a benefactor came forward: Henry Peek, a local landowner and prospective Tory parliamentary candidate. His offer of £1,000 towards the building of a chapel was subsequently inflated to a total of £5,500. Within two years the chapel was finished. Interestingly, while it was being built Peek wrote to a council member, Brodrick (later Lord Midleton), confessing his 'bitter disappointment' that in the dissolution honours at the end of Disraeli's premiership he had not received the expected peerage.[30] He had to make do eventually with a baronetcy and the marriage of his son to Brodrick's daughter.[31] Perhaps he thought that his munificent benefaction had enhanced his claims in the eyes of such Tory worthies as the Duke of Northumberland, Brodrick and Cubitt. Certainly the end result for Cranleigh was magnificent. The chapel was designed by Woodyer and built in red brick with bands of Mansfield stone and black brick and floored in Minton tiles. It is 103 feet long, in the shape of a 'T', the crossbar being originally an ante-chapel screened off from the nave by an oak reredos. It is impressively high – 50 feet – and with an apse built in what is sometimes called the French style. To the modern eye the building would have been somewhat gloomy, the more so as time went on and the clear glass in the windows was replaced by stained glass. The Archbishop of Canterbury performed the opening ceremony in July 1869. Tait's interest in education was second only to his (albeit temporary) involvement in the question of disestablishment of the Church of Ireland, debates on which were currently raging.[32] Following in the footsteps of his predecessor Longley, Tait made his way to the more peaceful environs of Cranleigh. It was a magnificent occasion. The theme was religion in school and in the home. The Archbishop spoke from the text, 'Salute the brethren which are in Laodicea, and Nymphas, and the church which is in his house' (Colossians iv, 15). Later Henry Peek spoke of his belief that 'education is of no avail whatever unless associated with religious teaching at school and at home'.[33] A fine array of the Victorian elite lunched in hall afterwards, the four hundred including the Bensons, the Brodricks, the Cubitts, the Northumberlands, Charles Buxton and W. H. Smith. The members of the council must once again have been busy making good use of their connections. For Merriman, the whole glittering occasion must have set the seal upon all his work thus far.

For the boys however school life proceeded on a more humdrum level. Cranleigh preserved, for several decades, that freedom and absence of rigid hierarchies and minutely organized free time that had been characteristic of most public schools in the middle of the century. An old boy remembered that 'there was little or no mapping-out of our leisure time'.[34] The breaking-up supper on the last night of term symbolized the ethos: 'chartered freedom prevailed' and there were songs, cheers and feasting until late at night.[35] One visitor in 1875 recorded that 'Cranleigh boys may wander where they please, and this freedom is characteristic of the establishment throughout'.[36] Games were ill-organized and masters continued to play in school teams until 1888. Even by that date there was a minimum of compulsion: in the winter, football was obligatory for only an hour per week.[37] A debate of the same period saw a vote against the proposition that 'compulsory games are beneficial', and even the proposer admitted that for senior boys the only compulsion should come from 'esprit de corps'.[38] Cricket was taken seriously enough for practices to be declared sacrosanct so that even detention should not interfere with them.[39] And the school magazine praised the game not only as 'good bodily exercise' but also as 'of great moral use'.[40] But these were merely hints of things to come. Boys found other things to do besides games. A school magazine article in 1879 suggested ways of passing a half holiday:[41]

> 'A ramble through the woods, a visit to the top of Pitch Hill, are excursions by no means to be despised, especially towards the end of term when primroses begin to peep and violets to bloom ... Butterfly excursions may be made ...'

Then, as something of an afterthought, the writer suggested that games might be played. The countryside undoubtedly offered attractions, and the visitor of 1875 saw how 'Cranleighans are not restricted to (school) boundaries, and in fine weather their distinctive blue caps may be seen far and near moving among the Surrey hedgerows'.[36] A Cranleighan of the 1860s, later to become a public school master at a time when schools were more highly organized, remembered the evidence of individuality, the pursuit of hobbies, the widespread idiosyncracies and even the proliferation of nicknames – features of school life which as he ruefully admitted had been almost regimented out of school life a generation or two later.[42] Of course there was a darker side; it was claimed later that games were character building, were good publicity for the school, kept boys out of mischief and used up their excess energy constructively. Perhaps because there was little organized sport, a tradition developed of 'gory, bare fist fights behind the gym' – fights in which a boy might become involved willy-nilly.[43] These fights had become traditional enough for one Old Cranleighan to call them 'official'.[44] In the early days, as a boy who was later a master remembered, the fights were winked at by authority and took place usually not on school premises, but at the crossroads below Mannings Hill.[45] There is a story of one such fight, classically between the school bully and a younger boy, which was chanced upon by Merriman who had a habit of appearing on horseback whenever boys were up to no good. On this occasion he did not interfere but stood aside shouting words of encouragement to the younger boy: the outcome is not recorded.[46] A tradition of fighting was probably common in most public schools at the time. An Old Salopian, visiting his old school in the late 1880s, 'on enquiring where the fighting alley was, and being told that personal combat did not happen nowadays, that games took the place of the ring, held up his hands in horror at the degeneracy of modern boys'.[47] But it is the freedom, rather than violence (which did not die out with the advent of organized sport) which is the notable characteristic that comes down to us from those early days: 'the glorious freedom of the 1870s', as the historian of another public school calls it.[48] Philathleticism had not yet arrived.[49] Merriman had never been to a boarding school. Quick's sojourn at Harrow had been brief but was at any rate long before the advent of athleticism. It was natural that at Cranleigh these masters should allow the boys to roam freely, miles away as they were from the nearest town. And no doubt too the boys used that freedom not only to fight but also to smoke. Cigarettes had not become common as yet; pipes were the vogue, though 'a pipe of the village shag could be as eventful as a Channel crossing'.[50] And maybe, 'through mere boredom', boys 'drifted into all evil and mischief'.[51] Anything to break the monotony, for as Frank Fletcher recorded of his own Rossall schooldays of the 1880s, 'they were dull. I remember that this puzzled and surprised my relations, who thought that school life might be unpleasant, but must be exciting'.[52]

Food at Cranleigh was certainly not exciting. With very low fees and with the need to pay off debts and develop the buildings there was little money left to spend on food. It is interesting that one undergraduate at Oxford in the 1840s could run up a bill of £900 in a year: more than the annual bread bill for 300 boys at Cranleigh in the late 1870s. The boys had a spartan diet. George Orwell remembered that, only a generation before his own at prep school, the boys had been given a slab of unsweetened pudding as a first course at dinner, to break their appetites.[53] This was the practice at Cranleigh. The meal was helped down by a glass of beer called 'swipes', as it was also at Cheltenham. At both schools the practice was discontinued in the 1890s.[54] The change to milk was received, if we are to believe the governors, with 'general approval'.[55] The meals, despite the beer and the breaking of appetites, still caused grumbles. In 1877 the scholars were banned from carving the joints, presumably because they had been too generous with the portions.[56] In 1888 even the masters had to be reminded that they should not 'refuse to carve anything that is sent from the kitchens'.[57] But at least there was meat at lunchtime. The evening meal was more of a high tea, with the school providing the basics of tea and 'toke' (bread), the boys supplementing it as best they could from their own resources. This practice of a very meagre evening meal continued into the 1920s, though in these later years at least there were cooked breakfasts. Extra food was always welcome. To supplement the dining hall meals, boys could visit the tuck shop which opened after Easter 1866 and remained in the same cottage premises in Horseshoe Lane until 1936.[58] It was run, under license as it were, by a Miss Ede aided by a small management committee of masters and boys. Miss Ede took half the profits and the other half went into the school games fund. So when over-earnest boys attacked what Charles Kingsley called the 'loafing, tuckshop-haunting set',[59] as when a Cranleighan wrote that the tuck shop undermined those 'athletic, intellectual, unselfish' attributes one expected to find in public schoolboys,[60] an obvious riposte was that the school, and especially school games, benefitted by its operation.[61] Prefects had another source of extra food. Being members of the village football club they could go along to the club-house, where meals were served. One boy remembered a birthday treat in 1886 when he took some friends there. Spectacular consumption of sausages was achieved, for although he himself could only manage four of those delicacies, one friend consumed eleven, and another thirteen.[62]

Chapel, games, leisure time and food were important; also vital was what went on in the classroom. The quality of the intake of boys, and the age structure of the school, mark off Victorian Cranleigh from its modern counterpart. There was no entry test, no 'quality control', and even Benson at prestigious Wellington had experienced an 'inauspicious commencement' when the very first boy he took into the new school claimed: 'I'm no sure, however, that I know anything'.[63] And Quick found that the first boys at Cranleigh were 'frightfully ignorant, though some of them had been at school for years'.[4] There was as yet no widespread system of preparatory schools and indeed nothing specific to prepare for, as the Common Entrance Examination did not yet exist. Nor was there a specific entry age. Like most schools, Cranleigh admitted boys between the ages of 9 and 14; the entry age was only beginning to settle at 13 towards the end of the century.[64] Even this rule was breached, as is evident from a glance at the age structure for 1885.[65] Among the 347 boys in the school then, there was a boy of 6 and another of 8. At the other end of the scale, there was a 'boy' of 20, who had been at the school just three years and was a scholar in the upper sixth. Promotion from form to form was on merit, not on the grounds of age: the oldest boy in 1885 was in Upper Fourth, though he had been five years at the school and placed originally in Lower Third. The forms were very simply organized from Lower 1 to Upper and so on through to Upper 6; boys who arrived at the school were placed in an appropriate form according to their age and academic ability. The lowest form after 1880 was not Lower 1 but 'the House' – this was a preparatory department catering for '24 of the youngest boys'.[66] Its purpose was not primarily academic but to create room for a slight increase in numbers in the school. It was the beginnings of the prep school: housed in 'the Old House' on the other side of Horseshoe Lane, it was known as 'the House', and run by Mr and Mrs Hardy, with the aid of a governess. The small boys were 'in all respects . . . members of the school'.

From the beginning, work was taken seriously enough for the Mathematics and General Subjects orders for the whole school to be printed termly. At the end of the first year H. J. Roby, a fellow of St John's who was secretary to the Commission on Middle Class Education, was called in to examine the boys in Latin, Divinity and Mathematics. For decades, the school 'held aloof from the Oxford and Cambridge examinations'.[67] Instead the practice continued of calling in examiners, usually from the universities, who assessed the boys' work, and whose annual reports were printed and were available on speech day. And a tradition of 'Collections' grew up which was, as a master of the time observed, 'an efficient and businesslike system'.[68] It involved a formal interview in Hall when masters read out comments on their pupil's work. The boys attended and the Headmaster recorded his verdict and added his own comments of praise or blame. The practice seems to have died out after Merriman, though it was revived again in the 1970s for scholars and exhibitioners only. Even in 1866 the curriculum was broader than the first examiner's reports would suggest. As had been promised in the prospectus, English, History and French as well as Latin, Divinity and Maths were regular subjects, while German, Greek, Land Surveying and Singing were available at extra cost. In the late seventies there seems to have been a (perhaps temporary) phase of teaching Pitman's shorthand: employers tended to like boys having it, and it was found useful in teaching boys to analyse words and sounds.[69] This was appropriate for boys who were generally destined for a practical, commercial or technical career, and for the same reason Science soon became a school subject. Merriman's mentor, Benson, had claimed to be a keen supporter of Science teaching in schools, reckoning that Chemistry in particular caught some boys' imagination, as well as proving useful for entry to Woolwich or some technical or commercial career.[70] At Cranleigh some lectures on elementary Science was introduced soon after the school opened. A liberal benefactor was the local worthy D. D. Heath, who had himself had a distinguished career at Trinity, Cambridge: he was up when the Wordsworths and Selwyns were making that college an intellectual centre in England and perhaps that gave him his interest in education. He was a generous supplier of bits of scientific equipment to Cranleigh, and in 1880 his new and fully-equipped laboratory came into operation at the school.[40] Meanwhile, on a more practical level, a metalwork shop had been established in the building still known as 'the forge' and this was followed by the appointment of 'a man, cunning in such matters, to teach medieval iron work'.[71] The craft was a common one in Surrey, though we do not know whether this man had been responsible for creating the chapel corona. This was an 11 foot high iron and brass chandelier carrying 54 candles, designed by Woodyer after one in a Belgian church, and hung in the chancel.[72] Metalwork and chemistry were felt to be suitable for Cranleigh boys, many of whom were expected to follow their fathers in a career in agriculture. Merriman encouraged this; he was himself, as a local newspaper noted, a 'practical farmer'[73] and came from farming stock. What opportunity his headmastership of Cranleigh offered him for 'practical farming' is not recorded, but certainly his boys carried off a fine crop of the scholarships awarded by the Royal Agricultural Society. They took four of the ten offered in 1878, and six in 1880. The Secretary of the Society praised Cranleigh as the leading school for agriculture in the country. Its fame spread as far as Italy, where its preeminence was recorded in the 1889 report of the Direzione Generala dell'Agricolture.[74]

The school's interest in agriculture died out when Merriman departed, to be resurrected briefly with the purchase of a farm after the second world war. But even for Merriman, agriculture and practical studies were not all. There was an academic side to this interest. Since the late 1830s there had been a growing movement in the country towards externally set and moderated examinations, and St Mark's College, Chelsea, which Merriman had attended, was itself a product of that movement.[75] From that movement, and with the stimulus and money provided by the Great Exhibition, there developed the South Kensington Examinations.[76] Some time in the early eighties Cranleighans began to sit for these exams. Some records survive: in 1888 the national pass-rate for the South Kensington Science exams was 69%; Cranleigh's fell below this at 63%. Those taking the highest grade had a very successful record however: 68.5% as opposed to 33% nationally.[77] But the school was not really geared to examinations. The headmaster must have been well-versed in the arguments for and against public examinations and he favoured instead assessment by external examiners. He justified this to parents, telling them that this method gave greater flexibility and freedom to the school to develop its own curriculum.[78] By the end of his headmastership, he was allowing two or three dozen boys a year to sit for the Cambridge Local Examinations at junior level, but still holding to the idea that they were incidental rather than a main object of the teaching in the school.[73] The same ambivalence is evident in Merriman's attitude to the universities. He claimed that 'neither himself nor anyone connected with the school looked upon it as a part of their duty to prepare boys for the universities'.[79] For one thing, the cost of a university education was at least three times the cost of fees at Cranleigh; generally boys from Cranleigh came from homes where this level was prohibitive and they needed either a scholarship from the university or some help from Cranleigh.[80] Occasionally a governor provided some money of his own for a worthy cause and in 1877 an anonymous donor founded the St Nicholas Scholarships to help boys in their pursuit of a university education.[79] The first university awards were won in 1872, two sizarships at Merriman's old college.[81] A trickle followed. It included one of the masters at Cranleigh who became one of the first thirty entrants to Selwyn, Cambridge, founded specifically to provide a low-cost but definitely Church of England university education. By 1893 one of Merriman's old boys had become President of the Cambridge Union: Peter Green had had a distinguished career at school and was to go on to become one of the finest parish priests in early twentieth century England.[83] More boys managed to go to medical school; teaching hospitals were generally less expensive than Oxbridge colleges. But the fact remained that at Cranleigh, for years to come and well into the twentieth century, most boys left school long before university entrance age, largely because 'parents were in such a hurry to turn their boys into money', as Merriman's successor lamented.[84]

University education was not the only way forward, especially in Victorian England. The aspirations as well as the financial resources of the parents determined that most boys were destined for business or commerce. Merriman's advice could be eccentric: one boy remembered telling the headmaster, on the last day of term, that he intended to study law. (It is interesting to note, incidentally, that this seems to have been the only occasion when the boy's future career was discussed at school.) 'So you're going to join the "Devil's Own"; a pity you can't think of anything else with your brains – goodbye!' With the benefit of this careers advice the boy went on to become a prominent Yorkshire solicitor.[85] Other Merriman boys went on to greater prominence without benefit of university education. Hudson Kearley became founder of the Home and Colonial

Stores and an MP; ennobled as Viscount Devonport he was first Chairman of the Port of London Authority and later Britain's food controller during the first world war. Writing with an almost Victorian turn of phrase the school magazine on his death held him up as a 'romantic example of what can be achieved by hard work', as one who 'rose from the position of a salaried clerk to the highest position in the business world'.[86] He had left Cranleigh at the age of 15, after a stay of four years. George May had left Cranleigh at the same age in 1886, joined the Prudential Assurance Company as a clerk and ended up as its secretary. He chaired the Economy Committee which recommended huge cuts in government expenditure and led to the fall of the MacDonald Labour government in 1931. He too was ennobled.[87] *The Cranleighan* had praised Devonport's qualities of 'hard work, confidence, integrity, and honesty of purpose'. The school might not turn out the 'golden-haired young god' on the Eton or Harrow model;[88] Cranleigh parents were not people who moved in the corridors of power or through the stately homes of England. But Cranleigh, like other – perhaps most other – public schools, was part of an upward thrust by the middle classes:[89]

> '"Manliness without coarseness, polish without complacency, nobility without caste' – under Hughes's definition, any public schoolboy might make himself a gentleman, though he owed his education to his father's trade in "unmentionables". And it was in the public schools, not in the officers' mess, Tattersall's or the Hurlingham that the new model gentlemen were being made . . .'

Indeed, many Cranleigh boys owed their education to their parents' 'trade in unmentionables'. The school was geared to the needs and ambitions of parents in the small towns and countryside of Surrey, Sussex and Hampshire. As had been expected, farmers were not over-keen to have their sons educated at Cranleigh. Only for a few years after its foundation did the largest single percentage of parents (24%) come from the agricultural sector, and only if included in that sector are land agents, hop growers and fruit growers as well as farmers.[90]

Even then there is a problem of definition: some farmers seem to have been 'yeomen', others were undoubtedly 'gentlemen farmers'. People involved in the drink trade were the next largest category of Cranleigh parents (11%). This trade was a larger employer of labour in south London and Surrey and these were the days before parliamentary control, mechanization and monopolies. The biography of Archbishop Garbett of York – whose two brothers were at Cranleigh – gives a pleasant picture of rural Surrey: the tiny village of Tongham on the Hog's Back, where the Garbetts lived, boasted three public houses and a good deal of drunkenness.[91] It is sometimes difficult to interpret the information on parental occupation given beside each boy's name in the school's entry books; sometimes the occupations seem unexpected for parents able to afford a boarding school education, albeit the inexpensive one available at Cranleigh. Among the first parents to send their sons to Cranleigh were a cordwainer, a civil magistrate in India, the manciple of Winchester College, the Master of the Lambeth Union, and an artist. Other parents in the nineteenth century included a lighterman, a barge owner, and the secretary of the Shipwrecked Seamen's Fund. This last is typical of the increasing numbers of managers, secretaries of companies and directors who sent their sons to Cranleigh as the years went by – and who by the inter-war years were the dominant sector. There were some more prestigious parents in the nineteenth century as well: the Surveyor General (Inland Revenue), a general, two major generals, the Steward to the Prince of Wales, and H.M. The King of the Ashanti.

The King of the Ashanti was hardly a normal Cranleigh parent but the story is worth a mention. His son, born in 1861, had the highly unlikely name of Kofi Nti. He was virtually taken hostage during Sir Garnett Wolseley's expedition in the Gold Coast in 1874 and the government in London decided to send him to Cranleigh. He was baptized in the local parish church, taking as his Christian name that of his godfather William Welch, a master at the school. He stayed until 1881, making some limited progress in the elementary skills of reading and writing, and was still in form two when he finally left at the age of 20. A contemporary has left a delightful picture of him:[92]

> 'Looking back from the cab the day I finally left school, I saw "Coffee" waving from a bedroom window in the Head's house, with Dr Merriman's two little daughters one under each arm. The contrast between their golden curls and his frizz, their pallid faces and his ebony one, was most striking'.

William Kofi Nti KariKari did not go on to ascend the throne or otherwise to add lustre to the name of his old school. This 'highly disreputable gentleman', as one government official called him, lived on a government pension until that was cut off by Joseph Chamberlain, colonial secretary, in 1897. Beyond 1917, no record of him exists.[93] What a life: prisoner of war, culture shock in Surrey, government service in Trinidad after Cranleigh, interpreter to King Prempeh in Sierra Leone, and finally a village layabout in the Gold Coast, living on charity. For all that, as one of his schoolfellows later remembered using the idiom of another era, he was 'a delightful nigger'.[94]

Kofi was exceptional. Most Cranleigh boys were English and most came from the south east. It was not, however, a thoroughly 'Surrey' school: indeed the proportion of boys from Surrey was never more than a half, until the second world war. But whether boys travelled from a far distance or lived quite near the school, boarding in the nineteenth century was a fairly full time occupation, with only two long holidays per year and very few exeats: apart from Christmas and the summer, the only time boys saw their parents at home seems to have been during a short exeat given over Easter. This must have been particularly difficult for one-parent families, and indeed one is struck in the school's entry lists by the number of widows who sent their sons to Cranleigh. As has been said, the Victorians 'made a serious business of widowhood. It was indeed a profession in itself'.[95] Fees were low at Cranleigh, which undoubtedly helped widows. The school fees rose from £30 to £37.80 in Merriman's time, and incidentally at a time of no price inflation, so the school was becoming more expensive.

Some of the widows who sent their sons were themselves teachers. But there were of course no women teachers at Cranleigh. Only at the 'House' after 1880 did boys come across women – Mrs Hardy and a governess – in the classroom. Indeed there were few women in the community at all. There were some maids but the masters tended to be bachelors. One old boy looked back on the 1860s: 'I remember very very little of that strong and shrewd yet very tender womanly influence . . . the utter lack in a boy's school life then of any softening and refining influences'.[34] There was, he admits, one exception. Mrs Lane had been one of Merriman's first appointments. For the first fourteen years of the school she supervised the health and domestic arrangements of all the boys. She died at the age of 61, and there was – understandably given her unique motherly role and given the fashion of the times – a considerable outburst of emotion. The whole school followed her coffin from the school chapel to the parish church, the whole village went into mourning, and in the school magazine a long poem was dedicated to her:

> '. . . And now the twilight deepens; and the bell
> Summons to evensong: once more we kneel
> And strive to speak the gratitude we feel . . .'

There remained Mrs Merriman – 'a delightful figure, but alas! a far-away one'.[97] Her hospitality, recalled by an Old Cranleighan, was extensive: tennis parties, picnics on the hills, her birthday dinner parties, her Christmas dance.[98] But, one suspects, it was more directed to the locals and the masters than to the boys. Few other ladies figure in the school's early history; there was an occasional visitor to take part in a concert. But otherwise, for the boys, it was a monastic existence.

It was a monastic existence but, as we have seen in connection with games, it was not yet a highly organized or minutely supervised one. Merriman's own claim was that he had not sought 'to mould any particular type, but to allow each boy to develop his own personality'.[99] This is a far cry from the stereotypes of regimentation, philathleticism and finely tuned hierarchy too freely attributed to schools of this period. There was no fagging at all at Cranleigh: indeed the age structure of the school and the academic determinants of a boy's progress through the forms did not encourage a rigid hierarchy.[100] Houses scarcely existed. A modern writer has suggested that 'the centrality of the house system as a key institution of the later Victorian public school is open to question'.[101] Cranleigh bears this out and indeed the popular stereotype of the house system and house loyalties probably, yet again, owes much to its undoubted importance at such schools as Eton, Harrow and Winchester. The house system at Cranleigh grew out of the dormitories which were supervised by resident bachelor masters. Some time in the mid 1870s the dormitories were grouped together, as the school grew, so that one master looked after dormitories 1 and 4 on the south side of the quadrangle, so he had charge of '1 and 4 South'; the boys in his dormitory sat together for meals. Similarly there were dormitory masters in charge of '2 and 3 South', '1 and 2 East', 'West' (which was more cramped, above the dining hall, and so never sub-divided), '1 North' and '2 North'. These curious names, originally denoting geographical position, have been retained to the present day although they have lost almost all their geographical significance.[102] Up until the first world war, 'dormitory masters' had to be bachelors, and there seems to have been no very great significance or prestige attached to the job. Often masters changed from one dormitory to another, perhaps because they were seeking slightly better accommodation. Their living quarters were cramped: they merely had a room or two off their dormitory. It is a far cry from the housemasters at the great schools who could make considerable profits from the running of their houses. At Cranleigh it was not until the 1960s that houses became separate entities with the full paraphernalia of studies, dormitories, common rooms, changing rooms and staff accommodation all within a coherent area.

One particular feature of school life was not missing from Cranleigh: beating. At first, this was administered only by the headmaster. 'Stimulating canes' and 'soul harrowing birches' were used only in extreme cases, says one commentator.[36] There is some evidence however to suggest that Quick had found Merriman rather too ready to resort to these particular sanctions.[15] By the mid-seventies the second master could also beat, but it was a sensitive issue during that period. There had been a scandal at Winchester in 1872 when a seventeen year old boy was given thirty strokes, leading to the 'great tunding row' which became something of a national issue.[103] At Shrewsbury in 1874 one boy received 88 strokes from the headmaster, who was to retire more than thirty years later to the village of Much Birch.[104] In 1877 a boy at Christ's Hospital had actually committed suicide after a beating.[105] It is understandable that there should have been some discussion in 1876 about whether the senior prefect could administer corporal punishment: it was decided that he might do so but only – as the edict quaintly recorded – 'in cases of bullying and bestiality'.[106] The authority of prefects was in fact slow to develop. By the mid-eighties they were being admitted into office by ceremony in hall, and they wore squares or mortarboards.[107] Of the first fifty prefects created by Merriman, fifteen were degraded (several twice over); one was drowned; one became the first OC to preach in chapel[108] and one became a master. Henry Caswell had been at Cranleigh for less than a year when in October 1866 Merriman took him on as a trainee teacher, and he remained at the school until 1891.[109] Sometimes prefects could be impressive in traditional ways: one boy remembered the senior prefect in 1883:[110]

> 'I can picture him now – walking up and down the classroom (during prep) wearing a mortarboard with a tassel, with a bright alert air, and a merry twinkle of the eye. I know we all respected him immensely as a fair and just disciplinarian . . . I also remember him as lesson-reader in chapel, resplendent in white surplice.'

Another favourite feature of the 'public school monolith'[111] is clothing. But the blue cap remained the only uniform item in Merriman's time; the village boys seem to have made something of a sport of acquiring such caps and thus apeing their 'betters' – a nuisance which at least one Cranleighan saw as something of an affront.[112] Games clothes were scarcely known, though it is comforting to read an instruction of 1879: 'All boys to change their socks after sports'.[113] This was common enough. At Aldenham a boy of the same period remembered that 'we in the lower game never changed',[114] and even at Harrow 'it was only in 1888 that a regulation dress became general' for ordinary games players.[115] Not until the advent of a new headmaster did the characteristics of the 'monolith' become evident at Cranleigh. The characteristics of Cranleigh during the Merriman years were a reflection of his own style, of the aspirations and expectations of the parents, and of the youthful nature of the school. It does not detract from Merriman's achievement which was prodigious. He had filled the school; its bank balance was in the black by 1887. He had sent out to other schools an impressive array of men to be headmasters: no headmasters of other public schools it is true, but of middle class and grammar schools. The list of masters who served under Merriman and who left then or during his successor's time to take up headships must be something of a tribute to Merriman and to Cranleigh:

1876 Revd H. W. Pate	Bristol Cathedral School
1881 T. Henderson	Bedford County School
1883 C. S. Logan	Newcastle Grammar School
1883 Revd W. E. Inchbald	Kingston Grammar School
1885 Revd A. W. Callis	King Edward VI Grammar School, Wymondham
1891 Revd C. G. Duffield	Appleby Magna Grammar School, Leicestershire
1892 Revd E. N. Adamson	Sunderland High School
1893 Revd T. Layng	Roysse's School, Abingdon[116] (1898 Maidstone Grammar School)
1908 Revd E. T. Lea	Steyning Grammar School
1911 H. C. Brooks	Preston Grammar School

There were several others, but the details are lost. What is clear is that Cranleigh had not broken through into the league of great schools, as had other recent foundations like Cheltenham, Clifton, Wellington; it had few connections with the landed classes apart from its governors, and it drew its clientele from a local rather than a national catchment area. It had remained what it was founded to be: a school for the sons of those members of the middle class who were not landed and not wealthy. Nevertheless the promotions gained by Merriman's staff indicate that he ran a respectable and worthwhile establishment, with a good reputation. Having secured this good reputation for his school, and having built up the numbers, Merriman decided to retire. He was still only 57 and had spent the whole of his married life at the school he had created. Leaving was going to be a wrench. He was deeply involved in local affairs: chairman of the gas company, a waywarden, secretary of the county agricultural association. He was a regular speaker at local meetings and in the parish church. He was a founder member of the governing body of St Catherine's School at Bramley and a manager of the local national schools. But, like his school, his influence and reputation were local not national. Perhaps his own background and contacts were never extensive or exalted enough to ensure him some plum living or ecclesiastical preferment. Few of his pupils went on to national greatness so his name seldom appears in the memoirs and biographies of late Victorian worthies, for his pupils were not writers of memoirs or the subjects of biographies. There was no character defect: Joseph Merriman was obviously a dynamic character with a commanding presence, the ability to inspire affection and fear, and of the stature of those 'very superior men' who as headmasters of more notable schools have become part of the history of Victorian England.[117] He deserves, belatedly, to join the ranks of the Percivals, Thrings, Haig-Browns, Saundersons – men who left their mark on Victorian public schools and, therefore, on whole generations of boys.

Merriman must have been aware that his contacts were limited and his chances of preferment slim. So when in October 1891 he received from his old college the offer of the living of Freshwater on the Isle of Wight, he decided to accept it.[118] At the end of the Lent Term, 1892, he preached his farewell sermon in chapel, and shook hands with each boy at the end of the service. A tearful farewell to the staff followed.[119] The Council members recorded their thanks, praising him in particular for 'the high moral tone which he had maintained throughout (his twenty-seven years) and . . . the careful management which had gradually relieved (the school) from a heavy financial burden.'[120] Not long after his retirement to Freshwater, his wife died; but with his larger family, the school, his links remained strong. Almost every year he returned to be guest of honour at Whit reunions, or travelled up to London for the Old Boys dinners. He died, suddenly, at Freshwater in 1905. A year later, a classroom block was opened in his memory. By then, however, Cranleigh was a very different school from the one he had nursed from an assemblage of eighteen boys to a thriving institution of over three hundred.

CHAPTER THREE

A Fully-Fledged Public School (1892–1908)

THE FLEMING REPORT, published in 1944, claimed 'that during the period between 1870 and the last war the Public Schools became . . . more conventional, stereotyped and complacent'.[1] It was, more specifically, during the years around the turn of the century that saw Cranleigh take on more and more of those characteristics which marked off the 'public schools' from the proprietory and private schools which still survived in large numbers. In the 1890s, the atmosphere of the early days evaporated. Gone was the freedom to roam, the casual attitude to games, the absence of hierarchy and uniform. If not inevitable, it is certainly understandable why Cranleigh should develop in this way. The pressure for such change did not come from the governors; the composition of the Council had changed little. Partly it came from the masters, many of whom had now been to public schools themselves, and more especially from the new headmaster. There was subtle pressure from the old boys who, rubbing shoulders with old boys from more prestigious schools learned the value of the old school tie and increasingly tended to look back on their own schooldays through regulation rose-coloured spectacles. Just as significant were the pressures of the market place; there were fewer farmers and shopkeepers now and the new breed of parent – the company director or ambitious business man – might be expected to hope for his son a conventional public school education, albeit still at very low cost. And the increasing competition from other schools may well have played its part.[2]

It is interesting to contemplate, however, that at precisely the time when Cranleigh was conforming to type, other schools were being founded in conscious revolt against that type. This 'progressive school' movement produced Abbotsholme in 1889, Bedales in 1893, Clayesmore in 1896 and King Alfred's, Hampstead in 1898. Of these schools a modern writer has commented: 'as one escapes from the stifling pressure of the conventional public schools around 1900–1910 it is the sense of freedom that is exhilarating'.[3] But as the century drew to a close at Cranleigh it was not the exhilaration of freedom that was evident, but rather the satisfying feeling that 'they were now one of the public schools of England, and had a right to call themselves such'.[4] Or, to use the categories of a recent commentator, Cranleigh had been a 'quasi-public school' which had gone through the process of 'becoming' and by the turn of the century had 'arrived'.[5]

Merriman's successor, who presided over the school throughout these years of transition, was a Surrey man – George Cantrell Allen. Unlike his predecessor he had been a public school boy. It cannot have harmed his chances when he applied for the post at Cranleigh that he had been a boy under Benson at Wellington. Even the august Merriman had breathed that name with reverence. Now Benson was Archbishop of Canterbury who came down soon after Allen's arrival to open the Chapel at St Catherine's school. He met his old pupil there, and in public described him as 'a beloved and immensely respected member of the school'. Allen was the grandson of a yeoman farmer, and the son of a draper of some means.[6] After Wellington he had gone up to St John's, Cambridge and then returned to his old school as a master under Wickham who had been his own headmaster during his last year at school, when he had been head boy. Wickham, a former don who had married Gladstone's daughter Agnes and who was later to become Dean of Lincoln, had gathered around him a distinguished staff. In the years to come they were to fill the headships of Eton, Lancing, Uppingham, Tonbridge, Sedbergh, Highgate, Ipswich, Trent and Cranleigh: 'a glorious record, never since equalled'.[7] Allen left Wellington for Dulwich in 1881, and was ordained in the following year. After a decade he applied for the headship of Cranleigh which was being advertised at a salary of £750 p.a. Only five others applied, all of them clergy. Three were already headmasters: Harrison at St Lawrence, Ramsgate, Forbes-Müller at Hereford County College and Welch at Archbishop Holgate's School, York. One was an assistant master at Wellington, T. F. Hobson, who was later to spend three rather unsatisfactory years as Warden of St Edward's, Oxford. The other man was the elderly Rector of Ongar. Three men were interviewed, with a strong recommendation that Allen was the man: he was duly appointed in November 1891.[8] 'Old Crow' or 'the Crow' as he was later called, was 37. In the Easter holidays of 1892 he and his family moved into the headmaster's house at Cranleigh. It was a school of 280 boys, lacking many of the traditions and facilities with which Allen was familiar at Wellington and Dulwich; he was young enough to contemplate a long headmastership putting its deficiencies to rights.

During Allen's own schooldays, his headmaster had shown little interest in games. The boys ran them, and Benson would sit in his study catching up on correspondence even while the school was involved in its big annual steeplechase.[9] But towards the end of Benson's time, and during that of his successor, things changed: it was a development common to many schools.[10]

> 'Between approximately 1860 and 1900 from diverse origins . . . there developed a broad measure of conformity with regard to the major features of athleticism; supportive ideological statements appeared, considerable investment in the machinery of games playing was made, compulsory games were introduced and an intense enthusiasm on the part of many pupils became evident'.

Games had been fairly casual during the Merriman years; now Cranleigh caught up with the general trend. As a member of staff at two great schools Allen had been witness, perhaps all unconsciously, to the developments in common rooms of public schools: 'the College fellows disappeared from their staff. In their place came a formidable body of "Blues"'.[11] So when Allen arrived at Cranleigh there was no one on the staff like the Revd Septimus Buller Phillpotts, one of the last Senior Fellows of King's, Cambridge, to have been elected under the old statutes.[12] He was a Cranleigh master in the early seventies, and remembered as 'tall, spare, long-legged; his mortarboard all awry; a squeaky voice with an inability to "woll" his r's, an ear so deaf to music that he could not distinguish "God Save the King" from "Pop goes the weazel"'.[13] That breed had gone, along with life fellowships and bachelordom at Oxford and Cambridge, and school common rooms where men stayed as far as possible away from the day-to-day pursuits of boys. The age of games enthusiasm – among masters and boys alike – had arrived.

Allen must have been particularly pleased that his arrival at Cranleigh coincided with the arrival also of the enormous shield awarded to the winners of the public school gym competition. Cranleigh boys had first entered this fixture at Aldershot in 1887, and came 21st. In the 1892 competition Nai Vin and F. Taverner beat Cheltenham, Clifton, Harrow, Tonbridge, Rugby and thirteen other schools. Interestingly, in that same Aldershot fixture the individual fencing section was won by an Harrovian – Winston Churchill. Oddly enough, twenty years later a Cranleighan was beaten in the semi-finals of this section by a kinsman of Churchill's – Oswald Mosley. Allen must have been delighted to step into such a goodly heritage. For the rest of the nineties, Cranleigh never fell below fifth place, and came first again in 1893, 1894, 1895, and later in 1913. Second place was gained in 1898 and 1899.[14] It was a significant and publicly recognizable achievement for a small school. Indeed, according to a recent historian of the public schools it was instrumental in placing Cranleigh in a significantly up-market bracket.[15] Status, he claims, is reflected more than any other way during these years in the "interaction" of a school on the games field – what other schools were played; what level of success was achieved. In these terms the most prestigious sport at Cranleigh was undoubtedly gymnastics, but in football and cricket in the '90s fixture lists were built up involving Horsham Grammar School, St John's, Leatherhead, Reading School, City of London School, Whitgift and Epsom. There were fixtures also with Guy's and Charing Cross Hospital, and from 1897 the MCC. In 1907 (though that seems to have been the only time) even Charterhouse was engaged in matches: Cranleigh won at gym by 250 points to 209½, though her 1st XI Football team lost to the Charterhouse 2nds 6–0.

And the sentiments within the school also denote the changing status and ethos of Cranleigh. In 1895 the school magazine began to carry an editorial for the first time, and in every issue but one until the end of the century, games figured largely in it. The editorial sometimes merely commented, as in 1895 on the school sports 'which form an inexhaustible topic from the time the final heats are run off until the decision of the final event and the award of the Dormitory Challenge Cup'.[16] Sometimes there was exhortation, calling for more runs, and in general more sport, as in 1896; and in 1899 lecturing[17]

> 'the School at large . . . (for) . . . it is in their power to very largely contribute to the success of the (football) team by showing an interest in its doings, and turning out to watch all matches and encourage the players by cheering'.

Individual Cranleighans wrote to the editor in similar vein. One boy demanded that 'the school be forced at least to be present' during football matches, with attendance ensured by 'holding a call-over at some time during the game'.[18] Another demanded that spectators spectate instead of playing about on the touch line or boundary.[19] Others called for more enthusiasm at house matches, and that 'idle half holidays' be spent putting in some cricket practice.[20] The Headmaster was able to announce proudly at Speech Day in 1896 that 'they had had a more successful year in football than for many years past', and that 'with regard to cricket, this year had, he thought, without exception throughout the history of the school, been the most successful'.[21] The mood was caught by outsiders, and a local benefactor presented £200, the income from the investment, to provide prizes for gymnastics and cricket performances each year.[22] And the headmaster contributed a football song:[23]

> . . . 'Now the moral of my story, as is plain for all to see
> Is that footer's but a game of Life, the same for you and me;
> When the goal is close before us, play the man and let the chorus
> Of our boyhood cheer us on to win the victory.
>
> Chorus: Oh! Its "Play up, School" and its "Buck up School!"
> Play the game and play together
> While we chase the merry leather,
> In the brave October/chill November/chill December weather.
> Buck up, School!'

The words were original, but the genre is familiar – one of the dozens of songs spawned in these years at schools throughout the country. None of them achieved the immortality of E. E. Bowen's 'Forty Years On', a Harrow football song, or of William Cory Johnson's 'Eton Boating Song'.[24] For romance and nostalgia the Eton song is unrivalled, which is presumably why Lord Rosebery gave orders that it should be played as he lay on his deathbed. But one of Allen's old boys captured those feelings of romantic nostalgia in his own way:[25]

> 'My prevailing and all-pervading memory . . . must be that of good friendships, many of which continued into after-life; bright winter days and sunny summer ones; white flannels; cricket; the outdoor swimming bath . . .'

Such nostalgia is a powerful force in English history, and unique to English literature. Merriman's old boys expressed the feeling frequently. Hugh Kearley (later Viscount Devonport) was a particularly loyal OC who asserted in the midst of a highly successful commercial and political career that 'he owed all his success in life to the School and to Dr Merriman'.[26] Another of the doctor's old boys, Francis Floud (later Sir Francis, High Commissioner in Canada and governor of the school) summed it up well:[27]

'He believed they could not find in history or ancient literature any sense of the romance of school which was so strong a force in the minds of most young and old Englishmen at the present time'.

He meant, of course, in the minds of those Englishmen who had been to public schools. By contrast Melvyn Bragg asserts, having interviewed men who attended state schools in his home town before world war one, that they uniformly 'referred to their schooldays as "terrible"'.[28] For public schoolboys the myth, if not the reality, was different. The romance of schooldays exercised a huge fascination, stimulated by the 'public school novel'. In 1905 and 1906 alone, six significant such works were published – Portman's *Hugh Rendal*, Vachell's *The Hill*, De Morgan's *Joseph Vance*, the Askews' *The Etonian*, Bradby's *Dick*, and Coke's *The Bending of a Twig*. This selection, says Edward Mack, 'marks the coming of age of public school fiction, generating, as it did, public awareness of a distinctly new category of literature'.[29] Vachell's Harrow on the Hill may have been a long way from Merriman's Cranleigh, but that didn't matter to OCs, especially when they got together in their OC clubs. The first reunion at the school took place on Whit Monday 1868, and that tradition continued for a century. The first dinner was held in London in 1881, and became an annual event. The first sports clubs, in football and cricket, were founded in 1886, and by 1898 the OCs were regularly playing the Old Etonians, Old Harrovians, Old Westminsters and Old Malvernians.[30] The OC Social Club was founded in 1894, there was a Provident Society in the early '90s, and in 1897 the OC Society itself was founded. Five years later it had 400 members, though this was only a small proportion of the 3,000 boys who had passed through the school, most of whom must still have been alive. Where were the 'submerged nine-tenths' asked the Headmaster with pardonable exaggeration at the OC dinner in 1905.[31] The OC dinner had its uses: within twelve months another 50 members had been recruited.[32] In Merriman's day, the dinner had largely been a rather personal gathering of his own old boys; now under Allen it was a more decidedly Old

Cranleighan gathering. It was an annual opportunity for the Headmaster to plead, promote, preach and report. In a significant speech in 1899 he told the OCs that in the latest entry to the school, 80% of the boys were the sons of OCs or had been recruited by OCs – 'a very wholesome thing'.[4] In 1900 and 1901 he responded enthusiastically to the patriotic call to arms from Lionel James, an OC who was war correspondent for *The Times* in South Africa, at a time when other OCs were being killed in the Boer War, and while the school was engaged in founding its own OTC. In 1906 Allen was able to announce the election of J. W. Williams as the first OC on the School Council.[33] But more generally, the OC dinner was a time for nostalgia and reminiscence and expressions of loyalty which Allen encouraged in 1897 when he declared[34]

> '. . . that it was not antiquity of foundation, nor large numbers, nor wealth of endowment that was the test of a great public school, but it was the spirit and the tone which the school breathed into its members, and, if the sons of Cranleigh lived true to traditions imbued in them there, the School could not fail to maintain the high position she had already attained, and, indeed, would advance to yet greater heights of success . . .'

And the OCs, for their part, gossiped and remembered, and maintained the links of friendship forged years before. Distance lent enchantment to the view. The OC of first world war vintage who remembered the 'evil reputation' of 'the Bullies' and 'the mob' in his house at school could also add: 'The odd thing is that when it comes to putting pen to paper and looking back, what is illtreatment and bullying – compared to Tom Brown's Schooldays we were milksops'.[35] The thrashings dispensed by Merriman were forgotten; instead 'Joe' was remembered for forgiving, and not thrashing, a young scholar who for a bet had rung the school bell at midnight.[36] Or he was fictionalized by F. S. Brereton OC, in one of his yarns for boys, *King of Ranleigh*:[37]

> 'Dr Layman . . . clean-shaven, save for a pair of whiskers, grey-haired, he presented a face which was the essence of kindness . . . save when there was cause for severity'.

Or 'Old Crow' was remembered as a public flogger who could also visit the san to speed a sick boy's recovery with words of cheer and liberal glasses of port.[38]

For Allen, Cranleigh was not all sport and thrashings, nostalgia and moral tone; work mattered. Games, he announced to OCs and parents at speech day in 1896, 'were not, in his opinion, of first importance'.[21] And on that occasion he was able to publish the news of G. H. Hardy's successes. Hardy's was perhaps the most distinguished mind ever trained at Cranleigh. The boy's father was first school bursar, who had founded 'the House' where he and his wife looked after junior boys. His son, born in 1877, was already as a boy of two writing down numbers up to a million, and factorizing the hymn numbers on the chapel board.[39] Prodigiously clever, he was placed in form III when he joined the school at the age of 10, and within two years he was taking first place out of twenty-four in the upper sixth. In July 1890 he was identified by an external examiner as producing 'exceptional papers for a boy of his age (which) give proof of great mathematical ability, as well as good teaching'.[40] In that same term he won a Winchester scholarship, taking first place in a field of 102 candidates.[41] So he was lost to Cranleigh, where there was simply not the stimulus or quality of teaching for such a clever boy, though even at Winchester he had to be taught in a class of one. Allen claimed him, justifiably, as part-Cranleigh, and declared a half holiday to celebrate his election to a major scholarship at Trinity, Cambridge. Hardy was to go on to beat his old headmaster by one by becoming fourth wrangler, and later a fellow. Hardy was not a typical Cranleighan; nor was Godfrey Taylor who in 1902 came first in England and the colonies in Cambridge Certificate Mathematics. The same boy went up to St John's, Cambridge, where he became the first Cranleighan to win a blue – in football. In 1980 he was still able to flourish Allen's post-card of congratulation, written half in English and half in Greek.[42] Godfrey Taylor, and his postcard, are nice examples of Allen's determination to train 'not only the boys' minds, but also their bodies'.[21]

The Headmaster was himself a classic, and this seems to have had its effect. He lamented publicly, in tune with the examiners' report of 1897, that there were 'several boys not learning any Latin'.[43] It must have given him pleasure that the debating society should vote in 1906 that 'a classical education is superior to one in modern languages' – a vote perhaps not unconnected with the fact that the headmaster attended the debate.[44] Certainly there was no emphasis on science and practical subjects at the school now; Allen had picked up none of the enthusiasm of his colleague on the staff at Dulwich, F. W. Sanderson, who as headmaster of Oundle was to revolutionize science teaching. The Royal Commission of 1895 was outspoken about the fact that farmers no longer sent their sons to Cranleigh because 'the teaching has not been adapted with sufficient care to that which the farmers desire'.[45] The school could answer that criticism: farmers' sons had never patronized the school in very large numbers; given the changing clientele of the school, and its development along very traditional lines, and the departure of Merriman, it is not surprising that there was a lack of interest in science, agriculture and technical subjects. What is more surprising is that the Commissioners noted that there was no 'sufficient laboratory' and that 'the chief teaching in the school is classical'. As an OC of the time remembers, 'science was practically unknown'.[46] Cranleigh was conforming to type, and even critics within the public school system in the 1890s were keener to attack 'cramming' and 'utilitarian specialization' than to uphold the claims of science.[47] There were exceptions, at Oundle and possibly Clifton, but in the main the public schools stuck to 'topics fit for gentlemen'.[48] A contemporary of Allen's, the Headmaster of St Paul's, F. W. Walker, summed up the attitude in his advice to a boy:[49]

'My boy, you are making a great mistake. If you go in for science, your future is quite uncertain. If you stick to your classics properly, I undertake to say that you will pay for your education in scholarships and be able to earn £400 a year within a reasonable time . . .'

Allen even saw fit to inject a little classical style into the school magazine: from 1896 lists of new boys and leavers were entitled 'salvete' and 'valete', or 'advenerunt' and 'decesserunt'. And soon after his arrival he wrote and published a school song – in Latin. 'Cranleienses Gaudeamus', with music by the director of music Richard Harris, was performed publicly for the first time in hall at a school concert in December 1893.[50] A boy signing himself 'Patriotic' was soon demanding that every Cranleighan learn it by heart.[51] That was the mood of the 1890s; by the 1980s the song was unknown to Cranleighans, and aired only at the annual OC dinner.

While the headmaster might laud the classics and the Royal Commission lament the absence of science teaching, a specific academic advance is evident at Cranleigh in these years: the increasing use of public examinations. Since 1877 the Senior Certificate of the Cambridge Local Examination had exempted boys from Responsions at the University.[52] This had not cut much ice with Merriman, who eschewed all public examinations and played down the element of university preparation in a Cranleighan's education. Now there was a change. In 1897, for the first time, eight candidates were entered for the senior examination, and this was to be the pattern for years to come. As yet, however, candidates were not entered for the Oxford and Cambridge Board examinations which 'like the Headmasters' Conference, marks one of the stages on the road of the public school towards educational supremacy in England'.[53] But neither of these features – Oxford and Cambridge examinations or membership of the HMC – was a necessary indicator of 'public schoolness' to a Victorian. Style, organisation, games mattered more. Ethos was more important than academic standards, and was to remain so for perhaps another half century.

Far removed from that ethos, and from Latin songs, examinations and the Surrey countryside, lay the parish of the Lady Margaret at Walworth in South London: 'some half-dozen short streets and three blocks of model dwellings. Yet in this seemingly small area dwell 11,000 people'.[54] So wrote Peter

Green, the OC who had had a glittering career at Cranleigh and Cambridge, and who was now an ordinand about to become the St John's College Missioner in Walworth. School and College missions had become 'fashionable', representing 'the service which the privileged classes feel called to give to the unprivileged' as a Charterhouse missioner put it.[55] There was a growing awareness among the educated, the middle and upper classes, of 'the gulf . . . which separates the lowest classes of the community from our churches and chapels . . . and from all decency and civilization'.[56] The decisions taken by public school and university men in the 1870s, '80s and '90s to found settlements in deprived areas 'stimulated one of the most powerful social influences of the next hundred years: the public-school social conscience'.[57] Cranleigh conformed to type. Since 1884 there had been some contact with the St John's College Mission – sending an occasional offertory from chapel, or entertaining a party of children to a day in the country.[58] In October 1894 Allen chaired a meeting at Walworth and a committee was formed of OCs and masters to fund a further missioner in the parish and to develop the links between the school and the mission. By 1898 the Bishop of Rochester was able to praise the school – and, gratifyingly, to link it with other and greater schools – by telling Cranleighans and their parents 'how much it broke the monotony of South London Church life to have these missions, which were especially attached to educational centres such as Charterhouse, Wellington, Cheltenham and Cranleigh'.[59] It broke the monotony of school life too. The year 1899 was not untypical. On the day after speech day, the school was invaded by 130 children from Walworth who attended a service in chapel, played games, went on rambles in the countryside, and ate large meals.[17] For Cranleighans it must have been an eye-opener; and what a contrast to the previous day, a rare photograph of which has survived, a period piece of boaters, Eton collars, white parasols, gowns and hoods.[60] And now these denizens of a different world, a world which few Cranleighans saw either while at school or later. The links between the school and the mission were fostered and maintained not so much by the boys, but by a small group of masters and OCs. In that summer of 1899 J. W. Williams entertained ten parishioners at his New Malden home: 'the party literally consisted of the poor, the halt, the blind and the deaf'.[17] In the autumn, the headmaster preached at Holy Communion in the Mission church. The boys of the parish were given a camping holiday at Bexhill by some OCs. The chapel collection of £1.17s. 1d. was donated to the mission in aid of a new organ. Two OCs were working part time at the Mission during that winter, and a third was contemplating giving up an evening a week to help. Donations came in from OCs as a result of hundreds of appeal letters sent out from the school. Not all OCs were enthusiastic however, and some fine comments are recorded from OCs who would not contribute:[61]

> '. . . no interest whatever in Cranleigh mission . . . things in the Potteries are so awfully bad . . . not being in complete sympathy with the scheme . . . the matter is of no interest whatever to me . . . I pay quite enough and more to the working man in rates . . .'

The Mission survived this lack of enthusiasm, though it never became a central feature of school or chapel interest at Cranleigh, and there was a worry in 1907 that 'the little band of Old Cranleighan workers has now dwindled to very small proportions'.[62] Perhaps Cranleigh parents, or OCs, were not comfortably enough established among the haute bourgeoisie for them to feel confident about themselves or their sons rubbing shoulders with the deprived. Probably the grander the school, and the more wealthy the parents, the more likely such a Mission was to flourish. Or perhaps the mechanics of the link between Mission and school were not conducive to arousing more enthusiasm among boys and OCs. The link continued, however, until the later stages of the first world war, when a new project was begun and St John's College put on record its 'deep sense of gratitude for the help rendered during three and twenty years of common work'.[63]

Meanwhile Allen had been busy introducing another feature of the modern public school, an Officers Training Corps. Drill –

not punishment drill which was another matter[64] – had been practiced in Merriman's time. Such *ad hoc* rifle corps had been common at many schools.[65] In 1886, three hundred and fifty boys had formed up in seven 'companies' with a band on the Common, to be inspected by Captain Herbert Sapte, the rector's son. They marched, wheeled and executed bayonet drill. A passer-by who saw the boys was moved to write to a local paper in fulsome praise: 'some of the elder boys forming Squad A went through the evolutions like regular soldiers, while I believe every boy on the ground enjoyed the whole thing immensely'.[66] Not until the end of the century did the suggestion emerge that a regular cadet corps be founded, though an opponent of the idea claimed that this could only be done at the expense of games success, as had happened, he said, at Bradfield where there was an excellent Corps.[67] Not many schools were so organized as yet. Eton, Wellington, Cheltenham and Marlborough were, but they had very strong military traditions. Indeed it is hard to find evidence for the claim by Rupert Wilkinson that 'the military characteristics of the Victorian public school are too striking to be overlooked',[68] especially since 'military' characteristics like hierarchy, regimentation and tradition were such late-comers at Cranleigh, and probably at many other middle class boarding schools. In the late 1890s however, at Cranleigh and elsewhere, such characteristics were becoming more common, and they had their effect. 'The change came around the time of the Boer War. Corps were then quickly founded where they had not existed before, and increasing proportions of boys enlisted in them'.[69] Again, Cranleigh conforms to type. The headmaster sent out a circular in the Easter holidays, 1900: the response was such that permission was immediately sought from the War Office to establish a Corps – at a time when the secretary for war was St John Brodrick, a member, and later chairman, of the school council. The first uniform was based on that of the 2nd Volunteer Battalion of the Queen's Regiment: dark green, with black facings and a Glengarry cap.[70] The ex-headmaster lent his support, speaking to the OCs about the 'imperial spirit'.[71]

The headmaster presented his own gun and swords to the officers of the Corps.[72] The school magazine carried up-to-date lists of Cranleighans serving in South Africa, and letters from them.[73] Soon in the chapel there was a marble tablet inscribed with the names of Captain Dowse, Lieutenant Onraet, Sergeant Leigh, Private Hutchings and Troopers Smeed and Young 'who in the faith which they learnt as boys within these walls laid down their lives for England'. The Corps grew, passing its original establishment of one hundred within a term. Cranleigh was brought into contact with other schools: the first entrants for the Cadet's Trophy at Bisley in 1901 came 8th, equal with the pair from the traditionally more military Cheltenham. The first team appearance at Bisley was in 1903, when the school gained a low but not disastrous position. In the public schools field day in 1901 Cranleigh's 'soldiers' fought alongside Carthusians, Marlburians, Wellingtonians and Rugbeians against boys from Eton, Harrow and Winchester. Here was that 'interaction' which Honey claims was so important.[74] In 1902 the OCs were addressed by war correspondent Lionel James OC, who told them that he 'was a red-hot man for conscription'.[75] He was asked by the headmaster to put his speech on paper so that current Cranleighans could hear the message, and join the Corps even if they did not eventually sign up for the colours.[76] Many of the boys who read that speech were to experience the full horrors of war in the great European conflict fourteen years later.

The Corps fulfilled its functions admirably: it was a means of discipline; it was an expression of 'patriotism' in an England currently at war; it was a means whereby the school could interact with other public schools; perhaps at its simplest it was a way of keeping boys gainfully occupied for several hours a week. And it was to become a permanent feature of school life, at Cranleigh and at most other public schools. The founder and commanding officer of the Cranleigh Corps was M. H. Pugh, Housemaster of East. He was a Johnian, who had arrived at Cranleigh in 1893 from Westward Ho!, and from 1900 to 1905 commanded the Corps. A man with 'very large feet and a very kind heart' as General Dunsterville called him,[76] he was some-thing of a character. One of his former pupils remembered that 'to keep in health he indulged in navvy work with spade, pick and barrow',[77] which explains why *The Cranleighan* recorded, in a gently ribbing tone, that 'he was fond . . . of mending roads, but owing to lack of suitable materials his efforts in this line were not always rewarded with conspicuous success'.[78] In fact Pugh had been Rudyard Kipling's housemaster at Westward Ho!, and he appears in *Stalky and Co* as the unfortunate Prout, whose large feet earn him such sobriquets as 'Hoofer', 'Hoophah' and 'Heffy'.[79] Pugh, thus calumnied as a young housemaster, remained at Cranleigh until 1905, after which he seems to have vanished without trace. He died in 1914, 'found drowned in the River Avon' as the burial register records. He may have suffered a breakdown, though there seems to be no significance other than a macabre coincidence that the original of 'Mr King' in Kipling's book – a man called Crofts – was also drowned, off Sark in 1912.[80]

In 1895 a Royal Commission declared that Cranleigh 'has, in fact, ceased to be a local school'.[81] This was not quite true: Cranleigh never had been a local school in the sense of taking most of its boys from Surrey, though it was and is true that most Cranleighans came from the home counties. Given that Surrey boys did not predominate, and that it had an increasingly 'public school' ethos, it was natural that its name should be called in question. Although it was still the 'Surrey County School' Allen pointed out to the governors that 'the name Cranleigh School had for a long time past been in use among the School's clientele'.[82] Indeed from the foundation of a school magazine that had been the case: *The Cranleigh School Chronicle* when it first appeared in 1871, then from 1878 *The Cranleigh School Magazine* and from 1900 *The Cranleighan*. And since his own arrival the headmaster had made sure that the *School Register* was headed 'Cranleigh School', and bore no reference whatever to 'The Surrey County School'.[83] The Council agreed that it was time to regularize this, and from 1897 onwards the official title was to be 'Cranleigh School' with 'Surrey County'

in parenthesis afterwards, a practice that was very soon dropped. The Council at the same time took another step: the
decision to apply for a Royal Charter. Lord Ashcombe and
Archdeacon Sapte along with another Council member, Mr
Cave, were to form a sub-committee and with the Visitor and
three representatives from St Catherine's were empowered to
take the necessary steps. Ashcombe undertook to bear any legal
expenses incurred. The Charter was duly granted, dated 8 June
1898. It legalized a 'Corporation of the Cranleigh and Bramley
Schools' consisting of at least thirty members along with certain
ex-officio members (mostly Surrey dignitaries), all of whom
'must be members of the Church of England'.[84] Oddly, this
provision did not apply to the headmaster or headmistress, nor
did the stipulation that lunacy, bankruptcy or apostacy would
disqualify. The Council was a corporate body in which was
vested the land belonging to the two schools; executive powers
were devolved by the Council onto the Finance and Management Committee of each school which met regularly, with a
smaller membership than that of the whole Council. According
to the headmaster the significance of the Charter was 'that they
were now one of the public schools of England, and had a right
to call themselves such "de jure" and "de facto"'.[85] So as well
as providing a legal base for the Council, the Charter represented an enormous psychological boost for the school even
though there is really no way in which it can be said to have
bestowed any further 'public school status' upon the school. So
the matter stood until 1959, when the charter was invoked and
certain rearrangements made.[86] Even then, its significance was
underscored: 'Public Schools may well before long find themselves in the political arena and our present Royal Charter
might well prove an invaluable protection'.[87]

J. R. Honey claims that 'some schools which had been
founded as specifically 'middle class' schools after 1850 had
arrived at an established place in the public-schools community by 1902'.[88] What he calls the 'effective public-schools community at its widest' in 1902 comprised 104 schools, of which
the top fifty might be divided into four groups. Group 1 (22

schools) includes the great foundations along with prestigious new-comers like Haileybury, Wellington and Marlborough. Group II (8 schools) includes Radley, Lancing and Felsted. Group III (20 schools) includes Cranleigh, along with such others as King's School Canterbury, Brighton, Epsom, St John's Leatherhead and Whitgift – all of which, as it happens, had catchment areas similar to or overlapping with Cranleigh's. Group IV included fourteen schools. Of these fifty top schools, ten appear on no Headmasters Conference list before 1902; indeed the Headmaster of Cranleigh was not elected to the HMC until 1916.[89] But the notable features of Cranleigh – most of them fostered by Allen in the 1890s – gave it the status of a public school of fairly high rank. This was the major achievement of Allen's headship. Other themes too are discernible during these years. One, the problem of declining numbers, was to continue and worsen after his retirement; the other, the whole problem of health and hygiene, ran its course and had almost been solved by the time of his departure.

CHAPTER FOUR

Health and Hygiene (1865–1914)

IT IS PERHAPS SURPRISING that more has not been written about ill-health and death in the Victorian and Edwardian school, for it is one of the features of the age which has changed out of all recognition. Part of this change shows up in the national statistics for life expectancy:[1]

Expectation of life at different periods

Age	Number surviving out of 1,000 live born males			
	1838–54	1891–1900	1920–22	1963
5	724	750	870	972
10	690	734	857	970
15	673	725	849	968

Of course the problem was worse in crowded industrial towns than in the country; worse among the working classes than among the middle and upper strata of society. Nevertheless the national statistics give some idea of the trends; and indeed even the upper classes often faced death and family loss. Tait, who while Archbishop dedicated Cranleigh chapel, had suffered the loss of five daughters in the space of five weeks, back in 1856.[2] If we look at any Victorian family, from royalty to the humblest in the land, we find records of those who died in childhood or youth. If we look at the frequency with which obituaries and death notices appeared in the school magazine and register, we see a pattern of fewer and fewer deaths, but more and more OC obituaries. Not every OC death was recorded, though probably the death of every boy was. The table gives some idea of the frequency with which Cranleighans were confronted with the fact of death:

	Boy's deaths (usually at school)	Master's deaths (at school)	Others connected with the school (matrons, governors etc)	OCs and ex-masters
1865–69	5	0	1	0
1870–74	2	1	1	0
1875–79	9	1	1	0
1880–84	5	1	1	2
1885–89	0	0	0	1
1890–94	2	0	2	10
1895–99	0	0	5	8
1900–04	1	1	3	10*
1905–09	0	0	5	12
1910–14	0	0	3	16**

* includes 5 killed in the Boer war
** includes 1 killed in the first world war

Note: the absence of death notices for the years 1885–9 seems odd, and may or may not be accurate; it may reflect the brevity of the school magazine in these years.

It was not merely that 'the strains of social mobility and the atrophy of the wider functions of the extended family caused (the middle class family) to eject its young into the care of auxiliary educational agencies' whatever the consequences.[3] The fact is that living anywhere in the 1860s was hazardous. It is understandable that the Victorians were open and articulate about death, even if they were not about sex. Twentieth century society takes a contrary view and while open and articulate about sex, prefers to cosmeticize and avoid the fact of death. Victorians had to face up to the hard facts. The mortality rate among boys of 10 to 20, for instance, was around 6 per thousand nationally in the 1860s. It had fallen to 3 per thousand by the end of the century, and the fall continued, to under 2 in recent times. It is true that at Victorian boarding schools 'epidemic diseases were so common . . . as to have been almost endemic'.[4] But schools reflected, in their health and hygiene, the situation in the wider world. Lady Diana Cooper records that after the turn of the century her family home lacked electricity and gas, and that there were no hot water pipes: hot water was distributed by a strange breed called 'water-men'.[5] That was in a great house. Even more serious problems existed. In 1877 the purchaser of a 'large and expensive house in the west end of Edinburgh' discovered, among other defects, 'that one of the cisterns was so placed that, in case of anything going wrong with the water-closet right above it, the foul water must fall into the cistern beneath – a general supply one'.[6] There was much debate, and little general agreement, on how to ensure sanitary conditions. The Revd Henry Moule preached the virtues of the dry earth closet, whereby a population of 1000 people could have the 'complete deodorization and inoffensive removal' of sewage by the use of 'two tons of earth (as) against 30,000 gallons of water a day!'[7] This particular debate was revived again in modern times, and it was a Rockefeller heiress who patented a 'dry-earth closet' in the 1960s – this time on ecological as well as environmental grounds.[8] At Cranleigh, the dry-earth closets were all removed at the end of the nineteenth century,[9] though lavatory doors were not affixed until 1963.[10] Admittedly this absence of doors had probably more to do with phobias about 'vice' than with health or hygiene.

The great debate on health and hygiene did not begin at Cranleigh until the 1870s. The winter of 1874–5 was a harsh one. One boy died, but the school was inclined to be thankful that it had escaped so lightly: it was said that one school had a mortality rate of 6%, and yet another had 25% of its boys down with scarlet fever.[11] Even so, the case of Edward Perkins had been bad enough. On Ash Wednesday, 10 February 1875, school had begun early, as was customary, with a period before breakfast: this practice would continue daily until the onset of the following winter. But the mornings were so cold and dark, and there were so many coughs and colds, that the practice was almost immediately abandoned. During the following weekend, the first in Lent, a fourteen year old named Perkins, who was in his fourth term at the school, was confined to the sick room; there was no sanatorium as yet, and the sick room was next to the servants' quarters adjoining the dining hall and kitchens. It was a bad case of scarlet fever, and on Tuesday, with his condition worsening, the doctor advised that his parents be sent for. A telegram was sent to Barnstaple, and the boy's mother arrived on Thursday morning. She sat by his bedside, and he died on Friday night. The parents decided he should be buried in Cranleigh, which is not surprising given the costliness of a funeral on top of the fact that the family home was a long way away.[12] On the following Tuesday the service took place in the chapel:

> 'Jesus lives! Thy terrors now
> Can no more Oh Death appal us'.[13]

The funeral procession wound its way down to the main gates, through the village, and on to the parish church. In the graveyard the body was interred 'close by the graves of those who had formerly been members militant of our body'.[14] For a whole week, the shadow of death had lain over the school. But worse was to come, even though the Headmaster was maintaining at speech day in July that 'the health of the school had been extremely good'.[11] The Michaelmas term passed uneventfully, apart from two accidents, the first of their kind, when a master and a boy both fractured their collar bones. Then, about three weeks before the end of term, a case of scarlet fever was diagnosed. A circular letter was hastily sent to parents, the school broke up early, and no further cases were reported. At the beginning of the Lent term 1876, measles broke out. By mid-February over fifty boys were affected, and an East dormitory was turned into an emergency ward. 'Inflammation of the lungs' followed, and affected two boys fatally. Another boy died just after the end of term. Parents were kept informed, and many wrote in to express their sympathy and their gratitude for what was being done.[15] The school doctor found for the first time that he was really earning his keep. Dr Albert Napper was one of the village characters; like Sapte and Merriman, he was a well-known sight on his horse about the area. Already over sixty, he had spent much time – with the rector's help – founding what was to be the first village hospital in the country.[16] His obituary recorded that 'he took much interest in sanitary questions',[17] and these were now a matter of great concern to him, as far as the school was concerned. With the support of a physician from Guildford, Dr Butler, he reported to the Council on the epidemic. There was an urgent need, they maintained, for a thorough investigation of the 'drainage, ventilation and other sanitary arrangements of the building'.[18] Recent propagandists for sanitary reform had proclaimed that the 'two cardinal difficulties', the obstacles in the way of better arrangements, were invariably 'indifference and expense'.[19] In the face of the recent epidemic, and the deaths, and an outbreak of further non-fatal cases in the summer term, and with the strong recommendations of the doctors, the Council could not afford to be indifferent. And they would have to bear the expense, which was considerable. Mr Lunn of Guildford, who knew the school's plumbing and drainage arrangements well, undertook a thorough investigation in the summer of 1876; the resulting improvements cost almost £200, or the annual fees for six boys.[20] Dr Napper made way for a younger man, and his son Mr A. A. Napper became school doctor.[21] He was required by the governors to visit the school every other day, and more frequently if so requested.

But disease struck again in 1880. An outbreak of scarlet fever affected about fifty boys, though none fatally. Although it remained a relatively important cause of death until the end of the nineteenth century, the virulence of scarlet fever was on the wane, and fatalities became rarer at school in the eighties.[22] In March 1881 Napper was given a gratuity of £25 'in consideration of the pecuniary loss entailed on him in consequence of his constant attention'.[23] His salary had already been increased, and now stood at 9/- (45p) per head per annum.[24] In the year 1880 a rather more significant event took place as regards school health, with the opening of a new sanatorium. Cubitt was again the benefactor: he paid for the purpose-built building, and gave it with the land on which it stood as a gift to the school, a gift now appropriately commemorated in the building which was converted from sanatorium into a boys' boarding house in 1961. The new sanatorium was of rather rustic red brick, with low slung tiles in Surrey fashion. It contained a sitting room, ward, single bedrooms and other offices on the ground floor. There was an isolation ward on the first floor, with a separate entrance and staircase. Hot water heating ran throughout which was a considerable luxury. The ventilation was contrived to avoid draughts – we can perhaps see the hand of old Dr Napper here. There were no fixed baths, but portable ones were on hand, and 'there can be no possible danger of sewage, as there are no w.c.s in the place, and the waste pipes all flow over open gratings outside'.[25] This is a reminder of the belief, which we shall meet again in the discussions about sewerage, that diphtheria and scarlet fever were caused by 'the smells arising from defective drains or sewers'.[26]

The new sanatorium did not mean the solution of all problems. In the winter of 1892 some cases of diphtheria were reported to the Council.[27] In fact the incidence of the disease was at its peak in the early nineties, even though the antitoxin had been first used in 1891.[28] The problem was exacerbated at Cranleigh when a parent claimed compensation from the school after his son had arrived home from school at Easter 1893, and the mother had contracted diphtheria and died. The governors were not disposed to accept any responsibility, but they did look carefully at the arrangements within the school. Again it was the drains that caused concern, and permission was given for major operations which in the end cost the school over £800.[29] In a small way Cranleigh proved the point that was being made about public health in 1867 that 'great epidemics are epochs of sanitary development'.[30] In 1894, when the total cost of operations had risen to about £1,000, the headmaster was able to report to the parents at speech day that 'the whole system of drainage had been entirely reconstructed since last year on the most approved modern principles', and that 'he thought they might claim now to be one of the healthiest schools in England'.[31] He spoke rather prematurely, for within a month or two scarlatina reappeared, and almost a hundred boys suffered from the effects, though none fatally. The outbreak had been countrywide which was some comfort, and indeed the Council were able to use it as an excuse for the 'falling off in the number of boys'.[32] The report for the subsequent year suggested a 'clean bill of health'.[33] Cranleigh had escaped relatively lightly. Neither Merriman nor Allen had faced the problems of their contemporary Thring at Uppingham who had evacuated his whole school to the sea at Borth. Even more dramatic was T. C. Fry's experience. He was dogged by the problem first as headmaster of Oundle in 1884, and then as headmaster of Berkhamsted in 1888; in both cases he (like Thring) ran up against local vested interests and found it difficult to accomplish anything by way of renewal of drains or water supply.[34] At Cranleigh the problem was never so great, and there as at other schools there were few fatalities after the turn of the century. In 1913 the health of the school was very bad in the Michaelmas term – influenza, measels, mumps, diphtheria, whooping cough, chicken pox and 'bad throats'.[35] But at least death did not follow in the wake. Influenza epidemics were common enough: during the world-wide one of 1918 the school was badly hit, with at one stage 260 boys in bed. Then, and on at least three other occasions – 1929, 1959 and 1976 – the epidemic was widespread enough to cause the boys to be sent home early or for the school to reassemble late.

Perhaps in the 1880s and 90s the governors ought to have looked more closely at the whole question of water and washing. The school began with a well dug at the main gate. Within a year the well had been sunk deeper, and a round pump house was built over it, with a thatched roof, and a horse whose sole purpose in life was to circle round and round pumping water up the hill to the school.[36] Not until two decades later was a public water supply available; for the remaining years of the century the school was able, at a cost of £70 p.a., to obtain 'ample supplies of fresh water' from the Hascombe waterworks.[37] The availability of a public water supply inspired the school with an idea for marking the Queen's jubilee in 1887. A fountain was presented to the village, and still stands on the common, its gothic design now much weathered. A big occasion marked its opening, with the school choir singing and the headmaster ceremoniously pushing the knob to obtain a cupful of water, though he found that the pressure was so great that he soaked his surplice instead.[38] Supplies of cold water are refreshing on a hot day, but they do not necessarily solve the problem of cleanliness. The sole provision for bathing at the school had been one plunge bath. 'Plunge bath' seems the most accurate description of its function as a place for a bracing dip rather than a good wash, since soap could not be used, 'nor water changed oftener than weekly'.[39] The Council gave permission in 1885 for the headmaster to investigate possible improvements in bathing conditions.[40] In the end, with the help of some parental contributions, and at a cost of £446 a concrete trough was built next to a large plunge bath which also served as a swimming pool.[41] Even then however even the prefects could only have 'hot water in the bathing trough (on) 2 days a week'.[42] This system remained in operation until after the turn of the century. Batches of boys arrived in the evenings for a bath and a plunge; the water was often left unchanged between one batch of boys and the next.[43] Until the age of 12 or so the little boys were washed by maids – hence their nickname of 'scrubs'. It was undoubtedly a significant moment for them when they could bath themselves, even in the company of a dozen or more boys in the same trough, and under the watchful eyes of the master of the week and a prefect on duty.[44] Since the trough was next to the swimming pool the cult of manliness was given full rein and even on the coldest days boys were required to go from their hot, or warm or tepid bath into the cold swimming pool; in the winter the first boys might have to break the thin layer of ice. Changes only came after the turn of the century. In 1907 new changing rooms were provided, with showers, footbaths and baths, enabling boys to 'change in luxury', although the water was often merely tepid.[45] These were used only after games, and in 1908 the evening arrangements for baths came under attack from the masters:[46]

> 'The crush of more than 20 naked boys in a single trough would shock many a parent were he to witness it. But they must hear of it . . . (We should) enable each boy to have a bath more privately than (is) at present enjoyed . . .'

Changes were made that year. Instead of the trough, nine separate baths were installed, and a hot water system reconstructed throughout the north wing. The plunge still happened at bathtime.[47] There were still occasions when warm water was in short supply.[48] But at least progress had been made, and no doubt health, propriety and cleanliness benefited.

Two of Merriman's old boys deserve some mention in connection with health and hygiene at Cranleigh. One was J. W. Williams, school benefactor and first OC member of the Council. His own son, J. C. Williams, was at Cranleigh from 1897 to 1902. Soon after leaving school, he died of tuberculosis, and this inspired his father to devote much of his time to studying the causes and prevention of disease.[49] In 1907 he made the fruits of his labours available to the boys at his old school. He delivered a series of health lectures.[50] The first was on 'the lungs and how to inflate them': this to combat the disease of consumption. The second was on 'intelligent physical culture' which involved an attack on professional sport, advised the eschewing of 'record breaking as such', and commended a recapture of the 'lost art of walking'. In the third lecture he dealt with 'questions of light, air and food', and denounced the use of 'pickles, hot sauces, sweet jams and drinks'. These were common enough themes in Victorian and Edwardian health culture. A prize winning essay of 1864 had listed as vital for physical fitness some very similar items: wholesome food, exercise, fresh air, rest, cold water and avoidance of 'injurious' foods like condiments.[51] Reading between the lines of the reports on Williams' lectures however, it is probable that his listeners regarded him as something of what a later generation would call a 'health freak'.

The other Merriman old boy also had medical interests; F. S. Brereton was a doctor and a soldier, though he was better known to the general public as a writer of books for boys. In one of these, an adventure set within a school, he describes

Cranleigh. The school was not named but its identity is obvious:[52]

> 'Suffice it to say that it is situated in Surrey, that it projects three parts of the way up a sloping hill, which is bathed by the sun on every side. There is not a musty spot about it, nor a corner nor a crevice in which injurious germs may hide. See it, then, a red-brick pile, clad with creeper, with its clock tower and its chimneys and pinnacles. Cast your eyes upon the surrounding country and admit, as admit you must, that never was there a more ideal position. For the village is a mile away. The school stands beautifully isolated. Fresh breezes sweep direct from plane trees and heather across its roofs and into its windows . . .'

It was a fine panegyric, more true of the school as Allen left it than of the school in F. S. Brereton's own day. Since then, the water had become purer, and sanitation and ventilation had improved. There were more classrooms and better facilities. And yet, at the same time, something had gone wrong, and the school was in decline.

CHAPTER FIVE

Decline (1900–1911)

In Allen's last report to the Council, October 1908, he informed them that 'the number of boys in the school this term was 173 as against 197 last term, which would mean a drop in income of about £250 for the term'.[1] In fact this drop was part of a much longer term decline, as the quinquennial averages show:

1880–84	340 (boys in school per term, on average)
1885–89	332
1890–94	273
1895–99	249
1900–04	233
1905–09	194

Numbers had dropped fairly steadily throughout Allen's headmastership, to almost half what they had been in the best of the Merriman years. On his last Speech Day, Allen tried to explain this phenomenon.[2] He told parents there was not enough money to spend on science teaching: though he maintained that more science teaching went on than they were given credit for. It is interesting that he should have identified this as a convincing reason for decline in numbers, and it reflects a renewed national interest in the inadequacies of public school science teaching. E. C. Mack maintains that in the decade before the war their lack of response to the need for science teaching or to the recommendations of the Bryce Commission or to the challenge of the 1902 Education Act show 'how far behind the times the public schools were slipping'.[3] But Allen argued that the reason for lack of science facilities was rooted in another problem: lack of money. And here was a vicious circle. Income had dropped because fewer boys were coming; fewer boys were coming because of the fee rise of 1894. As 'they foresaw at the time' this was bound to decrease numbers 'somewhat'. It is certainly true that the fee rise of 19%, which was only the second rise in the school's history and which took fees up to £45 p.a., came at a time when rising prices nationally were giving way to falling prices and falling costs.[4] In fact Cranleigh was much cheaper still than most schools; even after rises of 22% in 1911 and 18% in 1915 Cranleigh's fees were still only £75 p.a., as against Blundell's £114, Shrewsbury's £105, Brighton's £99 and Bedford Modern's £90. The increased fee income after 1894 had made possible some necessary work on the drains, though two years after that the Council was blaming falling numbers on the epidemic of that year.[5] Perhaps, indeed, it was somewhat ingenuous of Allen to seek the cause of decline in a fee rise of fourteen years previously. More probably there were other causes at work.

The explanation for the gradual decline around the turn of the century may well lie partly in factors operating nationally. T. W. Bamford notes 'a sudden change in public school growth' at this time, indicating that 'the change in public school vitality happened to coincide roughly with the Education Act of 1902', but he does not elaborate.[6] Certainly between 1901 and 1906 the number of children in maintained secondary schools rose by 136%; it was, as Halevy says, a 'social revolution'.[7] Perhaps a journal of the period was later identifying a trend when it noted: 'We shall be blind if we refuse to admit that the great county council schools will encroach more and more, as the years go on, on the privileges of the public schools'[8] In the wake of the Balfour Act of 1902 Uppingham's parents were warned 'of the consequent disaster if boys in the public schools found themselves left behind by the growing numbers who took advantage of the opportunities offered by the expanding provincial colleges and universities'.[9] And it can be no accident that a year later the Headmasters' Conference which had been founded by an Uppingham headmaster and was 'a league for defence, not a club for exclusion'[10] – took the precaution of introducing the common entrance examination. There is some dramatic evidence that public schools were feeling the draught. No new ones were founded in this period. And a number of 'quasi-public schools' collapsed instead of going on, as they might in an earlier period, to become conventional public schools: Blackheath School, Leamington College and Trinity College, Stratford, all collapsed in 1900–1902, as did the highly successful and academically distinguished Bath College in 1909.[11] And there is evidence too in schools which survived. 'Between 1890 and 1914 several even (of the great) schools suffered periodical shortages of boys'.[12] The phenomenon is evident at a whole range of schools, where there is evidence of falling numbers or smaller entry lists than for the last decade of the 19th century, though in most, but not all cases picking up again in the years before the first world war: at Mill Hill, Oswestry, Queens's (Taunton), Radley, St Edward's (Oxford), Shrewsbury, Tonbridge and Uppingham.[13] Of course in these and other schools all sorts of local factors applied, then and at other times: a weak headmaster, a recent epidemic, a scandal. Schools were extraordinarily sensitive and numbers could drop very quickly, especially in an age when the long term objectives of 'O' and 'A' levels did not serve as incentives for boys to stay. Radley, for instance, suffered periodic and dramatic dips in numbers in the mid 6os, the late 70s, the late 90s, with a long decline after 1908 and a sharp dip in the early 1940s.[14] Cranleigh had generally been more fortunate but by 1908 the problem was obvious. The explanation is less easy to come by. When Bradfield suffered a similar problem a few years later, the headmaster explained to the governors that the factors operating were: a general 'feeling the pinch' among public schools; a lower birth-rate among the middle classes; financial depression and a preference for expenditure on motor cars rather than on education'.[15] At Malvern in the same year the headmaster's theory was that 'it is not so much that fewer boys come to the school as that some boys are taken away earlier than used to be the case. Some parents are made nervous by the financial schemes associated with the name of Mr Lloyd George'. The historian of St Edward's, which experienced its bad times just a few years before Cranleigh, suggests that 'much, but not all, of this could be attributed to the competition from schools of a similar type, which had also used the prosperous eighties as an opportunity for expansion'.[17]

There is hardly enough evidence to allow confident generalizations about the causes of decline, but there are certainly enough indications to cast doubts upon Jonathan Gathorne-Hardy's statement that all was in fact well with the public schools in these years.[18] But certainly at Cranleigh particular factors were at work. Perhaps Allen's very success at giving Cranleigh the marks of a traditional public school had alienated it from some of its original clientele, as much as had the fee rise. The small tradesmen and shopkeepers, as well as the farmers, were not so well represented now among parents. Certainly the population of the south-east was growing; Surrey's increased by 68% in the first half of the century and by 160% in the second half even though during the latter period the northern part had been incorporated into London.[19] But the number of schools for the middle classes had increased as well via new foundations, migrations into the country and the reorganization of old foundations: since the founding of Cranleigh in 1865 parental choice had widened to include: 1872, St John's (Leatherhead) and Charterhouse; 1873, Battersea Grammar School; 1874, Queen Elizabeth Grammar School (Kingston) and Tiffin's (Kingston); 1875, Reigate Grammar School; 1880, Wilson's Grammar School (Camberwell); 1881, Whitgift (Croydon); 1885, Royal Grammar School (Guildford); 1897, King's College School (Wimbledon); 1899, St John's (Leatherhead) and St Saviour's and St Olave's (Southwark). This was an impressive range of choice, especially when one adds to it other established schools like Dulwich and Epsom, or Ardingly and Hurstpierpoint – which were in nearby Sussex and charged low fees.

One category of boy was coming to the school in the early twentieth century in greater numbers than at any time before or since: sons of clergy. Between 1900 and 1909, 46 such boys entered the school: the closest any other period has come to that is 27 for the years 1875–84. The year 1900 saw the incursion of

23, and though the general reason for this might be thought to be the low fees and Church of England correctness of the place, there is in fact a more specific reason. In 1899 one of Cranleigh's benefactors, Sir Cuthbert Peek (whose father had financed the chapel) was winding up the affairs of his brother, the Reverend Edward Peek, who had died in Lyme Regis. Edward Peek had run a small school there, St Michael's, catering for about 40 boys, mostly clergy sons. Sir Cuthbert proposed to transfer the endowment to Cranleigh as the best way of continuing his brother's work.[2] By the spring of 1900 about £2,000, which was less than the governors had hoped for, was made over to Cranleigh from the profit on the sale of the Lyme Regis property. Nineteen boys were also transferred to be educated at a fee of £32 instead of £45.[22] It was a mixed blessing for the school. It brought a temporary and needed infusion of boys, to be educated at low fees but with capital to make up for the loss of full fees; but there was no long term advantage to Cranleigh since the capital sum was not enough to establish an endowment for such a scheme to continue, nor was it likely that the link with Dorset and the west country could be maintained.[23] So despite this filip, the decline in numbers continued, from a temporary peak of 272 in the Lent term of 1900, to 213 in the Lent term of 1905.

In July 1908, when the fall had continued and there was a distinct prospect of numbers falling below 200 for the first time since 1871, G. C. Allen sent in his resignation. He was 53, and proposed to take up work as a parish priest in the living of Send, near Woking. He was retiring, he told parents, because 'he had always felt that 30 years was long enough for a man to be schoolmaster'. He continued, with more optimism than realism, that 'he was quite sure that whoever his successor was he would be a very fortunate man'.[4] Allen must have realized that troubled times lay ahead. Although not a member of the Headmasters' Conference, he must have realized that other schools were experiencing short-falls in numbers. Perhaps, after thirty years as a schoolmaster, he was tired. He lived until 1921; at least that was long enough to see a revival in Cranleigh's fortunes. And at least he could feel pleased that he had given the school those public school characteristics which made it undoubtedly one of the 'public schools of England', and which his successor but one, Rhodes, was to build on. It was partly a tribute to Allen when Rhodes was elected to the Headmasters' Conference in 1916. But for the moment, in 1908, the future looked bleak, despite Allen's public optimism.

The governors sent out about a hundred copies of a circular letter to the colleges of Oxford and Cambridge, and to other schools, advertising the post of Headmaster of Cranleigh School.[25] Only nineteen applications were received, and three men were invited for interview: one layman, an assistant master at St Paul's, and two clergymen, an assistant at King's School, Canterbury, and the headmaster of King Edward's School, Grantham. The headmaster, Keeling, looked most likely, but then the governors had second thoughts and readvertized. This brought in a further 52 applications. From these, their choice fell upon a 41 year old bachelor and layman, C. H. Tyler.[26] He came from a much more distinguished family than had either of his predecessors. His uncle was a brigadier general, his father a major general, and his grandfather had been governor of Victoria, Australia. He himself was an Old Carthusian, who had taken a first in classics at Pembroke, Cambridge. He had taught first at his old school, and then at Rossall where he became a housemaster in 1907. And, as J. W. Williams told his fellow OCs in 1909, 'Mr Tyler came not only with good testimonials for organization and intellectual attainments, but it would be good news to them that he also gained a blue for association football at Cambridge'.[27]

The Christmas holidays of 1908 were hectic ones for Tyler. He moved down from Rossall, pursued his courtship of Helen Hall whom he was soon to marry, and on the day before Christmas eve met with members of the council, who no doubt put him in the picture about the financial position and declining numbers of the school.[28] On 24 January he faced the school in chapel for the first time: the first lay headmaster, if not the first layman, to occupy the pulpit there. And he faced enormous problems within the school. By the end of the Lent term he had identified some crucial ones and explained them to the governors; dingy living rooms for the boys, unsatisfactory bathing arrangements, the 'deplorable' state of the library, the urgent need for new science teaching rooms.[29] The governors, faced at last with some positive suggestions for improvements which might reverse the downward trend in numbers, sanctioned the expenditure of some £600, and also gave the headmaster permission to advertise the school in whatever way he saw fit up to a cost of £25.[30] By the end of the year, the estimates had been raised, and they found themselves committed to an expenditure in excess of £1,100. This covered improvements in ventilation, renewal of classroom furniture, installation of a hot water system in the north wing, reflooring of the entrance hall, provision of more baths and some painting and decorating. In addition the urgent repair of the West roof and clock tower were carried out.[31] But money did not solve all problems. Poor Tyler, his wife now heavily pregnant, faced the departure of three members of staff in the summer of 1909 and discontent among the governors. Tyler had not been in the school eleven months when some were complaining that the expected upswing had not taken place, and in November 1909 one of them demanded an independent examination into 'the standard of education' at the school.[32] In December 1909 there were indications of low morale in the school in general, affecting performance on the games field.[33] Then, just after Christmas, the bursar resigned. The Revd Henry Crawford had been a master for thirty-one years, filling the roles of chaplain, housemaster and latterly bursar. There are no details of what had happened to precipitate his resignation, and illness may have been a contributory factor, but it looks as if he had a major disagreement with the headmaster. The OCs made a great fuss of him and he wrote to them of 'this time when such an awful break in my life has happened'.[34] He departed at the end of the Lent term 1910, and was not to return until he came to preach in 1913, some time after Tyler had left. Departing at the same time as Crawford was the Revd W. S. Borrow who was dismissed –

according to the boys – because of supposed over-indulgence in whisky drinking. When he left, there was a big demonstration of affection for him by the boys of the OTC (of which he was a captain) who fell in to the sound of a trumpet, marched to his study, and presented him with a pipe as a leaving present.[35] In the first four terms of Tyler's headship, six masters had departed; Allen had been able to boast in 1901 that 'only three masters had come and gone' in nine years.[34] By the summer of 1910, in Tyler's fifth term, the governors had become so concerned that they were beginning to contemplate the possibility of the school having to close down.[37] It is difficult to ascertain what they felt the real problem was. Certainly concern was expressed about academic standards, but in the external examiners' reports of December 1910 the only severe criticism was over the absence of good science facilities which the governors were urged to rectify.[38] Tyler had already drawn attention to this and was already engaged in drawing up plans.[38] The school's academic results do not seem to have dropped off,[40] and the usual small number of successes at Cambridge Locals was recorded, and several Cranleighans went up to Oxford and to London, or to the military colleges.[41]

Yet there is a feeling of concern and an undercurrent of agitation in the minute of masters' meetings, and in the notes made by masters of the week. There were continual naggings about the standard of work. Tyler was no 'flogger' in the Allen mould,[42] but was eventually constrained to suggest that boys should be sent to him for a caning if their work was bad.[43] And for the first time in the school's records, suggestions of 'vice' occur. This was not a subject much talked about openly in Victorian or Edwardian times, or much researched or written about until the 1960s. There was an occasional 'disclosure of indecent practices',[44] as at Wellington in 1861–2 but by the last quarter of the century veiled hints and warning were coming thick and fast in sermons and pamphlets. Clement Dukes, the school doctor at Rugby, published an influential book in 1883 on *Health at School*, which contained numerous hints to the authorities on ways of curbing sexuality among their boys.

Probably it was a growing problem, as the age of puberty seems to have been dropping steadily, and as schools such as Cranleigh acquired more older boys, who were therefore more physically mature.[45] No hints in any form however appeared at Cranleigh – or no record has survived – until Tyler's time. One boy later remembered that 'the discipline of the school was poor and morale very low. You can imagine that when I first went, at the age of 11, I was very frightened of certain things that would take place in the dormitories'.[46] And a master of the week, in the year of that boy's arrival, complained of the 'affectionate goodnights' that boys were lingering to wish one another before going up to the dormitories – 'a practice that seems to me an unwholesome one'.[47] There can only have been homosexual overtones, or an 'unwholesome' atmosphere in the school, for the master to react in this way. A year later another master hints similarly. There were often complaints from masters of the week that prefects were failing to turn up for bathtime supervision, but his concern was the opposite: 'on two occasions I have had to turn out of the bath a prefect who had dropped in to witness the bathing – a practice altogether undesirable'.[48] Indeed if this MW had read his Dr Dukes he would have objected to hot baths in the evening altogether, since they were 'capable of serious harm to many a boy by suggesting ideas and feelings which lead to practices that otherwise might never have been originated'.[49]

In the face of this vice (if vice there was) and low morale, Tyler was weak: 'a weak man, and no disciplinarian' as one boy of the time remembers.[35] Perhaps he was simply too liberal for Cranleigh, too much the expansive Old Carthusian. He was remembered at Gresham's, where he later taught, as one who had 'done so much to awaken the appreciation of art in the school', and he served there as President of the Society of Arts, and Librarian.[50] Undoubtedly a civilized man from a civilized background, his instructions to the prefects at Cranleigh were certainly highly enlightened:[51]

> 'To stop all approach to harsh treatment, of the younger by the elder, of the weaker by the stronger . . . to distinguish between

affronts to oneself personally, and offences against school discipline . . . to remember that discipline is maintained not only by
punishment, but also, and mainly, by word and manner . . .
above all to remember that faults to be corrected in others must
be avoided in oneself . . .'

No doubt Tyler was distressed that fagging, which had crept in
during Allen's headship, was 'causing a considerable amount of
hardship to many small boys'.[52] He took steps to curtail it, but
characteristically it took him over a year to sort it out.[53] This
indecisiveness is evident too when problems arose over school
uniform, which also seems to have made its appearance during
Allen's time. Masters objected to non-regulation coats which
were not the required blue or black. The rather tart minute
records that 'the headmaster expressed his opinion in favour of
colour, but no decision was come to, and the subject was
dropped'.[54] And this indecisiveness is recalled by an old boy
who remembers that Tyler 'expelled a boy for a very trivial
thing and when all the boys protested he reinstated him'.[35] The
picture begins to emerge of a man with all the right ideas, and
with a modern approach, but without the personality or deci-
siveness to carry them through, especially at a time when
school morale tended to be low as numbers continued to fall.

There were 168 boys at Cranleigh when Tyler arrived; in the
summer of 1910 the number had sunk to 154 – an all-time low.
Ironically there was something of an upswing in Tyler's final
term, which the new headmaster was able to cash in on – and
maintain.[55] In September 1910, with 157 boys in the school, the
governors set up a special sub-committee to investigate the
whole problem. They produced a very detailed report – unfortunately now lost.[56] A further small committee of three was
appointed, Lord Devonport having been called in to lend his
weight to the search for a way forward.[57] Its report is lost, but
evidently it decided that there must be a change of headmaster.
At the beginning of May, 1911, the Council considered the
report and resolved that it be shown to the headmaster.[58] On 5
May, having seen the report, Tyler sent in his resignation. On
15 May the governors stated, in a delicately phrased minute

which the headmaster received,[59]

> '. . . that while in view of the present position of the school it is necessary to make certain changes including the appointment of a Clerical Headmaster they cannot accept Mr Tyler's resignation without expressing their full appreciation of the efforts which he has made to improve the discipline and tone of the school and of his conscientious discharge of duties during the period of his Headmastership'.

There was no Speech Day that year. The school magazine recorded the departure of the Headmaster with a few polite words, after a much longer piece recording the coronation of George V. The same edition of the magazine was able to record, in some detail, the name and accomplishments of the new headmaster who was appointed before the end of the summer term.[60] Within a few weeks Tyler had vacated the headmaster's house. Within a year he had found a new job, as an assistant master at Gresham's. He remained there until 1930, then retired to Canterbury and latterly to Somerset where he died in 1945.[61] There is no record that he ever visited Cranleigh again.

CHAPTER SIX

Revival and Advance
(1911–1931)

EARLY IN JULY 1911, a fortnight after the coronation of George V and a few weeks before the departure of Tyler, the school council met to interview candidates for the post of headmaster.[1] There is no indication of how many applications had been received but a sub-committee had narrowed the choice down to three, all clerics: one was an assistant master at Lancing, and another at Cheltenham; the third candidate was headmaster of Ardingly. The governors went for this man, who had already proven his abilities as a headmaster, the Revd Herbert A. Rhodes, a bachelor of 42. The son of the headmaster of Uttoxeter Grammar School, he had been a boy at Shrewsbury under H. W. Moss. In 1888 he went up to Christ Church, Oxford, where he gained a football blue and captained the university team in 1892. He went on to teach at Felsted, Giggleswick and Christ's Hospital, and was ordained in 1899. For seven years he had been headmaster of Ardingly where he presided over 'one of the most important and successful periods' of its history.[2] Undoubtedly his reputation had reached the Cranleigh governors: he was a disciplinarian; his eyes were 'quick to penetrate the secret hiding-places of a boy's heart and mind'.[3] At Ardingly he had overhauled the time-table, given the prefects more authority and treated them as adults, and had been active in 'searching out anything that called for reform – or destruction'.[4] He had acquired the nickname of 'Searchlights' because of his prominent eyes and penetrating glance, and the name followed him to Cranleigh.

This small man, with a large personality, might just be the person Cranleigh needed. In the summer of 1911 he arrived at the school, accompanied by his elder sister Flo who was to reign with him as consort throughout the twenty years of his headship.

But in 1911 it was not at all clear to Rhodes that his tenure was certain to be a long one. The conditions of appointment included the usual one term's notice on either side and Rhodes sought – though does not appear to have received – a guarantee that if he carried on the school successfully his position would be guaranteed for three years.[5] He soon discovered, if he did not already know, that 'it was going to be a very difficult task to keep Cranleigh School alive'.[6] His own alma mater, Shrewsbury, had been a school of under 250 in his day, and he probably knew that it had experienced a decline in numbers in the early years of the century. Ardingly too had been a small school. Possibly the tide had already turned at Cranleigh but Rhodes immediately set about making certain of it. By the end of his first term he was clear about some of the needs of the school,[7] and fortunate enough to experience a significant vote of confidence from benefactors. The first sign of advance out of the doldrums was the offer from Sir Charles Chadwyck Healey, council member and patron of the local parish church, to fund the building of much needed science laboratories. Tyler had hoped from the beginning of his headship that such an advance would be possible; within a year of Rhodes' arrival, it was completed. The new buildings contained physics and chemistry laboratories, a lecture theatre and store rooms. They were built in the same neo-Tudor style as the main school buildings, and were opened in July 1912 by Sir William Ramsay, a Nobel prizewinner and discoverer of various inert gases. One OC who was present remembers that his last remarks to the boys were 'don't watch the clock and always give a little more than is expected of you'[8]. But his speech was not really the important feature of the day; what was significant was the great vote of confidence in the new headmaster and in the future of Cranleigh. The Lord Chief Justice, Lord Alverstone, who had been

Aerial view of Cranleigh School, 1982

1 Sixth Form Centre
2 Loveday House
3 1 North House
4 Headmaster's House
5 Speech Hall
6 Workshops
7 Chapel
8 Laboratories
9 Golf Course
10 Main Gate
11 Preparatory School

Marc van Hasselt,
Headmaster since 1970,
looking forward in 1982
to his last few years at
the helm

Dr Joseph Merriman, Headmaster 1865-1892,
with his staff in 1875

The Earl of Midleton, the Duke
of Connaught (centre) and the
Revd H.A. Rhodes, Headmaster
1911-31, at the Jubilee Speech Day,
July 1925

Bishop Loveday, Headmaster 1931-195
sitting beneath his portrait and greeting
one of his old boys, September 1980

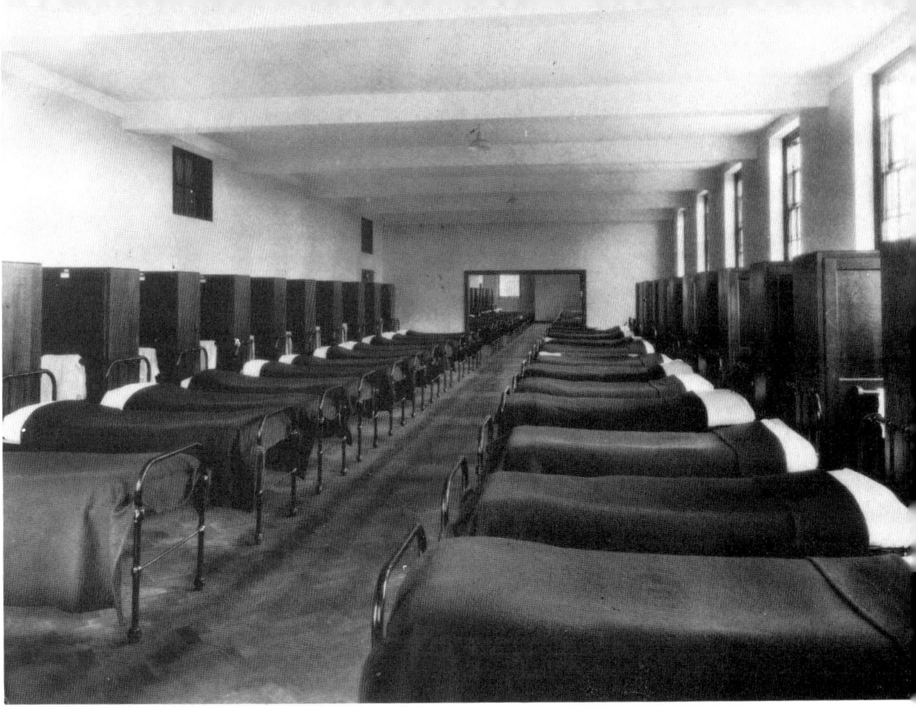

Dormitory containing beds for the whole house in the Connaught Block, opened in 1929; since sub-divided into studies and bedsits.

New-style living in the 1980s: a bedsit at the Sixth Form Centre created out of farm buildings and opened in 1972

A houseroom in the Connaught Block, 1930s

The social area in Loveday House, opened in 1981

The First XV in 1923

Cafeteria lunch in 1981; three previous Headmasters, Emms,
Rhodes and Loveday, look down on the scene from the back wall
(Reproduced by courtesy of *The Guardian*)

Michael Redgrave, a master at the school, taking the lead in his own production of *King Lear* in June 1934

A house play in May 1980: 1 North's production of Tim Rice and Andrew Lloyd Webber's *Joseph and the Amazing Technicolour Dreamcoat*

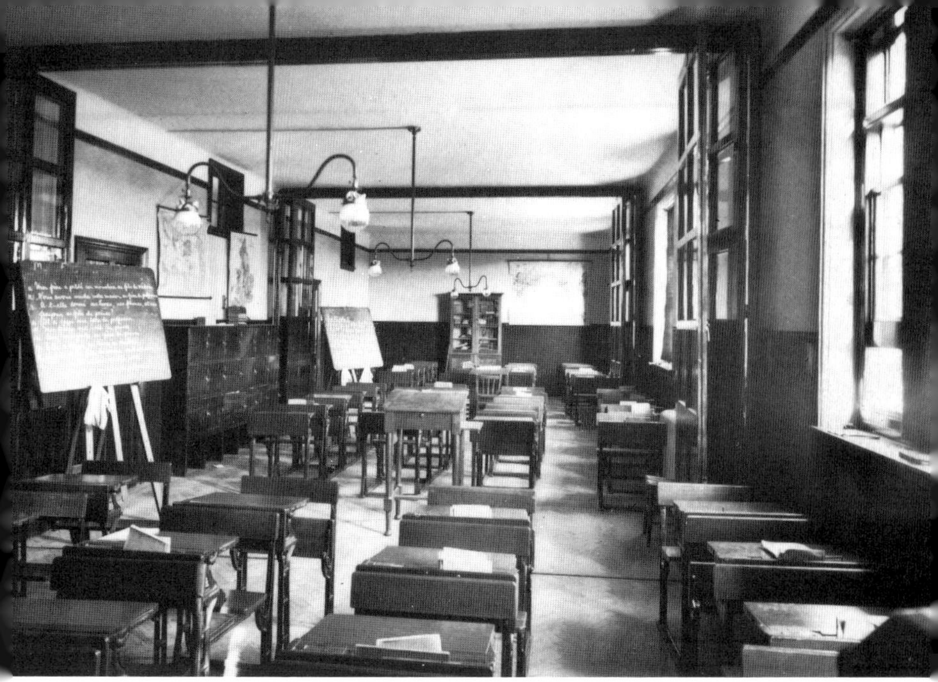

A classroom in the Preparatory House, as it was called when opened in 1912

The Second Master, K.S.G. Wills, taking a class in a laboratory in the new Physics Block, 1981

Cricket on the Common in the early 1920s

The new 'multigym' in 1982

up at Trinity with Cubitt, was present as were the Bishops of Winchester and Guildford, Lord and Lady Devonport, and the Surrey notables Sir Charles Bonham and Pandeli Ralli.[9] The opening was followed by a normal speech day, at which Rhodes was able to point to other signs of progress as well.

The other great venture which he had promoted during his first term at Cranleigh was the provision of a purpose-built preparatory school. At speech day 1912 he was able to announce the purchase of 17 acres of land opposite the main school gates and, noting that this 'comfortably rounded off the view', expressed the hope that benefactors would be found to enable the building of a Preparatory House. No Peek came forward on this occasion, but nevertheless the council decided to go ahead with the project.[10] It was decided to raise £11,500 by mortgage, of which £900 would pay for the land recently acquired, £7,000 would pay for the proposed building, £700 would covering the furnishing of it and the balance would be used to pay off existing mortgages, lay out the North Field for games and improve the sanitary arrangements at the school.[11] By April 1913 the architect was able to report that work on the new buildings was progressing well, and it looked as if the builders would finish within the contract time – the beginning of the new academic year. There was frenetic activitiy on the site during the summer months; workmen were active from 6.00 a.m. until 9.30 p.m. each day towards the end of the summer holidays, and the 'New House' was ready for occupation at the beginning of the Michaelmas term 1913, less than a year after the decision to build had been taken.[12] It was a fine building, a trifle gaunt perhaps at the top of the hill facing the main school, with its fresh red brick unsoftened as yet by any plants or flowers round about. But it was well fitted and furnished – certainly in the following years it was to prove invaluable in building up, and keeping up, the numbers in the school as a whole. The man who presided over the move to the new buildings, and the expansion of the new 'House', or 'Preparatory House' as it came to be called after 1916, was the Revd R. H. C. Mertens. He was one of Rhodes's first appointments, and remained as 'Master' of the preparatory school until 1934.[13] He was a high churchman like Rhodes, who devoted much time to the Cranleigh end of the school mission organization. He had a sister who was an Anglican nun at Wantage, and a cousin who was a member of the Community of the Resurrection. It was this cousin, Father Eustace, who gave confession to the young and devout Colin Stephenson, a senior school boy who later, himself a priest, became the Guardian of the Shrine of Our Lady of Walsingham. After confession, Stephenson was subjected to a lecture on birth control which was something of a pet hate of Father Eustace. He was given some pamphlets on the subject and then remembers: 'I experienced such relief (after confessing) that I can remember running down the hill from the junior school and several times jumping in the air from sheer light-heartedness'.[14] He was brought down to earth however, when his housemaster discovered anti-birth control pamphlets in his possession. Mertens does not seem to have offered auricular confession to his boys, but he certainly subjected them to a fair frequency of corporal punishment. He refined a system which he thought suitable for dealing with small boys: a system of 'Charlies'. Offences were totted up in the course of the day, which ended with a beating on pyjamaed bottoms in the dormitory by a clothes brush known as 'Charlie'.[15] Mertens, one of Rhodes's main props during his years as headmaster, is immortalized in some Heath Robinson drawings in the Prep School.[16]

Rhodes had seen the needs of the school under three main heads – buildings, land and finance. The new science labs and the prep school met his first point. Generous donors again helped to meet his second. Hugh Cubitt bought the land at the back of the school which had come on the market, though it had been rented and utilized by the school for some time. This land, the North Field, was then given over to the Council – another astonishing example of his generosity, and a particularly important one at this time when it served as another vote of confidence in the future of a school which had recently seemed to come so near to closure.[7] In 1912 the St Andrew's Fields –

behind the church on the common which was demolished in the 1970s – were leased and laid out with money from the OCs; in 1913 the fields lying to the west of 'Sanny Lane' were purchased, later to be known as the Sanny and Clare's Oak pitches.[17] So Rhodes's second objective, the acquisition of land and consolidation of the school estate, was well on the way to realization. His third objective was finance. Despite generosity of benefactors, the school needed resources to help pay for some of this land, and the repairs and improvements which Rhodes considered urgent. Perhaps one of the most important decisions during Rhodes's early years relates to fees. They had been raised by 22% in 1911 and now stood at £55 p.a. A survey by the governors in 1915 however revealed that Cranleigh still lagged behind comparable schools, and indeed it is interesting to see what schools were regarded as comparable: Aldenham £71, Berkhamsted £65, Epsom £78, King's, Canterbury £85.50, St John's, Leatherhead £88.50.[18] The council took the plunge again and put up the fees by 18% in 1915, and by 15% in 1918, and by 24% in 1920. These rises just kept ahead of the price rise which had come to England with the war, after a long period of relatively stable prices. And the school felt no deleterious effects, for indeed numbers rose. In January 1912 there were 168 boys in the school; by December 1914 there were 287, and following the 1920 fee rise there were 365.

At the Old Cranleighan dinner in January 1914 the chairman was the Revd Thomas Layng, who had been second master at Cranleigh in the 1880s, had gone on to a headship and was now Chaplain at Clifton. He was a man whom Canon Peter Green praised highly for his enormous and beneficent influence on boys,[19] and indeed it is interesting that he now made as a keynote of his speech 'the intimate friendship and the easy familiarity between master and master and between master and boy' which had characterized Cranleigh. His speech, and that of the headmaster in reply, were not merely full of the usual platitudes but – on this occasion – breathed a feeling of confidence.[20] Cranleigh was on the up again, and Rhodes was 'full of enthusiasm' for its present and its future. And as Rhodes well knew, the council and management committee minutes were now filled with schemes and plans for improvements, upon which the governors were looking favourably. The change over less than three years had been remarkable, and was the result of a number of factors. One was the increasing numbers of boys – something that looked set to happen anyway during the last few terms of the Tyler regime. As in the decline in numbers, so with this revival: a lot of other schools seem to have had the same experience. The fee rises meant that the school continued to move up-market in its clientele, a development evident in the 1890s and early 1900s: the difference now was that there seems to have been no shortage of clients, in itself a vote of confidence in the school. Another factor was the generosity of benefactors – the OCs, Chadwyck Healey and Cubitt; this in turn stimulated greater confidence within the governing body and a willingness to spend not only money that had been given but also money raised by mortgage. But perhaps the factor which should be the main focus in attempting to explain Cranleigh's revival in these years must be the headmaster himself. Rhodes seems to have succeeded, within a very short space of time, in projecting confidence, enthusiasm and a sense of security – all of which had been lacking in the Tyler years. At the OC Dinner of 1914, breathing confidence, Rhodes 'referred to the jubilee of the School in 1915 and expressed the hope that Whit-Monday of that year would witness the largest assemblage of OCs that Cranleigh had ever seen'.[20]

Of course it was not to be. In the last hot July days before war broke out a Cranleighan in London wrote of his longing:[21]

> 'To see the hills fade in the fading light
> From Hascomb round to Winterfold.
> High over Gatley's trees the evening star
> Burns white. Yet still the clanging bell will jar
> Too soon upon this peace'.

Little did he know how significant those words were soon to become. No-one knew, not Rhodes at the OC dinner, nor that Cranleighan in the city in June, nor the boys at the school:[22]

'During that summer term of 1914 before the war the weather seemed to be always fine, with cricket on the Jubilee and matches on the Common. The clouds of war were gathering but I think that most of us at first regarded the trouble in Serbia as just a third Balkan war . . .'

When the school returned in September, three of the masters were already on active service, and three weeks later came news of the first OC to be killed, Lieutenant Colonel Percy Maclear, aged 39. He was the first of many. And for the boys at school there were to be ever present reminders of the conflict: names published of casualties; photographs of the fallen hung in the chapel corridor; the 'Last Post' sounded each evening by the main doors. More masters went off to serve, including J. S. Purvis, one of Cranleigh's most versatile masters who was to return, with his health much impaired, after the war. He it was who wrote a poem, published anonymously in the *Daily News*, which Ernest Raymond claims seems 'to capture an English soldier's native patriotism with simpler or more perfect words than any other lines'.[23]

'I can't forget the lane that goes from Steyning to the Ring
In summer time, and on the downs how larks and linnets sing
High in the air. The wind comes off the sea, and, oh, the air!
I never knew till now that life in old days was so fair.
But now I know it in this filthy rat-infested ditch,
Where every shell must kill or spare, and God alone knows
    which,
And I am made a beast of prey, and this trench is my lair –
My God, I never knew till now that those days were so fair,
And we assault in half-an-hour, and its a silly thing:
I can't forget the lane that goes from Steyning to the Ring.'

Purvis was also something of an artist, and his sketch book of ink drawings contains two scenes which seem to capture the transition from peace to war. One shows the trees and roofs and pinnacles of Cranleigh School on a tranquil autumn evening in 1913; the other shows a stretch of the western front and is dated 15 September 1916, the day on which tanks first appeared on the western front and one of which figures in the scene.

School life, as the war progressed, was affected by inconveniences rather than anything more dramatic, though there was the occasion when a Zeppelin passed over on the way to raid the gunpowder factory at Chilworth in 1915.[22] The domestic routine was altered when the possibility of such raids meant that the school had to lie in darkness at night – though since there was no electric light as yet, the arrangements were not so complicated as they were to become in the second world war. In 1915 the master of the week recorded rather tartly that 'Saturday night's bathing was a little difficult as it is impossible to bath without such necessities as towels, lights and water'.[25] We may be sure that the boys did not feel too put out by this particular problem. Food rationing was a more serious matter, though it did not affect the school until 1917.[26] Vegetables grown on part of the North Field helped to supplement the wartime diet. Much needed kitchen improvements however were delayed because the effort and materials were required by the Ministry of Munitions.[27] So the war years passed, and the pictures in the chapel corridor accumulated, and the obituaries in the school magazine grew more numerous. In one of those hot summers before war broke out, the Cranleigh OTC had paraded before King George V in Windsor Great Park, and the boys had rather disgraced themselves on the way home by emptying their water bottles over a particularly objectionable porter at Guildford station.[28] Now many of those same boys were at war in earnest. So were some of the boys and many of the OCs who read in the first wartime school magazine that those who were not old enough yet need have no fear, for the war would last long enough and 'we shall have an opportunity of showing our patriotism'.[29] All too many died. The final total was large for so small a school. In all, 803 Cranleighans had served in the forces, which was probably at least one third of all Cranleighans alive at the time. Of those, 133 were killed; 108 decorations were won, and 57 OCs were mentioned in dispatches. Fifteen of those killed left Cranleigh after the outbreak of war.[30] Among those honoured was Major-General Sir Charles Townshend, awarded the DSO and the KCB, some compensation for the misfortunes he suffered (or was responsible for) under General Nixon in Mesopotamia.[31] Notable too was R. W. H. Moline, son of an OC and a master at Cranleigh before the war, who was twice wounded, taken prisoner, mentioned in dispatches, awarded the MC – and who became Archbishop of Perth in 1947. Humbler men served as well: four of the five Northover brothers fought and three returned wounded. Four members of the Norris family served; two never came back. To commemorate them all the school set up a war memorial fund. In July 1921 Field Marshal Sir William Robertson unveiled the stone pillar donated by Lord Devonport and erected outside the main school doors; it dominated the main drive, and was inscribed with the names of the fallen. The school magazine greeted the appearance of Cranleigh's own 'cenotaph' in words which do somewhat suggest that these 'memorials were designed and dedicated with overtones of paganism and Arthurian romance rather than of Christianity'.[32] 'So commemorated here they stand', declared *The Cranleighan:*[33]

> 'the good, the bad – now equal beyond the reach of praise or blame. What they might have been or what ambitions to become they held, they took with them. This is the fulfilment ordained for them. But this we know: here is not one who has not sealed for ever his affection for this place and his willing sacrifice to make possible a greater Cranleigh. In the commemoration of our benefactors these are not forgotten. For here is not one who did not show the love than which there is no greater'.

So a war begun in excitement and emotion was remembered with emotion. Cranleigh joined in the mourning of the nation; six months earlier, with similar emotions but with greater pomp, the nation had laid to rest the 'unknown soldier' in Westminster Abbey. 'They buried him among the Kings'; he may have been a Cranleighan.

While the war was still in progress an event took place within the school which was to have a profound effect on its whole future. 'We are actually playing the despised Rugby', the school magazine declared.[34] As far back as 1896 'a Rugby Fifteen got together by the masters did battle with a school team and, after an interesting game, suffered defeat by eleven points to six'.[35] The man who now worked the change from football to rugby was J. G. Fawcus who had been a master at the school since 1912, was a considerable sportsman himself and founded the Cryptics Cricket Club.[36] He ran the school cricket and was aided in introducing rugby by a young man who arrived at Cranleigh in January 1916, the term rugger started – L. C. Gower. It was he who became 'the architect of Cranleigh rugger'.[37] Gathorne-Hardy describes him as 'an ex-Welsh International of "meagre – indeed non-existent scholastic attainments"'.[38] It is not true that he was an ex-Welsh international though he had played for the university seniors while up at Downing, Cambridge, which he left without having taken his degree: so it is true that he was no great academic. *The Cranleighan* obituary actually, if somewhat tastelessly, poked fun at his teaching:[39]

> '. . . he used to demonstrate the difference between rotation and revolution of the earth by standing on a desk with a small globe, passing it round the electric light and turning the globe at the same time. Charles almost invariably got muddled as to which was rotation and which was revolution.'

Another ex-pupil remembered his 'struggling to keep ahead in his instruction in geography, English and arithmetic'. His classes were sometimes enlivened by his accusations that some unsuspecting youngster had 'broken wind'[40] which perhaps helps to explain why Rhodes referred to him as being 'a little on the "rough" side'.[41] Whatever he lacked in social graces and scholastic attainment he made up for in skill as a rugger coach. On most afternoons, after lunch, he presided over the ritual of games organization.[42] Everyone was designated 'white' or 'blue' (for the shirt they would wear) and told which pitch to go to. The only exceptions were those who were NTC, or 'not to change' on medical grounds: 'scrimshankers', Gower tended to call them. While the lesser mortals went off to play their rugger under less experienced coaches, Gower himself presided over the top game. The pace he set was relentless: scrum practice after morning school; afternoons on St Andrews with Gower himself (only 26 when he arrived at Cranleigh) instructing, cajoling and occasionally praising. E. W. Swanton has described Gower's creed: '"simple things well done – and at speed"; the perfect giving and taking of passes, incessant backing-up, relentless pressure'.[43] Under Gower Cranleigh made use of a seven forward pack,[44] except on one notorious occasion when in a game against Blundell's Cranleigh began a man short. It was found at the end of the game that two separate replacements had been sent on leading to a Cranleigh 16-man victory. The school magazine commented: 'It was the one topic of conversation all through the holidays . . . The miserable thing must have set all England on the guffaw'.[45] From 1916 until he left in 1931, Gower trained first fifteens which won 109 of the 165 matches they played, scoring 4029 points to 1709 scored against them. Only in very recent times has the record been equalled: the most successful rugger quinquennium in Cranleigh's history was in fact 1971–75 when B. D. Gowen's training led to an almost 80% success rate, compared with just over 70% successes in Gower's first five years. Results tailed off in the twenties. During Gower's last five years the success rate was less than 60%; he had seen this coming and thought that 'the standard of Rugger has improved all round in the Public Schools' and he could not refrain from adding, 'especially in schools where a holiday is given for beating us'.[46] But what has never been equalled, since the 1920s, is the high scoring, the success of individuals especially after they had left school, and the heights of enthusiasm about the game within the school.

High scoring was a feature of the early years. In one season – 1920–21 – the first fifteen scored 524 points in 13 matches, with only 89 scored against them: and their opponents included the Harlequins, Sandhurst A team, Mill Hill, the OCs, London Welsh A team, Epsom and Downside. Only the Harlequins beat them by the narrow margin 13–15. In 1919, King's, Wimbledon was beaten 136–0; in 1921, St John's, Leatherhead fell to Cranleigh 60–0. So naturally Cranleigh began to see its old boys make good in the world of rugby, and from 1933 to

1937 'the Old Cranleighans were the most successful Old Boys side'.[47] This success was stimulated by the raising of £8,000 and the opening of a sports ground and club house at Thames Ditton, a ceremony performed by the President of the Rugby Football Union, Vice-Admiral Royds. It was at a boom time for club rugby. In the twenties, 231 clubs were formed, 78 of these in the south east; in the thirties another 121 were added.[48] It was particularly popular among old public school boys, and over 50% of the England players in the inter-war years were from such schools: little wonder it has been called 'an exclusively middle class sport'.[48] Cranleighans were well represented among that number and the record is impressive:

M. A. McCanlis	E	1914–24*	International	1931		
M. S. Bona-ventura	1N	1916–20	International	1931		
H. P. Jacob	1N	1917–22	International	1924	1930	
A. Key	1N	1917–27*	International	1930	1933	
C. W. Suter	W	1924–28	Trial Cap	1936		
S. R. Couchman	2N	1924–31*	Trial Caps	1935	1936	1938
F. J. Reynolds	1 & 4	1926–33*	International	1937	1938	
C. O'N. Wallis	1 & 4	1927–32	International	1935	(Ireland)	

* denotes attendance at Prep School, hence long time span at Cranleigh. In addition, 53 OCs played for counties in the half century after 1919, though mainly in the pre-war years. It was a fine record, and one that did not go unrecorded in the press thanks to the journalistic activities of one very loyal OC, E. W. Swanton.

But there was another side to the story. If the high scoring and the OC successes mark off those days from a later period, so too does the emphasis on and enthusiasm for rugger within the school. It has been claimed that the dominance of team sport in public schools was just beginning to fade in the 1920s; this was certainly untrue of Cranleigh. In the organization of the school, in its reputation in the world at large, in the conversation of boys and the respect they accorded to or withheld from one another, and most especially in the memory of old boys and in their vision of what school was about, rugby in the 1920s played a role neither it nor any other game had achieved before or has achieved since or – we might predict – will ever achieve again. There is something never to be recaptured in the simple *Boys' Own Paper* emphasis on team spirit, sportsmanship, and winning that soaks so much of the rhetoric and colours so much of the memory of the 1920s. And the other side was put by one boy in 1930 who made the plaintive cry, 'I am certain a time comes when everyone here, whatever his Rugger status, becomes heartily sick of the game.'[49] The headmaster, for all his fondness for games and his sombre-suited presence at every first fifteen match, had declared long before the advent of rugger that 'while he yielded to no one in his keenness for other things, they must keep work on the top'.[50] This was greeted by cries of 'hear, hear' from a generation of OCs less dedicated to the cult of sport than later generations were to become. Indeed such was the tenor of some popular journalism about the school's rugger that the school magazine was constrained to protest in 1926, no doubt with Rhodes's blessing, that 'if an impression exists that . . . the School pays an excessive attention to games, then the sooner that impression is corrected, clearly, definitely, and once and for all, the better for us'.[51] By the end of 1930, when Rhodes's own time at Cranleigh was drawing to a close, he set about gently easing Charles Gower out: 'I do rather feel that a change would be good for him perhaps as well as for us'.[41] Gower was just 40 when he left; curiously he received no fond farewells in the school magazine and it was not until 1964, when he died, that he was written up there as 'the architect of Cranleigh rugger'.

But if it was rugger which gave Cranleigh greater national prestige, it was the advent of new buildings towards the end of Rhodes's headship which gave the necessary space for expansion, better facilities and the accommodation to match its enhanced standing and higher fees. It was a time when the middle classes were experiencing 'something of a golden age'[52] and this helped to keep the school full, but necessitated an expansion of facilities to meet the rising expectations of the parents who sent their sons. On a salary of about £400–£500, which was a modest middle class income, a family could probably afford a house of its own, a car, new electrical appliances such as vacuum cleaners, and a slightly higher income could pay for a servant or two, and for a son's education at public school.[52] For comparison, it is worth noting that it was a good time for schoolmasters as well: Rhodes was earning £1,400, the bursar £800 and the average master about £600. Despite the rather spartan life-style of the boys in the school,[53] there is an air of confidence and prosperity about mid-twenties Cranleigh. And the governors were alive to the mood. They spent £1,176 in 1924 on conversion of two houses on the common as masters' accommodation.[54] In 1925 they raised the fees from £115 to £135. But they also took a far greater decision: to borrow the sum of £30,000 in order to provide new dormitory and house room areas and to make other improvements.[55] The projected expenditure soon rose to £50,000, and the services of an architect were engaged in 1926 to realize the plans. They chose Sir Edwin Cooper, an old acquaintance of Lord Devonport, who had been chairman of the Port of London Authority when Cooper was engaged to design its headquarters building; he had also designed two premises for the Devonport School of Pathology and Nurses' Home at Greenwich. Lord Devonport agreed to pay his fees, and further agreed to add a speech hall to the proposed plans. The project involved doubling the length of the school's frontage by adding a whole new block in Neo-Georgian style. It was to join the old buildings on the west side, linking up with a revitalized servants' block which lay just to the west of the dining hall. This new range of buildings would include dormitories, houserooms and changing facilities and to its west (and, in the end, slightly apart) were to be speech hall and a headmaster's house.[56] Then another benefactor stepped forward, Mr J. W. Williams: he offered the money to re-model the classrooms on either side of the main entrance hall: the beams there were to be encased in plaster (creating a slightly curious barrel-ceiling effect) and the rooms furnished with some fine shelving, to create a library and reading room.[57] Another benefactor, the Earl of Midleton (formerly Brodrick) offered new entrance gates to replace the rather agricultural ones then in position.

Another area that needed attention was the chapel. This was important to Rhodes, who was a high churchman, and during whose regime the services were more ritualistic than before or since; a red sanctuary lamp glowed before the altar, always a sign of fairly 'advanced' churchmanship. As soon as he arrived at Cranleigh Rhodes introduced fully choral communion services which took place on most saints' days on many Sundays.[58] It was a much used building with two services daily, and in addition holy communion on Sundays and saints' days. An incomplete Hedgeland organ had been installed in chapel as far back as 1869; Hedgeland, a London organ builder, had a son at the school. Not until 1875 was the instrument completed; it had cost just over £600.[59] In 1896 it was improved by the addition of a 'pneumatic machine for lightening the touch', with an 'hydraulic machine for blowing purposes'.[60] The hydraulic blower had to be supplemented on big occasions by the services of shirt-sleeved boys manning the handle. In 1924 a new Director of Music arrived, Maurice Allen, 'an organist of outstanding ability'[61] who was to become director of music at Wellington in 1937. Given Allen's arrival and the centrality of chapel services to the life of the school, it was natural that amid the expansionist enthusiasm of these years Rhodes should propose a new chapel organ, which the governors sanctioned if it were paid for by voluntary subscriptions.[62] Appeals were launched, and in 1927 Purvis arranged a Pageant on the south field. This involved hundreds of boys as well as girls from St Catherine's, and £200 was raised towards the required £2,000. Despite hopes that the new organ would be ready in time for the opening of the new buildings, it was not until July 1930 that it was ready for dedication by the Assistant Bishop of Jamaica; the old Hedgeland was sold for £160 to the parish church at Longdon, near Tewkesbury.[62] The new instrument was powered by electricity, which had reached Cranleigh village in February 1929 and was supplied to the school in the course of that summer.

By August 1929, although the organ was not complete, most

of the building work and alterations had been finished. As well as the new block, library and reading room and gates there was a new armoury, a refrigeration plant in the kitchen, and electric light throughout the school. And in the midst of all the building the governors had sanctioned some salary increases for masters and for the school doctor, and within a year were to launch a scholarship scheme costing £290 p.a., the top scholarship being worth just under half fees.[63] At the end of 1929 a small fee rise came into operation raising fees from £135 to £145.[64] The total cost of the improvements was in the region of £90,000.[65] And Speech Day, on 3 August 1929, saw the grand opening of the new buildings by Lord Davidson of Lambeth, recently retired from the Archbishopric of Canterbury. The great new range of buildings, with a 'high standard of finish . . . more American than English'[66] was named the Connaught Building after HRH the Duke of Connaught, Queen Victoria's third son, who had first visited the school in 1880 and who on his second visit for the Diamond Jubilee speech day in 1925 had permitted his name to be associated with the proposed buildings.[67] It was a great day for the school, which had come a long way since that gathering of notables at the opening of the new science block seventeen years before. It was a day, Lord Midleton declared, 'which seems to mark the final step in the development of a local school with a modest outlook into one of the great public schools'.[68] There had in fact been many such days: there had been the opening of the chapel amid a great crowd of dignitaries in 1869; there had been the advances of Allen's time including the grant of the school charter and the gradual development at Cranleigh of all the characteristics of the typical public school; there had been the opening of the prep school and the laboratories in 1912/13 which seemed to mark a new beginning for the school; there had been the election of Rhodes to the Headmasters' Conference in 1916, an event which passed almost unnoticed amid the calamities of the Great War; there had been the growing fame of Cranleigh's rugby. Moreover there had been the development of Cranleigh's catchment area, as 'after the First World War the history of central Surrey became set on a new course'[69] with more migration from London, and the growth of what later came to be called 'commuter-land'. Almost half the parents now described themselves as managing directors or company secretaries, and nearly 60% of the boys lived in London or Surrey. The population of Surrey alone now stood at one million; it had been a quarter of a million when the school was founded, and just over half a million at the turn of the century; and it was no longer a population dominated by farmers and small tradesmen.

It was a fitting moment for Rhodes to contemplate resignation; he could survey a headmastership which, despite the First World War, had been a time of almost uninterrupted progress at Cranleigh. He was now over 60, with time to undertake a second career as a parish priest at Kingston, near Lewes in Sussex. He remained there until 1944 and died in 1956. He had lived long enough to see his successor retire from the headship and to visit the school in the time of his successor's successor, who had been born while Rhodes was Headmaster of Ardingly. In the autumn of 1930 the governors accepted Rhodes's resignation, 'with deep appreciation of the great work he has done during the 20 years he has been Headmaster'.[70] A few months later they appointed his successor, another Salopian who was also a bachelor and a cleric, but who was nearly half Rhodes's age. And at Cranleigh – as indeed in Britain – a new era began.

CHAPTER SEVEN

The Life of a Schoolboy
(1919–1929)

CRANLEIGH IN THE TIME OF RHODES grew and progressed; rugby flourished, and new buildings were planned. Occasionally the world outside impinged: during the First World War, or the influenza epidemic of 1918, or the 1926 General Strike, or the Great Depression which began in 1929. But for the schoolboy, then as now, great events outside the walls of school were of less significance than the routine of the place, the day to day pattern of events and routines, mild excitements and occasional dramas. Writing of his fictional 'Bamfylde School', R. F. Delderfield notes that 'now and again, of course, she was jolted out of her complacency . . . But as soon as the bell rang the inner rhythm of the place would assert itself'.[1] As at inter-war Bamfylde, so at Cranleigh. It is the 'inner rhythm' of the place and the routine and life style of the ordinary schoolboy which concern us here. The modern generation feels perhaps that it knows the story already, from Delderfield's *To Serve them All my Days* or from James Hilton's *Goodbye Mr Chips* or even from the yarns of Frank Richards. Even the stories of Billy Bunter tell us what a public schoolboy looked like, what he did, the language he used; George Orwell summed it up:[2]

> 'You are at Greyfriars, a rosy-cheeked boy of fourteen in posh tailor-made clothes, sitting down to tea in your study on the Remove passage after an exciting game of football which was won by an odd goal in the last half-minute . . .'

But it is all highly romanticized; and the ambience, in terms of the clientele if not of the masters and housemaster, is that of the

100

grand school. The average public schoolboy of the nineteen twenties neither sat in tailor-made clothes nor sat in a study. The truth is more mundane. What was life actually like for a schoolboy at an ordinary boarding school? And such is the continuity and, in the past at least, the conservatism of such institutions that we might be speaking of the 1890s or even the 1940s as much as of the 1920s.[3]

The new boy probably travelled to school by train. He was about 13 years old, for the entry age had now settled at around that age. He had successfully negotiated Common Entrance, though that was not difficult to do in the twenties if the school had any beds which needed to be filled. He wore his bowler hat for travelling, and a neck-chafing Eton collar, with a blue serge suit or dark jacket. Catching the train at Waterloo, he was one among many boys milling round the London stations in mid-September, some of whom wore even more distinctive school uniforms, and all the new boys – whatever school they were heading for – feeling apprehensive about public school life, which they knew only from the pages of *The Magnet* or *Tom Brown's Schooldays*. If the Cranleighan had been to the 'House' then the route to Cranleigh was familiar and he would know many of the faces when he arrived. His friendships might go even further back than that to Hesketh, Miss Tapp's pre-prep school in the village, whose green-capped little boys represented a lower form of life than even the prep school boy. So if he were lucky he might find himself among old friends, or he might find he knew nobody. 'No one spoke. I had a lonely walk up Pitch Hill', is one boy's melancholy recollection. Or worse, the new boy might commit, all unwittingly, some solecism and be punished even on his first day; or he might be greeted at the main entrance, as one boy was, by having his bowler hat jammed down hard over his ears. And there might be other hazards to encounter, though they varied from house to house and from time to time. Sometimes there was an initiation rite called BRA, or 'Boot Room Afterwards', which meant a miserable session in the boot room being smeared with polish or perhaps being knocked about. And there might be another initiation rite: standing up in the dormitory for a new boys' 'concert' and singing a song, and being pelted with fruit or soap. Not many had the savoir faire of one new boy, slightly older than the others, who instead of the usual offering of 'Greensleeves' or 'God save the King' gave a spirited and unexpurgated rendition of 'Eskimo Nell'. These were the 'rites of passage'; thereafter the new boy, while still a junior, was a new boy no longer and to him would soon fall the responsibility of doling out the same treatment to the next generation of new boys.

But initiation rites, when they happened, were moments of high drama for a small boy. Life was more usually dominated by the unchanging rhythms of school routine and house room custom. The house room was where the boy lived and moved and had his being; from there he went out to face chapel and lessons and games and corps. Cranleigh still described itself* in the *Public Schools Year Book* as being run on the 'hostel' system. Houses were not coherent geographical entities: in effect a house was a dormitory and a house room. West, 1 North and 2 North were the 'out-houses' because they had their house rooms in huts at the back of the school; what they lacked in heat they made up for in convenience for they were not also used as classrooms, as were the house rooms of 2 & 3 South, 1 & 4 South and East. East was different, though, for it contained all the dayboys, who outnumbered the boarders there. It was the rough house. But all boys, whether from 'in' or 'out' houses, slept in dormitories around the quadrangle. Getting-up time was early, and the new boy had to be washed and out of the bathroom by 6.55 a.m., to make way for his elders and betters seeking hot water for shaving. Getting out of the bathroom meant in many cases getting away from the washbasins which stood in the middle of many of the dorms, as did chamber pots in some. By ten past seven the new boy was out of the dorm, still struggling perhaps with his stiff collar, and wearing flannels and dark jacket for normal schooldays. He had not made his

* throughout the twenties

bed: this was left to an army of maids under a major domo who ensured precise folding over and tucking in. The boys had their own domestic discipline when flannel parades ensured that all garments were present and correct, stacked and stowed neatly in compactums – the massively solid wardrobes provided by the school. Then, down in his house room, the new boy met a formidable array of customs and rules. A position at a large table was allocated to him; there he would work, though he must place nothing on the table but his books and perhaps a magazine. While he worked there during the long 1½ hour prep in the evening, he was not allowed to look up. There were detailed rules about 'looking up' which varied from house to house, and they were relaxed a little latterly when it was felt that an absolute prohibition on looking up might be bad for the eyesight. The trouble with relaxing the rule was that people took advantage; that was a cry frequently heard from the prefects when any relaxation of rules was contemplated. People would look up not merely to rest their eyes but to look meaning-fully at someone else, or to watch idly what was going on. The punishment for this and other prep misdemeanours was 'SO', or 'standing out', when a boy had to leave the room and stand outside facing the wall.

After prep the boy went up to a long dormitory, ill-lit by three gas mantles. Once a week there was a bath ritual. A squad of boys trooped down in dressing gowns, round the cloisters which at that stage were unglazed and open to wind and cold, to the swimming pool.[4] Round the pool were a dozen or more slipper baths; so the boy had a hot, or luke-warm bath there first, followed by a dip in the swimming pool in the centre of the room. When the water in the pool had been changed (once a week) it was clear and very cold; towards the end of the week it might be warmer, but was distinctly cloudy. That was the one hot bath of the week; showers after games were cold, or at best luke-warm. Then, after the bath, up to the dormitory; the lights were eventually extinguished by a servant, Mr Dogherty or 'Dirts', who solemnly processed, unspeaking as always, round to each gas mantle. Later, in the darkness, the Headmaster himself might make a silent perambulation of the dormitories. Sometimes, before or after lights-out and if the bachelor house-master or tutor was absent from his room adjacent to the dormitory, there might be some scrum practice. The 2 North dormitory, with its iron bars in the roof, lent itself to various types of gymnastics or endurance tests. To be caught might mean being punished by 'drill'.

Drill was perhaps the most characteristic of all the Cranleigh punishments. It took place each afternoon in the quad under the direction of the prefect of the week or the sergeant major. A drill was a half hour session, with four consecutive sessions being the maximum. Attired in games kit, cap and blazer, the miscreants were required to run round the quad with arms upraised, or do other physical exercises, depending on the ingenuity or sadism of the person in charge. Most boys were given drill at some stage; some had it frequently. It could be imposed by a master or a prefect; it was an automatic punishment if a number of 'standing outs' or SOs had accumulated in the house room. And as if drill were not in itself sufficient punishment, the culprit knew that his drill went towards a house total, published weekly until this was abolished in 1929. For less serious offences within the house fines were imposed. For leaving gear around in the changing room or leaving books about in the house room the fine was 1d per article. In a typical week the house funds might be augmented by some 5/- from this source. For more serious offences, there was beating. Sometimes it was administered, very effectively, by Rhodes himself, especially for bad work. Less usually the housemaster might beat. But most frequently beating was carried out by the senior prefect or house captain. Sometimes, 'informally', a prefect might apply the slipper in the dormitory. And there were cases of drills being 'beaten off' – the offender reckoning that a few minutes suffering under the cane was preferable to a few hours in the quad. Whether this violence imposed from above had as its inevitable counterpart violence from below is open to discussion: certainly there was plenty of violence at the boy level. As always when adolescent boys get together there was bullying, or simply good natured ragging. Even if it led to bruises and black eyes the schoolboy code of honour prevented 'squealing': the house captain might intervene with an off-the-record dressing down for the bully. Sometimes there were fights with an audience, and in a school that taught boxing the boys had acquired the basic skills. 'Behind the gym' might be the challenge thrown out, which would guarantee an audience and a relatively fair fight. But they were less common than they had been in the 19th century.

The boy in the house room did not of course spend most of his time being punished or fighting. He did spend a good deal of his time in 'lock-up'. On half-holidays and at weekends in the winter months, boys were confined each evening after call-over to their houserooms. There was little to alleviate the boredom. A house gramophone with a limited supply of records was a help. Sometimes in a fit of enthusiasm a prefect might get permission to spend some of the fines money on new records; sometimes the machine broke down and the boys had to make their own music. On one occasion a housemaster had to intervene when his over-zealous prefects ruled that playing musical instruments, like the banjulele, or whistling during lock-up, were to be banned. For little boys – the bottom quarter of house – there came an unwelcome diversion in the form of fagging. It was never a highly developed system at Cranleigh, had not existed at all until around the turn of the century, but was to survive until the 1960s. Some of the fagging was for prefects: running errands, brushing clothes, cleaning shoes, fetching hot water for shaving. Otherwise it was a generalized form of fagging involving cleaning up the house room, tidying the changing room and so on. But the houses were not coherent enough for the classic kinds of fagging written up in so many school stories. It was only now, after the First World War, that the houses were so called; before that the quite accurate description 'dormitories' was used. There were few studies. The housemasters wielded little power and influence compared to that of the headmaster; those who were bachelors lived in cramped, inadequate quarters next to the dorms; married housemasters lived out. There were no green baize doors; few housemasters did much in the way of entertaining their boys. House spirit and house identity could mean little off the sports field. In each house there was certainly a strict order of seniority. And there was a curious ambivalence. Friendships between older and younger boys undoubtedly happened; it would be surprising if in that monastic community there were no romantic attachments. Colin Stephenson tells of how shocked masters were when a preacher in chapel spoke from the text 'See that you love one another', since 'housemasters . . . spent a lot of their time and energy trying to ensure that we did no such thing'.[5] Little evidence survives of such attachments, and no doubt they served a function on occasions by protecting the younger boy from bullying or ill-treatment. At the same time, prefects often complained that seniors were being too familiar with juniors in general, and consequently 'losing respect'. The finely balanced power structure was too delicate to allow such informality which might undermine the necessarily hierarchical nature of the house. Privilege was important. 'Goods' – boys sent up to the headmaster for good work – might be allowed the special privilege of going to their lockers during prep. Seniors might not be prefects but might have certain little areas of responsibility – looking after the billiards money or the drill book, or being librarian, or supervising the tuck box room. Prefects could take a short cut to the baths at night; non prefects were not allowed hands in pockets, or jacket buttons undone. In all these marks of hierarchy and privilege, the rules and customs at Cranleigh were far less complex and time-hallowed than at many schools. Its variations in dress were not so bizarre, its boys not so wealthy, its buildings and accommodation not so grand, as at some schools. Too often the small number of schools with rich traditions, wealthy foundations, splendid public buildings and geographically separate houses equipped with studies, resident housemaster and family, and their own dining rooms, are taken as typical. They are not. Far more common was the Cranleigh style.

But at Cranleigh, as at almost every boarding school, prefects were important. The number stayed fairly constant: most houses had about fifty boys of whom three or four were house prefects and one or two were school prefects, of whom one was house captain. One of the house captains was also Senior Prefect, and in the twenties there was a run of very strong boys in that position. He, along with the prefectorial body, was responsible for discipline not only in the houseroom and dorm, but also in the dining room and outside the school: they were more likely than masters to apprehend boys for not wearing their caps, or for breaking bounds; they would discourage boys from visiting public houses – though they might visit them themselves: the Windmill was a favourite stopping off place during a walk up Pitch Hill. Sometimes prefects – more especially house prefects – were ineffective and had to run with the crowd. Sometimes prefects – especially school and senior prefects – were young men of considerable power and influence. One such was even able to influence the headmaster not to patrol the school on the last night of term so that he and his friends could have a late-night farewell supper together in the library. For some, prefectship meant entering – at least tentatively – the adult world of responsibility and relationships with adults, especially with headmaster and housemaster. For others, no doubt, being a prefect meant little more than acquiring the odd, but highly-prized, privilege. This is true of the modern school as well, even though it is a place far less rigidly hierarchical, and with less automatic respect given and demanded.

Over and above the status of different boys and the gradations of privilege, there were the school rules, and the minutiae of regulations governing most aspects of life: clothing regulations, for instance. There was the headgear of bowlers for travel, caps for the winter terms, boaters for the summer. There were house and colours caps for games. In hot weather, everyone had to change into flannels and blazers before afternoon school; ties or cravats had to be donned during school hours or for meals, but might be discarded at other times; blazers could only be discarded with permission. The hazards of permissiongettings could be formidable: to obtain an exeat the headmaster was involved, and poor work could lead to his saying 'no'. Making a telephone call required a chit from the housemaster and perhaps a long wait while the lady who controlled the tiny school switchboard wrestled to obtain a line. Regulations and chits were encountered at every turn, and boys knew well the risks and hazards of forgetfulness or wilfulness. In a way, it was a cosy, well-regulated world, based on order, hierarchy and prescription. Food was as ever a diversion but at mealtimes, ritual prevailed. The master of the week, the prefect of the week, the beakies or jims (servants) and the head jim all had their part to play: the ritual slamming of the door, all standing at their house tables, no talking, the saying of grace, the sitting down by order of seniority. After the war food was better than it had been, especially when in 1927 tea was upgraded somewhat from the traditional plain fare of tea and toke (bread) which had had to suffice between lunch on one day and breakfast the next. The midday meal was the main one, and was perhaps better than the nicknames for the dishes would imply: dead man's leg, cat pie, burst boil. And there was always plenty of toke. Boys could supplement the teatime diet with potted meats, spreads and jams. With a chit from the bursar, a boy could approach the cook who might be prevailed upon to supplement the meagre tea by cooking a rabbit that a boy had recently snared, or frying some bacon acquired from home. For some adventurous spirits there was a dining club which took itself off to the woods to consume food imported by a day boy. And as ever there was the tuck shop – still in the little cottage on Horseshoe Lane where it had been founded in 1866. Miss Mould presided, serving hot drinks, shakes, toffees and cakes which could be consumed in the garden if the weather was fine, or in the stables next door if wet. Sometimes an old boy would make an appearance, and squander some of his new-found wealth by treating any boys who happened to be queueing at the time – to cries of 'sportsman'. School order was not entirely forgotten even in these more relaxed surroundings: Miss Mould had a swear box, and an incautious comment was charged at the rate of 1d for each offensive word; and prefects, when they arrived, went to the top of the queue. The 'plebs' or 'scrubs' could have a long wait. Then, once a year, there was a major break in routine. Ascension Day was traditionally a holiday, after the service in chapel in the morning. One housemaster had a tradition of taking the whole house off to Abinger Hammer, walking there and back and stopping for refreshments. Another more adventurously took the whole house sailing on the River Wey, with a lunch at the Farncombe Manor Hotel. Repeated year after year perhaps the novelty wore off a bit, but it was a break in school routine.

Of course much of the school routine centred on the classroom. There boys met with a great variety of masters. Some were frankly vulgar: Hayter who called every boy 'stinker' and so acquired that as his own nickname; Gower with his tight discipline, unkempt appearance and idiosyncratic teaching. There were more cultured men: Max Machin who took a London doctorate, was an archeologist and classic, and taught at Cranleigh for 35 years; 'Tum' Purvis, 1 North housemaster, who had a lively mind and was something of a polymath – he took holy orders in 1932 and left Cranleigh in 1938 after a quarter of a century's service to end up finally as a Canon of York and reviver of the cycle of medieval mystery plays there.[6] Purvis was out-ranked in seniority by Antrobus, who taught under Allen, Tyler and Rhodes and who was still in the 1920s dressed in the formal attire of a vanished era. There were the Winsloes, brothers and OCs, one teaching cricket and the other running the bursarial department. There were the clergy: Rhodes himself; and Mertens who was master at the prep school; Crowhurst who became second master and who like Purvis was a late ordinand; Thomas who went on to be Master of Llandovery; and more fleeting figures like Pickford and Riley and Simpson. Simpson was a biologist and an eccentric, who obtained permission from Rhodes for the boys to smoke in the dissection room to cover the smell of formaldehyde. He went off later to become a no doubt wildly eccentric headmaster in the West Indies.[7] There were other masters whose Cranleigh careers were short: some were thought to be homosexual and the abrupt departure of one or two tended to confirm this suspicion for the boys; one had a drinking problem, and another had a tendency, undiscovered by the boys, to run into severe debt. Another was disapproved of by the headmaster since not only was he a 'rabid socialist', but also had a New Zealand accent. It was, on the whole, a relatively stable staff: the Winsloes, Crowhurst, Aldridge, Moore, Purvis, Clare, Gower, Herbert (at the senior school) and Mertens, Wells and Johnstone (at the House) were on the staff in 1919, and still at Cranleigh in 1929. In those ten years the total number of staff has risen from 26 to 29. There were other survivors for most or all of the twenties: the medical officer, Dr Walker, the physical training instructor, Captain Mills, the bandmaster, Mr Whaley, and the sanatorium matron, Miss Pocock. Academically, it was not a distinguished staff. His Majesty's Inspectors of Education, who conducted an inspection of the school in 1921 (and subsequently in 1935, 1952 and 1961) were tactful but firm in expressing their opinions: the staff were keen, and much involved in all aspects of school life, but they were not intellectually distinguished and their teaching methods were frankly old fashioned. But then, the quality of the boys they taught was not high either.

In order to fill the school Rhodes had accepted many boys of very low academic attainments. There were no entrance scholarships or leaving exhibitions which might act as bait to brighter boys. Rhodes had done his best to shake the boys up soon after his arrival by introducing fortnightly orders, and indeed for some years the results were published in a printed booklet. On the basis of these orders the headmaster addressed the whole school once a fortnight: the 'bads' were caned if their work did not improve, and the 'goods' received mild privileges. In 1921 a House Challenge Cup was instituted to give the boys an incentive in work similar to those on the sports field. The situation however did not improve much throughout the twenties. Most boys in fact did not stay for a full five years so many never took the external examinations: for those who did, it was now the Oxford and Cambridge Board, which had been substituted for the Cambridge locals during the war. But most boys at Cranleigh in the twenties were destined for business, which they often entered at the age of 16, making Cranleigh still a fairly young school.[8] Only a couple of boys a year went on to university; a few more went to medical school; rather fewer went into the army.

For the average boy, the ethos of the school and his own ambitions conspired to place academic work fairly low on his list of priorities. Games were far more important. Here, rugby dominated. But there were other games as well: cricket was popular though school teams never reached a very high level of proficiency, despite Fawcus's coaching, and unlike the rugger teams were more often than not beaten. The same was true of the hockey, despite coaching from Sholto Marcon, an international who joined the 'House' staff in 1919. Shooting and boxing were quite popular among the minor sports; tennis was still regarded as rather a soft option. Major and minor sports, chapel, corps, classes, prep and lock-up meant that the boys were well supervised. There was time for the odd poaching expedition, or for the occasional illicit cigarette – though even a boy who had been given an exeat would be beaten if caught smoking outside the school in a cafe or in a bus. Sometimes there was a drinking party, though this usually cost too much for it to be a common occurrence. Pocket money was only 4d per week for the small boys, rising by stages to perhaps 1/6 a week for sixth formers and slightly more for prefects. Besides parents were not rich, and were considerably stricter with their boys than those of a later generation were to be, so little extra pocket money found its way illegally into boys' pockets. And since the village was usually out of bounds, opportunities for spending were severely limited – at least the tuck shop did a roaring trade.

So the rhythm of school life proceeded in the twenties. In 1926 the General Strike provided a diversion, and the school was kept informed of events in the outside world by a news bulletin written and duplicated by Purvis. In 1927 there was the excitement of the Pageant, when on three successive July days boys could mingle with girls on the south field as 300 performers laboured to raise money for the new organ. Occasionally, as in 1929, there was an epidemic: it was measles that year, and half the members of each house were laid low, necessitating the opening up of extra 'wards' in dormitories, and the amalgamation of dormitories of healthy boys from different houses, leaving the boys with that sense of greater freedom and novelty which schoolboys can evince from any disruption of the normal routine. And each boy's own routine was probably interrupted at some time in his school career by a stay at the san – for some unfortunates this could last up to a whole term, by which time the novelty must have worn off. The regular and common complaint of chilblains, not surprising given the cold and damp environment of the winter months, afflicted most people. But boys are resilient creatures, who seem to have survived for a whole term without having their games clothes washed. This was in order to save the expense of having to demand duplicate sets; so their games clothes could not be laundered, only rinsed out by the boys themselves (in cold water) if they were so minded. The result may have been somewhat offensive but no more serious than that, it would seem.

So the Cranleigh boy of the 1920s lived his school life – a life so like that of his predecessors for many decades, and for several decades to come. And it was the kind of life lived by thousands of boys at other such schools – small, rather Spartan boarding schools which lacked the social cachet of some of the greater and larger public schools, but which nevertheless shared many of the characteristics. The monasticism, the hierarchy and the lack of choice were common, and so different from the style of the modern boarding school. The Cranleighans of the twenties were a different breed from their successors in the sixties and onwards. And they lived in a different world as well. It was a more settled world, at least for the inhabitants of the south east who knew little from personal experience of depression and unemployment. It was a world that had been shaken by the Great War, but which in so many ways assumed it could continue as if nothing had happened – the British Empire was even larger than before, domestic servants were still cheap and plentiful, prices were relatively stable and the 'Baldwin Age' denoted, at least ostensibly, stability, solid virtue and 'safety first'. Churchgoing was less popular now, but public rituals and public life, and even the recently established BBC, proceeded upon the assumption that England was still in most senses a 'Christian' nation. Most of the boys who left Cranleigh in the twenties went into business. Few great names emerged from those generations, except for that galaxy of games talent – Alan Key, Clive Wallis, Stanley Couchman, Jeffrey Reynolds, H. P. Jacob, Reggie Mathys, Norman Martin and others – whose activities and achievements were given such wide publicity by their journalist contemporary Bill Swanton, who did so much to spread the name and fame of Cranleigh in the thirties and subsequently.

For the ordinary boy at school, games loomed large, perhaps larger for him than for his predecessors or successors. For the headmaster, work mattered; for men like Purvis and Machin the things of the mind were important. But for the average boy, whatever his interests or talents, there was always the backdrop of life in a boarding community, with its demands and its routines. His focus each day was the dormitory and the house room. And the ordinary, everyday concerns of the twenties, as seen through the eyes of a prefect, was well summed up in a passage taken at random from a house log book for the week ending 8 October 1926:

'House Room:

The general state of the house room this week has been very untidy, owing, chiefly, to the people on the room failing to report.

Drills:

The house were 2nd in drills this week and this is a great improvement on last week's performance. 7 hours.

Fines:

These amounted to 4/9.

This week a chess club has been formed by Waugh 2 and already there are several sets of chessmen in the house.

This week a new boy named Jacklin arrived and was placed in the second form.

Samuels 1 and Pearce 3 have lent some thirty records to the house, which are a great asset to the house stock of gramophone records.

The old house gramophone was purchased, by auction, by the senior table under the organisation of Trent for the sum of 25/- which goes towards the House Funds.

NB   The senior table is in a very untidy condition this week.'

The report is signed by the house prefect of the week, countersigned by the housemaster who has added the comment: 'There is far too much SO at present'. So ended an ordinary week in the life of a house at Cranleigh in the Michaelmas Term 1926.

CHAPTER EIGHT

Changed Times (1931–45)

IN THE SPRING OF 1931 an Old Cranleighan, Sir George May,[1] was drawing up a report which was to have profound consequences for Cranleigh and for the United Kingdom. The May Report was a response to the financial strains from which the country was suffering, along with the rest of the world, in the wake of the Great Depression. Its recommendations for creating a balanced budget led to the formation of a National Government, a split in the Labour Party, and a policy which eschewed what have come to be called 'Keynesian' solutions. While these dramatic events were running their course at Westminster and in Whitehall, and throughout the western world, a new, young headmaster was settling in at Cranleigh.

In February 1931 the governors had selected three possible candidates to replace Rhodes.[2] One was William Cavill, a bachelor of 42 who had been headmaster of Hymer's College, Hull, since 1927. He had several strong claims as he had taught at Ardingly under Rhodes, and like him was an Oxford football blue. In fact he was to remain at Hymer's until 1951. The second candidate was Thorold Francis Coade, a married man of 34 who was an assistant master at Harrow and who, on failing to secure the Cranleigh headship, went on in the following year to become headmaster of Bryanston where he remained until 1959. The governors' choice in fact fell on the other candidate, a man of Coade's age and with in many ways a similar kind of outlook.[3] David Loveday was a bachelor, and the only cleric among those shortlisted. 'An engaging young

115

Salopian', as David Newsome calls him,[4] he read Classics and Theology at Cambridge, where he became friendly with the Master of his College, A. C. Benson. Benson, son of the Archbishop, had taught at Eton where he had been a house-master before moving to Magdalene. He looked after his undergraduates and developed a particular fondness for Love-day, 'a rather haggard and wild looking creature' but 'rather interesting and mature for 19'.[5] To the distress of both of them, Loveday had to bid Benson farewell at the end of 1915 when he took a commission with the Oxfordshire regiment,[6] returning to Cambridge after the war where he prepared for ordination and became part of that intimate circle – Dadie Rylands, Owen Morshead, Bernard Manning – around Benson, who was nearing the end of his life and in his infirmity found Loveday 'unfailing in kindness and tenderness'.[7] If the governors were looking for a contrast to Rhodes, they had obviously found one in this young and 'un-clerical' clergyman.[8] Despite the fact that David Loveday was a cleric, the contrast with his predecessor could hardly have been more marked. Rhodes had been sombre, elderly, almost stolid in appearance. Loveday was tall, spry, and with a caustic wit. Generations of boys were to hoard examples of his eccentricities and phrases. How his entry into assembly was preceded by the cry 'School!' at which everyone rose to their feet as the headmaster entered followed by the senior prefect 'carrying a rug so that David might be comfort-ably warm in his chair. Presumably it was draughty in front of the stage'.[9] How one boy was asked at lunch to contemplate 'the aesthetic difference between a disembodied and a sucked plum stone', and invited to look at a housemaster's plate and then at his own to perceive the difference; 'I have never forgotten the lesson!', writes the plum vandal.[10] How Loveday delighted in the odd and curious: the clergyman called Raper who was unfrocked for rape; the master whose wife had a loud unpleasant voice and whose telephone number (two or three digits in those days) was the number in *Ancient and Modern* of the hymn, 'The voice that breathed o'er Eden'.[11] Loveday was a man of strong opinions, a man of intense loves and dislikes. The boys appreciated, from the moment of his arrival, that changes must be on the way.

Loveday faced a huge task in a school that was tough and uncultured. Rhodes himself had had to spend his last days at Cranleigh, after the end of the Lent Term 1931, dealing with a particularly nasty bullying incident. Loveday, whose own schooldays had been 'extremely unhappy',[12] was determined that Cranleigh should not be that sort of place. But the sort of place it might become was determined partly by the events of the outside world. During his second term the school magazine announced that 'the numbers of the school are up, so that at present we are not suffering as are some of the public schools in these very trying times'.[13] In 1932 however the masters offered a voluntary salary cut.[14] By 1934 the governors were publicly lamenting the 'difficult times' which had led to a fall in numbers from just over 300 (which figure had remained constant throughout the twenties) to about 230.[15] The consequent fall in fee income further undermined the economy of a school facing long-term debts left over from the building operations of the twenties. Such slender financial margins as there were had to be utilized – as the minute books attest again and again – for the alleviation of hardship and the provision of scholarships and bursaries. Loveday laid great stress on people, not on the physical surroundings or the school's plant. It was characteristic of him, but it was also the only possible approach, for it was obvious that there could be no major building operations at the school for some time to come. Loveday also emphasized work;[16] his first speech to the OCs set the tone:[17]

> 'The reputation of Cranleigh at the moment is of a school where the boys are happy, well looked after, and where rugby football flourishes. We have a high reputation in the athletic world. But the standard of work is not high, and that has become widely known.'

But how to effect a change? The financial resources were not sufficient to enable expansion of the scholarship programme, and indeed it had to contract. The new scholarship scheme had been launched during the great expansion of 1929, but the sum available contracted annually throughout the thirties. At Loveday's insistence it had stood at £840 worth of scholarships offered in 1932, but the total offered for 1936 was only £370. However the number of preparatory schools sending boys who won scholarships was impressive: 52 in all during the thirties, including such musical places as Christ Church Cathedral Choir School, the choir school at Salisbury and St Michael's, Tenbury. It was on Loveday's insistence that music scholarships were made available.[18] A wider spread of schools was represented on the scholarship lists in the thirties than in the late forties and early fifties, testimony to Loveday's considerable initial impact. Within the school he was anxious to encourage the housemasters, who had previously played a very subsidiary role in the attracting of boys to Cranleigh, to seek out good boys, and to do some 'empire building' for their own houses.[19] The new approach was symbolized also in his insistence that end of term reports should be fuller than the one-word comments that were the norm, even for housemasters, in Rhodes's day.[20] Lists of boys who won scholarships began to appear in the school magazine.[21] Masters were encouraged to take time off to keep up their contacts with Oxford or Cambridge Gaudies or reunion dinners.[22] For the boys too a new approach was obvious: Loveday abolished 'bads' and the canings associated with them; indeed he was no flogger in the Allen or Rhodes tradition.[23] And drill, a somewhat useless and pointless punishment, tended to fade out in the mid-thirties into something more useful – like cleaning rifles; though one up-holder of the old order was moved to protest at this pandering to 'little Willie – "so highly-strung", you know!'[24]

Another clear indication to the boys that the old order was changing was in the arrival of new masters. The HMI's report of 1935 noted with approval that a third of the masters were now under 30, and while they still felt that there was insufficient academic distinction they acknowledged that 'the staff is stronger and more effective' than in 1921.[25] One new man of note was Michael Redgrave. He was just 24, and had been taught by Loveday at Clifton before going up to Magdalene.

He arrived to teach modern languages and also, as the head-master encouraged him to do, to 'carry out experiments in theatrical production'.[26] He was a breath of fresh air – in the classroom and in 2 & 3 South where as house tutor he was active in entertaining boys, holding play readings, and supplying food after lights-out. He deserved his nickname, 'The Red', in more ways than one.[27] His main impact was of course on school drama, and it was an impact that has lived on long after his brief two-year stay. Drama assumed an importance never before known at Cranleigh, or perhaps at any other school: boys were involved, as were masters, in acting and building, fetching costumes, being stage hands, creating the set; school routine was disrupted and new topics of conversation appeared. The list of plays, with Redgrave as 'director, manager, designer and star actor'[26] is formidable:

July 1932	*As You Like It*
March 1933	*Samson Agonistes*
June 1933	*Hamlet*
December 1933	*The Tempest*
June 1934	*King Lear*

His last production at Cranleigh was reviewed in *The Times*, *New Statesman* and *Nation*, as well as all the local papers. About 1,200 people in all attended the three performances. Masters acted alongside the boys – Jacob, Purvis, Gordon-Potts, Broad, with Redgrave himself as Lear. G. Wilson Knight wrote a flattering review, noting in particular a point that must have pleased Redgrave and Loveday and which is an important comment on any school drama:[21]

> 'It is a curious paradox that a small boy can intuitively appreci-ate a fine point of production whose exact reason he may not understand for another twenty years. What the producer knows intellectually the audience receives intuitively'.

After that triumph Redgrave left schoolmastering to join the Liverpool Rep: 'I do not doubt that the future will justify his choice', wrote Knight.[21] Tyrone Guthrie was less encouraging: 'I do feel you'd be rather a mug to leave Cranleigh'.[26] But at least he left behind him a tradition of acting and of major school productions which was picked up and carried on by J. S. Purvis. He had produced plays before but the atmosphere in the school was more receptive now, and his fine eye for detail, his own acting skill and his immense care with costumes and production secured the tradition Redgrave had started.[28] Not that everyone was impressed. There were the inevitable complaints that drama was overrated. As one correspondent complained, the school magazine had always carried pictures of rugger teams, but now only 'some wretched photo of a school play, in which not a soul is recognizable'.[29] Another felt that accounts of school matches 'provide far more interest for the majority' than accounts of dramatic productions.[30]

Loveday himself was no great devotee of sport. 'A remarkably dull game' was said to have been his comment on arriving on one occasion at a rugger match during half time.[31] Ironically, after a run of very poor seasons in 1929–31, the first fifteen now experienced something of a revival and the seasons 1932–4 were very good. Thereafter however they lost more matches than they won up until the outbreak of war. Other games flourished as never before. Symbolic of the change was the appointment in 1933 for the first time of separate captains for tennis and fives.[32] Cricket had not had the successful run during Rhodes's time that rugger had enjoyed and the headmaster had never been satisfied with the standard reached.[33] Things had improved somewhat since the 1910 season when *The Observer* reported a record of 14 runs in 16 games. 'The competition for the average bat must have been very keen', commented Mr Punch.[34] The season of 1930 had been worse for the cricketers than the rugger players, with 10 matches drawn, 4 lost and none won. Not until 1940 was the number of games won greater than those lost or drawn. But what particularly worried the master in charge, Blackshaw, was the lack of enthusiasm in the school: 'never have I seen less voluntary support and fewer spectators than at Cranleigh'.[21] But although since the war Cranleigh could boast its own cricket ground, after half a century of using the common in the village jointly with the village club, no marked improvement in standards occurred.[35] Perhaps it was still over-shadowed by rugger; perhaps it was now overshadowed by other games. For as well as more tennis and fives, there was now golf as well. In fact in 1931 two OCs had 'covered themselves with glory' in the Halford-Hewitt, being narrowly beaten by the eventual winners, Harrow.[36] Now, for the first time, boys could play; the masters decided in 1936 to throw open their course to paying members.[37] And for boys of even more individualist temperament cycling was allowed, if they first joined the Ornithological Society.[38] Then in 1936 the scheme for the building of some squash courts was revived. An appeal went out to Common Room and to OCs, and the response was so good that two courts were built and opened within the year.[39]

One of the enthusiasts behind the building of the squash courts was Gordon Gordon-Potts, who had come to replace Redgrave in 1934. Loveday was fortunate that hard times which limited expenditure in schools also threw on the market men of high calibre who were tempted by the security of schoolmastering. Schools were in a buyer's market, and Loveday chose well when he appointed Gordon-Potts, who had been educated at Oundle and Brasenose, had taught at Eton, and was 28 when he arrived at Cranleigh. 'The finest type of English public school master',[40] he remained at Cranleigh until war broke out. His energy and enthusiasm were felt in many areas of school life: in shooting, drama, debating, athletics, and French, German and maths lessons. He applied his knowledge of surveying to laying out the common room garden and planting trees round its tennis court. In 1935 he became Charles Blackshaw's tutor in East and he is remembered rather as Redgrave was:[41]

'There was a pleasant, restful and perhaps rather unschool-like atmosphere in his room. I don't know why such a thing should stick in my mind more than another: perhaps it was the enormous amount of chocolate biscuits we used to consume while he used to read, strangely enough, Siegfried Sassoon's *Memoirs of an Infantry Officer*'.

Not only because of Gordon-Potts but taking its tone from the headmaster as well, there seems, not only at Cranleigh but elsewhere, to have been a slowly growing 'atmosphere of trust between master and boy'[42] during these years. Gordon-Potts played a part in that and Loveday thought he would soon lose him since he was 'clearly marked out by his forcefulness of character, fertility of ideas and untiring industry for a Headmastership'.[43] It was not to be; Gordon-Potts and his brother Michael both fell in action in June 1940. The common room trees still stand.

Other masters came and went. F. H. Warre Cornish, a distinguished classic, was lost to Eton after only four terms because there was not enough senior classics teaching to give him. Dr Simpson, that biologist, cleric and eccentric who 'seemed to be much more interested in dissecting frogs than in chapel affairs'[31] went off to a headmastership in India. R. A. Henniker-Gotley became headmaster of Sebright after eight years at Cranleigh. E. A. Clare left in 1937 after twenty years; his services as a cricket coach are immortalized in the field renamed 'Clare's Oak'. Maurice Allen, Cranleigh's director of music since 1924, was much prized by Loveday who gave him the housemastership of 2 North in 1936; but Allen still had musical ambitions and went the following year to be director of music at Wellington. In 1938 an interesting quartet of new young masters arrived. A. W. Young from Hertford, Oxford, and G. P. Maguire from King's, Cambridge, were to give long and distinguished service to the school until the mid-seventies. The other two arrivals did not stay so long. Herr E. Steinke was the last German assistant; he left after the year, leaving behind only sinister rumours that his interest in photography was no mere hobby but was rather more connected with German Intelligence. The other new arrival, Luis Cernuda, was a young Spaniard who was later to achieve fame as one of the representative poets of that unhappy period in his country, from which he had fled. One of his poems, *Nino Muerto*, might well be a lament for a boy who committed suicide at Cranleigh in the summer term of 1939. All in all, it was an interesting common room.

Loveday could feel pleased by the way things were going despite the letter of complaint to the *Daily Mail* by a Cranleigh parent, who fortunately did not name the school. He objected to the 'quite inadequate' meals served to his son, who was therefore forced to have frequent recourse to the tuck shop.[44] The charge was hardly fair: food seems to have been of a good standard in the 30s. Certainly the incident did not stop the school going ahead with the building of a large new tuckshop (in what is now the Art School) which opened in 1936 and was run by Bill Mason who had been school cricket coach since 1915; he was to remain running the tuck shop, in different premises, until 1957.[45] Other diversions also made the life of the boys more pleasant. In the mid thirties the school had its own dance band, 'The Blue Liars'. The dramatic diet of Shakespeare was varied by Gilbert and Sullivan and by a performance of a musical written by Purvis featuring a very stupid Cranleighan and called *The Pill*, 'a title less equivocal than it would be today'.[46] There was 'Atha', a society which from 1931 showed films to the school, thus alleviating the dreariness of lock-up at the weekends.[47] There were end-of-term concerts which even the tolerant Loveday had to put a stop to when a particularly risque skit was performed, hard on the heels of a parental complaint about the 'moral tone' of one of the houses.[48] But it is a mark of the way the school had developed that in 1938, in the seventh of a series of articles on various public schools, the *Daily Mail* could carry a large headline 'Cranleigh is Music Conscious'.[49] The article was flattering about the school's music, new buildings, golf course and sports record, and the writer waxed almost lyrical when he described the boys' accommodation:

> 'No one has seen Cranleigh until he has visited a Cranleigh dormitory on a day when sun streams through the windows . . . There is a wide space of polished flooring down the middle of the dormitory. I stood at the end of one of the dormitories and the 'raspberries' (blankets) on the beds stretched away from me in a never-ending pink haze across the shining floor.'

And the headmaster himself was active in getting the school

better known. In 1933 he was Select Preacher at Cambridge and in the same year preached for Dean Inge at St Paul's. In 1937 he revived the office of Visitor; happily the current Bishop of Winchester was C. F. Garbett, a Surrey man whose brothers had attended the school.[51] Throughout the thirties Loveday invited a distinguished series of preachers: headmasters, deans, bishops – including the eccentric Winnington-Ingram of London who delighted in pillow-fights in the dorms with the boys, who played along with this harmless foible.[31] Dean Inge on the other hand 'looked on small boys with obvious distaste',[31] but he preached at Cranleigh and gave Loveday's supper party afterwards the accolade of a mention in his diary which was crammed with accounts of many more prestigious social occasions.[52] Loveday could feel that the school was becoming better known, especially in areas other than the rugger clubs of the south east. In 1934 he proclaimed that drama had made the school 'a place of culture'.[30] In 1937, when four Oxbridge awards were won, he was able to boast that it had been 'the most distinguished year in the history of the school'.[51]

A premonition of the shape of things to come appeared in the pages of the school magazine in 1933. Sholto Marcon,[53] the hockey international who taught at the prep school, was on a year's temporary secondment to Kurt Hahn's school, Salem, in Baden, Germany.[54] In a letter back to Cranleigh Marcon described Hahn's arrest by Nazi officials and the subsequent troubles which disrupted school life, especially the student-fomented unrest over the demands by some to wear Hitler Youth uniforms. More sinister yet was his description of the party official who visited the school and 'alluded to the Jews on the staff'.[29] Presumably the Cranleighans who read the letter hardly gave it a second thought. It was not until 1938 that the school was forced to take note of events on the continent of Europe. On Tuesday 20 September, while plans were being laid for a second visit to Hitler by Britain's Prime Minister, Neville Chamberlain, the housemasters at Cranleigh were having one of their regular meetings; they were discussing air raid precautions.[55] Plans were made not only at Cranleigh but across the nation as trenches were dug, blackouts prepared and gas masks distributed. On the last day of September, however, Chamberlain flew back from Germany with 'peace in our time'. The euphoria soon faded; in January 1939 the first house-masters' meeting of the new term discussed not only some points about games clothes and scholarship examinations but also the necessity for air raid precautions, and a sub-committee was set up to deal with them.[56] In March, Germany invaded Czecho-slovakia in breach of the Munich Agreement and a week later housemasters and OTC officers were making plans for fire fighting.[57] The fire fighting squad was set up under two mas-ters, Pope and Phillips, while two others, Maguire and Stevens, were responsible for raising a First Aid Party, instructed by lectures by Mr Hillman Attwell, an OC chemist in the village. At the end of the hot summer term the school made plans for a new form, the 'Naval and Military', as an appropriate academic response to the needs of the times. The school broke up for the holidays with none of that blythe ignorance of the possibility of a world conflict that had characterized the genera-tion in that other hot summer of 1914. As on that occasion, war broke out during the holidays, and masters began to return to school early to undertake the task of preparing it for war. The building, standing exposed on a hill, needed blacking out, a huge task undertaken before term began by H. P. Jacob and not finished until October. Hundreds of windows had removable blackout screens or curtains made for them, while on the dorm windows above the library and on the glass on the north side of the quad, blacklead paint was used. The school telephone exchange, and the casualty clearing station at the sanatorium were sandbagged. When the boys returned most of the changes had been effected, and they found restrictions about the use of water and a new domestic routine requiring them to make their own beds. They found a whole new school had joined them as well. During the summer term Loveday had presented the prizes at Carn Brae near the coast, and had arranged that in the event of war they should come and seek the greater safety of Cranleigh. They came, settled in the tuck shop as their main headquarters, and stayed until March 1946. Reviewing the first term of the war, the school magazine was stoical:[58]

> 'When we returned this term, we were rather stunned by the realisation of war until we were accustomed to the blackout and the altered timetable and the youthful voices of Carn Brae echoing down the corridors. For besides the news of the war and the dug-outs, to which we have long been inured, these have been almost all the visible changes in Cranleigh'.

Of course school routine had asserted itself, but more changes were on the way. In May 1940 a school section of the LDV was formed.[59] There was a Gas Squad and, after December 1940, an Air Section of the OTC. There was instruction in unarmed combat or UAC, a welcome diversion from the usual PT. There was the Utility, or 'Ut', Squad for the younger boys who were charged with the responsibility of collecting waste paper for the war effort. There were house allotments by the pavilion which produced a meagre supply of vegetables. There was holiday work, in which half of the school helped local farmers to bring in the harvest. The golf course and south field were 'put out to hay' and harvested by the boys. From Michaelmas 1940, during the Battle of Britain, the dormitories were moved downstairs for safety and in addition each house had an air raid shelter connected by telephone link with the headmaster's shelter.

There were, as in peacetime, alarms, excursions and moments of excitement. On the lighter side there was the summer fete in 1940 which raised 100 guineas for Red Cross Funds. But the war came nearer: there was a machine gun attack on Godalming High Street; a bomb fell on Bramley station; although no damage was done to school property, 1000 bombs fell in the Hambledon Rural area during September 1940. Later in the war flying bombs, falling short of London, proved they could well have been an effective secret weapon for the Germans had not their bases been quickly overrun: one fell on the parish church hall and another on Gatley's Field adjoining the Jubilee which exploded while the boys were on holiday in the summer of 1944. The Headmaster was at home and he woke to find his bed covered in plaster and some slight damage to school buildings. And the war came nearer via the BBC: in dimly lit houserooms on winter evenings, with perhaps a blue bulb giving dim light if Mr Jacob thought the blackout not secure enough, boys could listen to the latest news and hear the voice of Winston Churchill exhorting the nation. There was the excitement of the victory at Alamein, which sent one boy off to ring the chapel bell in jubilation.[60] But for most of the time the war meant an altered school routine, lack of sleep because of airraids or ARP duties, the monotony of a wartime diet and the chore of securing and taking down the blackout. It also meant a diktat from the housemasters in 1942: 'One official bath per week to a depth of 5 inches', with the admonitory rider, 'no avoidance of washing'.[61]

The war had a serious effect on staffing. 'No other school had so large a proportion of their regular staff on active service'.[62] For the first time in the school's history a female teacher was employed, with warnings of dire consequences if boys should take the opportunity to misbehave.[60] Of a staff of 25 in 1939, 14 departed for active service and two – Pope and Gordon-Potts – were killed. There was a sharp drop in numbers in the school, as parents decided to keep their sons with them, or opted for 'safer' areas of the country. The headmaster felt, as he pointed out to one worried mother, that 'it is our duty to hold together and stay where we are in as safe an area as any in these days'.[63] Many parents were not convinced, and numbers fell from 237 in 1939 to 214 in 1941. The numbers at the prep school stayed constant at around 75 but the numbers of dayboys in the senior school grew, from 27 at the beginning of the war to 37 at the end. In 1942 the governors launched a programme to help increase numbers in the school.[64] Eighteen scholarships were to be available, to a total value of £1,000. A fund of £800 was established for the headmaster to use at his discretion in cases of need. There were small fee rises for dayboys and an increased contribution from Carn Brae, to help offset the cost of these schemes. In fact the worst was already past; Surrey no longer seemed a potential battle-ground, and numbers rose steadily for the rest of the war to 300 in 1945, which almost equalled the best years of the Rhodes regime in the late twenties. Meanwhile the headmaster had managed to deflect any suggestions that the school buildings should be requisitioned; early in the war it was named as a possible radar establishment but this was housed at Whitley instead.

On 8 May 1945 the school was given a day off to celebrate a moment long awaited – Victory in Europe. Festivities in the village culminated in a great torchlight procession, a bonfire on the common, and the ceremonial burning of the swastika flag. Later, causing less excitement, came the end of the war against Japan. So Cranleigh had survived a second world war, and in 1949 a second war memorial was opened: a 'sanctuary' and roll of honour in the Reading Room.[65] On the roll of honour were the names of 136 Cranleighans who had died in action; the oldest had left the school in 1901, the youngest in 1942. Among the names was that of Pilot Officer Sir Iain MacRobert who had left East in 1935; his brother also fell in action. The response of their mother, Lady MacRobert, was to send £25,000 to the Secretary of State for Air with the request that it be used to purchase a Stirling bomber which was to carry on its fuselage the name 'MacRobert's Reply'. Dr Ian Jacklin died heroically in shark-infested seas, swimming round to give succour to the survivors of a torpedoed ship. Others survived. Ian's brother, Edward, went on to head the Rhodesian Air force; George Kitching later rose to the Vice-Chief of the Canadian General Staff. This time, Cranleigh's war poet did not remain anonymous: Bernard Gutteridge served in the East, reached the rank of major, and published his poetry during and after the war.

But now the war was over, and although national service and rationing continued, changes were on the way. Perhaps Old Cranleighans had been right,when visiting the school during the war, to ignore the superficial changes in routine and to say 'The old place doesn't change a bit'.[62] But the post-war world was going to be different, and the great international and national changes would bring different attitudes and changes more profound within the public schools. While Loveday could not foresee what changes would come, he pointed out in his last wartime Whitsun sermon to the OCs:[67]

> 'Before each generation lies the task of plucking up and destroying the weeds of indifference or self-satisfaction, laziness and self-pleasing which are the perpetual menace of a common life unless it is informed by high ideals and impregnated by a lofty spirit.'

And, as the Revd Harry Williams said to his fellow OCs exactly a year later,[68] 'No doubt God's in His Heaven at this first post-war Whitsun, but all is by no means right with the world'. In Cranleigh, as in the world, the problems and challenges of war were replaced by the equally stern and challenging problems of peace.

CHAPTER NINE

Progress and Problems
(1945–1960)

IN AUGUST 1945, after a landslide victory at the polls, Britain's first majority Labour government took its seat on the Treasury bench in the Commons. Oliver Lyttelton, sitting on the opposite front bench, was appalled at having to listen to a rendition of the *Red Flag* and noted: 'My complacency melted in a minute. I began to fear for my country'.[1] That was something of an over-reaction, but nevertheless it was clear to many that Britain would never be the same again; that it was impossible to pick up where we had left off in 1939; that old styles and habits could not be resumed. 'Britain has undergone a silent revolution', declared the *Manchester Guardian*.[2] Not surprisingly it was a time of gloom for the public schools. Miss Wilkinson – 'Red Ellen' – was Minister of Education. A Royal Commission appointed in 1942, which included in its membership such august public school figures as Robert Birley of Charterhouse and Miss E. M. Tanner of Roedean had come out in favour of a measure of integration between the maintained and independent sectors.[3] But the problems facing Attlee's government were huge: economic difficulties and the task of reconstruction at home; emergent nationalism and increasingly threatening Communism abroad. These meant there would be little time, money or enthusiasm to spare to deal with the 'public school problem'; Butler's Education Act had already reorganized secondary education in the maintained sector. It was to be left to future Labour governments to tackle the independent schools. But the nation's problems, particularly the economic aftermath of war,

130

made themselves felt in every independent school in the land. Westminster borrowed a quarter of a million pounds from Lloyds.[4] Cranleigh turned to the trustees of Queen Anne's Bounty, the secretary of which was an OC, Sir Mortimer Warren.[5] The hope of a loan of £55,000 was not fulfilled and all the school managed to achieve was a reduction by the Commercial Union of the interest rate on their loan from 5½% to 4½%. The boys within the school may have been unaware of these financial deliberations, but they were well aware that things had changed: not necessarily, it seemed, for the better. The school magazine's editorials in the immediate post war years captured the mood: 'Letters consist almost entirely of complaints . . .';[6] 'Instead of the carefree, happy-go-lucky existence of four or five years ago . . . there is now subdued and restrained activity';[7] 'If we are to be independent we must be financially strong . . .';[8] '. . . the hard times through which this country is passing . . .';[9] 'If in the old days there was more intolerance and hardness in the School, there seemed more fire and keenness . . .';[10] 'Men have thought that the world was about to end many times, but never before have means been contrived with which to achieve this catastrophe . . .'.[11]

And yet, by many different indicators, these post-war years were a time of progress for Cranleigh, despite the austerity and gloom, and even before that 'unprecedented tide of prosperity rolled over the country'[4] in the late fifties and sixties. Between 1945 and 1960, numbers in the school increased by 22%, and that from what was an already high level of 300 achieved at the end of the war. This was an increase comparable to or better than that in schools similar to Cranleigh in size or catchment area, except those which had been dislocated by war and resumed their growth from a lower base line after 1945.[12] Fees during the same period rose by just over 123%, much in line with fee rises at other schools. In Loveday's last five years as headmaster, fees averaged £227 compared with £149 during his first five years: an increase of 52% Expenditure on scholarships meanwhile increased by 92%, fulfilling at last the hopes cherished by Loveday in 1931–3 but dashed by the economic climate of the times. Staffing ratios were better now too; the master-boy ratio in the early thirties had been 1:13.1; now it was 1:12.6. This was better than the average. In maintained schools the ratio was 1:20.6, and in other public schools the average was 1:13.7.[13] However the average age of the staff was much higher now than it had been in the thirties when the Inspectors noted the infusion of new blood. In 1947 there were twenty-two members of staff, of whom thirteen were of pre-war vintage: the headmaster himself and Messrs Aldridge, Garrett, Hall, Hopewell, Jacob, Machin, Maguire, Stevens, Tucker, Upcher, Wood and Young. The Inspectors in 1952 thought the staff still not as well-qualified as it might be, but 'there is distinction in one or two quarters, promise in others, and there is little sign of real weakness'.[14] And it was a growing staff: by 1955 there were twenty-eight.

Expansion is not evident in buildings during these years. At the time of the school centenary, the then bursar surveyed the post-war period. He listed all the improvements made in that twenty years, at a total cost of around a quarter of a million pounds.[15] But there had been only limited progress during Loveday's last years and for that period he was able to identify only:

1947   Purchase of High Upfold Farm
1949   War Memorial alcove in Reading Room
1952   Grass laid in Quadrangle

Obviously the most notable of these was the purchase of the farm.[16] It lay on land adjoining school property on the north side and came up for auction in 1946. The governors decided to put in a bid of up to £14,000 for the farm, buildings and 81 acres of land.[17] Having purchased it, a further £7,200 was spent in 1947 on livestock, dairy equipment and other machinery, with an estimated expenditure of £1,672 for more livestock, fencing and implements.[18] It was an enormous investment for the school, equivalent to about 122 boys' fees. It was financed not by appeal, but by mortgages.[19] About 100 acres of land now came under cultivation: eighteen acres was to be pasturage and winter oats, potatoes, peas and rye grass were planted.[20] Within a year a thirty strong dairy herd (non-pedigree tubercular-tested Ayrshire heifers) was installed, a bull purchased, and by the winter of 1947 fourteen heifer calves had been born. The school magazine waxed almost embarrassingly lyrical:

> 'The dairy cows grace the fields, and the small calves frisk around their pens. The young bull feeds happily in his box, giving an occasional bawl when he thinks the cowman is not coming quickly enough with his food.'

The promised poultry never materialized but in 1949 forty-eight pigs were bought.[21] An agricultural society was formed to organize trips and lectures, and in 1948 an agricultural sixth was added as a specialist group alongside the 'naval and military sixth'.[22] The academic impact on the school was not as impressive as might have been hoped. A survey of boys in 1949 to discover their favourite subjects revealed English, Geography and History well ahead of the field with over 12% of the votes each, while agriculture came thirteenth out of eighteen with 1.6%, Zoology 15= with .8% and veterinary science 16= with .4%.[23] This highlights a problem: what was the purpose of the new venture? Was Cranleigh to make a bid to become again, as was claimed of her in Merriman's day, the leading school for agriculture in the country? Surrey was no longer the rural backwater it had been in the 1880s. Boys at Cranleigh did not come from farming backgrounds, only a few a year intending to go into farming, and besides the modern route involved academic qualifications and further education at a university or agricultural college. A writer on Surrey in 1970 could point to the farm as an interesting 'unusual feature' of the school,[24] but neither the governors nor the headmaster and staff ever articulated a clear statement of exactly what place the farm should have in the life of the boys and the school. As financial losses mounted year by year, the governors grew increasingly worried about its role in an academic institution as well as about its financial viability. During its first ten years, losses totalled over £12,000, and as much as £2,000 in one year alone

(1952). Even in a good year, 1948, losses were £383 as against an expected profit of £860.[25] It never could be seen as making a profit even though it supplied milk to the school at a price advantageous to the farm. Over the years, various justifications of its role were adduced. One argument was that it protected the whole north and north-western side of the school from encroachment by village housing; it didn't require a farm there to do that. Another was that it provided fresh milk and vegetables for the school, but there was no financial advantage to the school in this, given the overheads of running the farm. From an educational point of view it was argued that it gave training in farm management; or that it was a 'selling-point' for that or other reasons when parents visited the school. All these points were made in the late forties and early fifties, but no coherent policy was ever worked out: Loveday's successor faced the problem from the moment he arrived, and was as unable as his predecessor to provide really convincing good reason for the school to go on losing money every year. But this was to be merely one of the problems he faced, and when he left in 1959 it was still unsettled.

So although the decade after the second world war was, by many indicators, a time of progress for the school, the most evident symbol of that progress – the acquistion and development of the farm – indicates some of the problems faced by public schools in this period and some of the ambivalence with which they faced the modern world. The outward forms and practices at most public schools continued as if there had never been a war, and only a certain defensiveness and an occasional attempted rapprochement with local education authorities indicated that there was a Labour government in power. Some of the more exotic displays of school dress – at Cranleigh boaters and striped blazers – had been casualties of the war years and did not return. But in many respects the schools of the late forties looked very much like the schools of the late twenties or thirties. In an 'era of long-range plans',[26] in education and elsewhere, public schools were not forward-looking; Cranleigh did not attempt to foresee future trends or keep in the van of educational and social experiment, as schools were forced to do in the 1960s. The attitudes to the farm are indicative of this at Cranleigh. So too was the decision not to encourage the admission of coloured boys.[27] The discussion on this matter resulted from the request of a high commission in London for a place for a diplomat's boy. Of course at the back of the governors' minds there was undoubtedly the fear that Cranleigh parents would be surprised to see coloured faces among the school's population. But there was another aspect as well. Most boys came as a result of having been put down for the school years before, and also having been prepared for the Common Entrance examination at prep schools in England or abroad. Applications from coloured parents tended to come in very late, and often the boy concerned had not been prepared for the public schools' syllabus. With a little more imagination – as was shown many decades later in the 1970s – such problems could have been overcome, but one must take into consideration the climate of the age and also the fact that Cranleigh could not realistically expect to attract the sons of kings, princes and maharajahs who patronized some of the English public schools, and who usually make an appearance in the school stories of Frank Richards and the like.

Perhaps it is a pity also that the governors rejected Loveday's suggestion that Cranleigh might buy the lease of Hesketh. This school, 'Miss Tapp's' it was called, was one of the few places in the area where pre-prep education was available.[28] Of course both of these decisions could be justified: Cranleigh was full and its entry lists looked healthy. There seemed every reason to suppose that the trend was upwards, since the birth-rate indicated an ever growing school population until well into the eighties – a faulty projection, as it happened, since the school population began to contract in the mid-seventies.[26] But it was evident that despite post-war austerity (or possibly because of it) parents still 'sought out schools in the private sector'.[26] Some were, no doubt, trying to avoid the possibility of failure at the new 11+ examination and fought shy of secondary modern schools. More significantly, the south-east of England was, and increasingly, populated by parents who wished for and could afford a private education for their children whether for its academic benefits, or for convenience, or out of simple snobbery. Given the failure of the Labour government to tackle the 'public school problem' there was scarcely any incentive within the independent schools to change or to construct new patterns of education or contacts with the maintained system. Yet, as the school magazine had commented in its editorials in the post-war years, times were changing, and this was reflected in the state of morale within the school. There were good things of course. Examination results in 1948 were the best to date. Boys were going up to Oxford and Cambridge who were to go on to distinguished careers: Christopher Dearnely in music, Anthony Caesar in the church, David Calcutt in law, Richard Hastie-Smith in the Civil Service, Peter Hazell in schoolmastering. In 1948 R. F. Barrow became a fellow of Exeter College, Oxford; in 1951 the Revd H. A. Williams was elected to a fellowship at Trinity, Cambridge. Nor was success confined to the things of the mind. In 1948 P. D. Cameron and J. M. Langmead were runners-up in the Public Schools Squash Doubles. And in the decade after the war the first fifteen – but not the hockey or cricket teams – experienced a run of good seasons, and that is usually taken as some kind of indication of the state of morale in the school. So is food, and there the picture did not look so bright. The school had managed rather well during the difficult war years.[29] But in 1946 the housemasters asserted that 'the boys were underfed' and there were warnings from the school doctor that physical activities would have to be curtailed if the amount of food were not 'materially increased'.[30] It was a bad omen in a Britain where the war, despite shortages and monotony, had actually stimulated an improvement generally in the nutritional value of the food schoolchildren ate, and at a time when the welfare state was making significant strides in ante-natal and child care.[31] The problem at Cranleigh rumbled on: it was discussed in 1951[32] and in 1953, by which time the headmaster, evidently rather tired of hearing complaints from boys, directed that any questions about food and diet should be raised with housemasters and not with him.[33] Rationing ceased in the nation in 1954 but the problem continued.[34] Perhaps it only finally ended with the introduction of cafeteria feeding in 1972.

There were other indications of low morale or discontent: complaints about bad behaviour at the Richmond sevens rugger competition in 1949; a storm in the same year over the garb in which 2 North played a housematch;[35] complaints that 'support given to school teams . . . was deplorable'.[36] But every institution has such moments of self-doubt. As the last wartime restrictions were lifted, and as slowly and then with increasing rapidity an affluent society developed in Britain, eyes at Cranleigh began to look to the future and to the schools Centenary in 1965. It was at this moment that David Loveday retired. Before him lay another career, first as archdeacon of Surrey and then as Bishop of Dorchester. Cranleigh, like the nation, was bound to experience great changes in the fifties. The very nature of David Loveday's headmastership ensured that, for his was a very personal control, and it was he to whom, above all, the Inspectors pointed in 1952 when they tried to analyse the school 'knit together as a compact community' with none of 'the centifrugal tendencies observable in some schools'.[14] A change of headmaster at this juncture was crucial: it was unlikely that any other man could step straight into David Loveday's shoes, or indeed would want to exercise such personal and centralized control over the place that was a feature of both the Rhodes and the Loveday regimes. Loveday's early-thirties concern for creating a school with more autonomous and adventurous housemasters had not been maintained,[37] perhaps because of the pressures of wartime, perhaps because of decline in numbers, or perhaps because of Loveday's own growing experience and his strong personality and flair.

In April 1954 the new headmaster arrived, having been elected unanimously to the post.[38] Henry March came from a school very different from Cranleigh: at Charterhouse, where he had been head of modern languages and a housemaster, he was used to much greater house autonomy, more boys and higher academic standards. March attempted to diagnose the 'problems' at Cranleigh.[39] He saw the basic problem as low quality of intake; although the school was full the candidates for entrance scholarships were poor, the examination results at senior level were weak, and all too many boys left school early.[40] Any solutions to the problem in academic terms would take a long time to work through the system and perhaps even longer to get across to prep schools, whose patronage of Cranleigh was rather less enthusiastic than it had been in the mid-thirties. Even though the scholarships were more valuable now the number of prep schools sending candidates had not risen appreciably; and of course Cranleigh's own prep school provided a larger percentage of the intake now than before the war: it had grown from a school of under fifty in the early thirties to a school of eighty-plus in the mid and late fifties. The governors realized that a message that might get through more quickly to parents and prep schools would be an improvement in the facilities and buildings at Cranleigh. Almost immediately, the builders moved in. By 1955 the Junior School was first to benefit with a new gymnasium, kitchen and library; the old kitchen area provided space for three new classrooms, and extra washing and changing facilities were provided. It was the first significant development at the Junior School since its opening in 1912, and there was some hope that now, as then, it would stimulate renewal at the senior school as well.[41] By 1956 it had a fine new swimming pool as well, and the beginnings of an orchard on its approach road to mitigate the rather gaunt appearance of the buildings at the top of the hill. Changes at the senior school began with the headmaster's announcement to housemasters in December 1955 that 'art would begin quietly next term'.[42] March, like the ill-fated Tyler, was enthusiastic about developing this side of the school. Economic pressure had forced art out of the timetable in 1931 when Clinton, the talented 'drawing master' departed.[43] The old tuck shop building which had housed Carn Brae during the war and junior school overflow after it until the opening of their new buildings, would provide a spacious setting for the new subject. But perhaps it began 'quietly' because the introduction of art at other schools after the war had been greeted in some cases with outrage, as might happen in the rather tough environs of Cranleigh.[44] At any rate, the event went unrecorded in the school magazine. Rather more publicity was given to another advance of 1955: new biology laboratories were opened behind the 1912 science school by Sir William Penny, leading atomic scientist and the father of two boys at the school.[45] Other new buildings soon followed. In 1956 a set of semi-detached houses (Lowerfold and Horseshoe) was built in Horseshoe Lane as masters' accommodation; for the same purpose the Old House was converted into flats. The West cloisters were rebuilt in 1957 and a new dormitory constructed for West in the following year. In 1959 a new swimming bath and changing rooms were opened as a memorial to the fallen of World War Two, and as a first stage in the building programme connected with the centenary appeal.[46] Further buildings were on the drawing board, depending on the success of that appeal which by 1959 stood at £60,000.

There were other signs that Cranleigh was 'obviously progressing':[47] games flourished. During the new headmaster's first three years, the 1st XV won 33 of the 37 matches they played, and in 1955 had the only unbeaten season on record. At Speech Day 1956 the headmaster was able to record the athletic feats of H. B. Thorpe who had become the first Cranleighan to run the mile in less than 4½ minutes. He talked also of a 'steady improvement' in work.[48] But already there were some signs that all was not well. In June 1956 the services of the bursar were dispensed with; he had been at the school for less than four years and had 'lost the confidence of the Council and of the Headmaster'.[49] In 1958 – and perhaps it was a straw in the wind – the headmaster unsuccessfully opposed the acceptance of an offer by an OC to repaint the honours boards in the gym; March considered they were 'not in keeping with modern ideas', but the governors thought otherwise.[50] A year later the governors were expressing concern about the emphasis on music which the headmaster was fostering.[51] By then, however, it was becoming very clear that things were going wrong.

As early as June 1955, just a year after March's arrival, the second master sought an interview with the chairman of the governors. They were a formidable pair. H. P. Jacob, the second master since 1954, had been at the school under Rhodes, and was one of the outstanding senior prefects of the 1920s. He had been 'the most successful'[52] of Gower's pupils on the rugger field, and although no great academic had gone up to Oxford where he represented the university in rugger and hockey. He joined the staff at his old school in 1930. The chairman of the governors, C. G. Windle, had been a contemporary of his at school. Windle had recently taken over the chairmanship from Sir Francis Floud, who had moved to the more prestigious but less onerous chairmanship of the council. Windle was also a current Cranleigh parent in that summer of 1955 when Jacob approached him. The second master complained that the headmaster was ineffectual, indecisive, and made no impact on the school.[53] Windle subsequently took soundings from some fellow OCs who were also governors, and from 'some very senior masters'. They confirmed what the second master had said. In July Windle, accompanied by Floud, interviewed the Headmaster and told him of the complaints. March asked for time to consider what he called, with some prescience, the 'indictment'. He then saw Floud, a month later, who passed on to Windle and the other governors his feeling that he was satisfied; Windle agreed to back the headmaster though he confessed later that he still had 'mental reservations'. There the matter rested for three years and the headmaster might well have thought it was dead and buried. The affair blew up again in 1958 however, this time in public. The senior prefect had cut chapel and declared himself an 'atheist'. Jacob reported the matter to March who, while angry, was inclined to leniency. Jacob disliked the headmaster's handling of the affair, and his lack of consultation with himself and other staff. He resigned from the secondmastership, though he agreed to stay on for the moment as an assistant master. Criticism of the headmaster was now out in the open however, and in November Windle warned March of mounting discontent. On 13 December 1958 the *Illustrated London News* carried a long, well-illustrated article on the school: it was flattering, a part of a series on public schools and as such was good publicity. The school magazine was moved to complain, however, about the power of the press: '. . . it gives great food for thought that a magazine, however good, can wield the power to make such a difference to a school's prestige and self-esteem'[54]. Perhaps the writer had in mind a rather more damaging article in the press. On 16 February 1959 the *Daily Express* published an expose of the troubles at the school, under the large headline, 'So it's "Good-bye Jake"''. Whoever had tipped the newspaper off it picked the story up and pursued it. A reporter visited Jacob, who was still living in his school house, and also met the ex-senior prefect who had now left the school but was having tea with his own former housemaster 'just 50 yards down the road from Mr Jacob's home'. The effect of the article, which simply told the story of Jacob's resignation from the second mastership in the previous year, and his impending resignation from teaching altogether, was devastating. On 6 March Windle received a letter from one of the housemasters: all the criticisms of the headmaster were true, the letter claimed, and reiterated the points made by Jacob to Windle four years previously: that the headmaster was ineffective and was making no impact on the school, that he was indecisive, and that he was presiding over a school where morale among masters and boys was sinking. 'That letter was for me the end', Windle later claimed. A week afterwards, on 14 March, the governors met and agreed unanimously that the headmaster should be invited to resign as from the end of the Lent term; were he to refuse, he would be dismissed. It was also agreed that Jacob should be appointed as acting headmaster. These extraordinary decisions were to be put to a specially convened meeting of the Council for ratification; meanwhile, Windle saw March and apprised him of the situation. Without awaiting ratification by the council, March sent Windle his letter of resignation: however he would go not at the end of the Lent term, but in the summer. Meanwhile the headmaster and his supporters had called upon some outside aid: Robert Birley, March's headmaster at Charterhouse and past chairman of the HMC, and Archbishop Fisher, an ex-officio member of the Council and chairman of the GBA.[55] On 19 March Fisher wrote to the governors making it clear that to demand the headmaster's resignation as from the end of the Lent term was to imply some gross moral turpitude. A hastily summoned meeting of governors on the 25 March accepted this, but was torn with dissension about the role in the whole affair which had been played by OC governors; one member felt there were too many matters 'labelled "Old Cranleighans only"'. The full meeting of the Council met a fortnight later in London: nineteen members attended, thirteen sent apologies, and three sent apologies along with letters of resignation. It boded ill, and it was a rough meeting. Much displeasure was expressed by Council members who were not Cranleigh governors and who had been dismayed to receive first intimation of trouble from reports in the press. However the Council managed to vote unanimously to accept March's resignation as from 31 August, and with rather less enthusiasm they agreed that Jacob should become acting headmaster for a year. While the second meeting of governors had been taking place in London on 25 March, equally dramatic events were unfolding at Cranleigh. It was the last day of term, and common room gathered for its final meeting. The headmaster, as was customary, delivered a short speech to the one master who was leaving – Jacob. In it he admitted that 'while it was possible to say goodbye to a colleague, it was not possible to say goodbye to a friend'.[56] The common room was unaware of the reversal of roles that was soon to take place. On 14 April a letter went out to masters and parents telling them the news of the headmaster's resignation; it was felt wise to delay the news of Jacob's appointment until 27 June. Nor was the suspense yet at an end, for it was not until 14 December that the announcement of David Emms's appointment as headmaster was made.[57]

It was a painful time for many; members of common room

felt insecure and Windle tried hard to reassure them. The school had received unwelcome publicity[58] and there was to be no entry for Cranleigh in the *Public School Year Book* of 1960. Moreover the new headmaster could not expect election to the HMC until its members were happy about rearrangements of the Council and governing body. A special subcommittee was appointed which reported back to the Council, and emendations of the Charter were sought which would give each school on the foundation – Cranleigh and St Catherine's – its own governing body and chairman, with a separate chairman of the Council.[59] To symbolize the changes, an outsider, Sir Arthur fforde, was obtained through the good offices of the Archbishop of Canterbury to act as Chairman of the Council. It must have been a painful time too for March, as he lived through his last term at Cranleigh, aware that in spite of all, his headmastership had seen the school become a more civilized place with better buildings and larger numbers. At the end of the term he went off to teach temporarily at Marlborough. The final irony came in 1964 when Charterhouse found itself in need of a temporary headmaster and appointed Henry March to the position. At Speech Day in 1959, Jacob paid handsome tribute to his predecessor:[60]

> 'He will always be remembered here as a man of high ideals who gave of his best to the school. Under him there grew up a new and lively interest in the arts generally, yet he understood and encouraged the sciences. To me, personally, he always showed the greatest kindness and consideration.'

Privately, to the governors, he was less enthusiastic; he thought the music department over-staffed, that morale was low, the school directionless, masters slack, discipline flabby and PT neglected.[61] He admitted that fundamental changes would have to be left to the new headmaster.

It is tempting to see the painful events of the late fifties at Cranleigh as being in some senses outside the control of the leading actors – March, Jacob, Windle. There are parallels with the developments of 1900–1911. Then, a new headmaster was faced with problems which perhaps a stronger man might have coped with; Tyler didn't, and took the blame. Looking at the post war years in public schools Jonathan Gathorne-Hardy stresses 'the complexity and diversity of the picture before us'.[4] Superficially, schools like Cranleigh might seem to have been travelling along the same well-worn groove in that decade after 1945; but it is obvious, if difficult to quantify, that new forms of wealth, egalitarian social pressures towards good schooling for all at secondary and tertiary levels, and even the advent of television, were bound to influence the development of public schools. Perhaps there was at Cranleigh, and other schools, a lack of direction in that decade which required tougher leadership than March could give if things were to be put right.[62] Meanwhile Jacob held the fort, the Appeal continued to call for more money with the Centenary just five years away, and the school awaited the arrival of its new headmaster. David Emms was tough, but he was also young. The combination seemed to be just what Cranleigh needed, and indeed ensured that the school would ride the storms of the sixties with more stability and less upset than at many schools.

CHAPTER TEN

Firm Government and the Permissive Society (1960–1970)

'THE MIDDLE AND LATE SIXTIES were among the blackest years in public school history. The schools were under attack from many directions. The Public Schools Commission was an overt political threat to their existence. Academic competition from the grammar schools hotted up. A new youth culture questioned their internal stability. Costs rose steeply, bringing with them sharp rises in fees . . . It was a bad time . . .'

So wrote Philip Venning in 1972.[1] With the longer perspective available now that the sixties are becoming history, we might wish to pre-date those changes and upheavals and see them beginning in the early sixties. Appropriately enough the musical 'Fings aint wot they used to be' opened in London in 1960. Cranleigh was likely to feel the wind of change before many other schools; 'Swinging London' was likely to affect her equilibrium sooner than that of schools more remote geographically or more traditional socially. Yet Cranleigh in the early sixties was peculiar; the school had gone through some years of turbulence already, and the new headmaster arrived in 1960 with a mandate that could not have been stronger: firm backing from the governors to do what had to be done, and with security of tenure in almost any eventuality. So Cranleigh's centenary was to come and go, and the 'pendulum years'[2] to begin and end, without the school being thrown off course, or turned upside down by the young revolutionaries. Nor did the revolutionaries within the Labour party, which had been

145

mustering its arguments against selection and privilege since the mid-fifties,[3] interfere directly with the school. Or perhaps the revolution was led from within and from the top, for the new headmaster was only 34.

David Emms arrived at Cranleigh in the summer of 1960. He had spent the previous nine years as an assistant master at Uppingham; this, his whole teaching career to date, had been preceded by a spell in the army, and at Oxford where he gained a rugger blue. He was Cranleigh's first rugger playing head-master which no doubt got him off to a good start with many, especially the OCs. He was well aware that he needed a good start. During his last term at Uppingham, and in a year when no Cranleigh entry appeared in the *Public School Year Book*, he had requested an Inspection of the school and the Ministry of Education had promised early compliance.[4] Even before they reported, Emms had begun to see the problem areas. Most obvious, though not necessarily most significant, was the ques-tion of buildings. Some progress had been made in March's time, though more especially at the Junior School. Long-term plans involved further building at the senior school as part of the Centenary effort. On his arrival there was one building operation already in progress: the science laboratories were being extended, with physics gaining a new building linking the old 1912 labs with the new biology block. The expansion was long overdue; many other schools were similarly backward in their provision for science teaching. To help remedy this the Industrial Fund for the Advancement of Scientific Education in Schools had been set up in 1955 and was generous in its grants to independent schools in an effort to encourage them to send out more scientists. Cranleigh had managed to gain a contribu-tion at the lower end of the range: £6,000 towards the £16,000 cost of the new building.[5] So progress was already in train on the academic side. As far as boys' accommodation was con-cerned there had been little progress since 1929. At his first speech day in October 1960, the headmaster outlined the problem: that the houses were too big, and that their physical surroundings and accommodation were inadequate.[6] In the new year he was beginning to feel more profoundly that all was not well in the houses.[7]

The problem was partly a legacy from the past. Until the first world war houses scarcely existed and masters were appointed to look after 'dormitories'. Even the great expansion of 1929 did not affect the basic nature of the houses, which were still simply dormitories and houserooms with no geographical coherence. The Inspectors noticed in the houserooms an atmosphere 'of perforce rather rigid discipline'.[8] The problem was compounded by the fact that there was only one bachelor housemaster, and he was the only one resident with his house: the other five housemasters lived in Horseshoe Lane, hundreds of yards away from their boys, and represented within their houses by tutors who were usually young bachelor masters. Coming as he did from the firmly house-based Uppingham, and with as his only other experience of boarding school the equally house-based Tonbridge where he himself had been a schoolboy, it is easy to see why Emms was perturbed. He expressed his worry in small ways that are highly demonstrative: he suggested that parents of new boys should be contacted personally by housemasters, and not via a circular letter sent out by the bursar.[9] He felt, as Loveday had done thirty years before, that the allocation of new boys to houses was not personal enough; the links between housemaster and prospective parent should be stronger.[10] It cannot have pleased him to read in a house magazine the comment by an American exchange student: 'something which appalled me when I first came here was the weak student-teacher relationship. Here masters are rarely in real contact with the boys'.[11] If Emms could afford to ignore that as a mere youthful protestation, he certainly could not ignore the evidence of the 'amorous life of adolescents', as a recent writer has called it.[12] The same writer claims: 'I find it quite impossible to imagine anything more sexually obsessed than a restrictive boys' public school in 1890 (or 1930 or 1960)'. Naturally, evidence is hard to come by, and such as there is tends to be highly coloured.[13] There seems little doubt that homosexuality was often 'fashionable', to use Emms's own word. When some evidence came to light at Cranleigh, Emms addressed the school in no uncertain terms[14] – though perhaps with less explicit detail than that recounted by OCs who were boys in the school at the time and later entertained a journalist to an account of what had happened.[15] He had to deal with the problem again two years later, and again addressed the school.[16] He had to deal with fears that some boys were making undesirable visits to the prep school.[17] It could all be seen as symptomatic, not simply of repressed teenage sexuality, but of faulty or inadequate house arrangements. At the end of his first term, Emms was able to announce some progress towards getting the houses right. A new house was to be opened in the sanatorium building which had been given by Cubitt in 1880, and which was now unnecessarily large for the attenuated functions it had to perform.[18] Cubitt House opened in September 1961 with accommodation for 60 boys and a bachelor housemaster. The boys were decanted from other houses, thus easing the pressure in the main school block. It was very much in line with the recommendations of the Inspectors, who had placed at the head of their list of priorities more studies and better accommodation for the boys.[8] It remained a top priority with the governors.[19] In 1963 plans came to fruition. Two housemasters, K. S. G. Wills and L. Marshall, replanned the house areas, creating as far as was possible geographically coherent houses. Emms saw this unscrambling, this final move from the 'hostel' to the 'house' system, as part of a larger strategy. 'For Cranleigh to be based on eight small boarding houses, all of them separate and three of them 'out', would appreciably improve our public image', he wrote.[20] After 1961 there were six houses; in 1964 work began on a seventh. It would be the second of the out-houses and the first purpose-built house in the school's history. It was to set new standards in accommodation for boys, culminating in the luxury of eight study-bedrooms.[21] The new building was taken over by the boys from one of the houses in the main block, 1 North, thereby creating more space for the remaining houses as well. The housemaster who had run 1 North for five years already moved into the staff accommodation which was linked to the boys' side and which – unlike the Cubitt counterpart – was suitable for a married man. The eighth house Emms had written of came into being partially with the opening of the sixth form centre in 1972, and fully with the building of Loveday in 1980. A plan, suggesting once more the re-naming of all the houses except Cubitt, was shelved and has never been revived.[22] By the centenary year Emms could feel that the surroundings were coming right; apart from unscrambling of the houses the list of other additions was formidable: in 1961 the 6-classroom Rhodes block opened by the gym, and a further classroom adjoined the gym on the site of the old fives courts; in 1962 carpentry workshops were opened and a house in Horseshoe Lane – 'Birdbrook' – was purchased to provide temporary accommodation for boys; in the same year the armoury was extended and in the following year changing rooms and showers were installed in the gym.[23] But when Emms surveyed this scene of continuous expansion of facilities he realized that behind the bricks and mortar and more important than those lay the question of human relationships and the nature of authority within the houses.

In his first few years as headmaster, Emms felt that the smack of firm government was needed in the school: partly this was a result of the traumatic times through which the school had passed; partly the feeling sprang from the headmaster's own temperament. During his first term he reported 'considerable evidence of lack of good discipline' to the governors.[24] First he tackled the externals: pointed shoes,[25] short mackintoshes, drain-pipe trousers and bright pullovers were banned.[26] 'Fancy' haircuts were outlawed; 'a little squareness is an excellent thing', the headmaster told parents in 1960.[6] But these were outward manifestations. Nevertheless they were rules, and rules have to be enforced, and it was the house authority structure that was and is primarily charged with enforcing them. Here Emms saw problems. Housemasters, he felt, were trying to cope with too many boys: the average size of a house was 70.[24] In this situation was it possible to claim, as Dancy of Marlborough was doing a few years later in his apologia for boarding education, that a housemaster could know 'his' boys better than anyone else, including their own fathers?[27] And what of the prefects in a large house where the housemaster lived out? Emms felt the prefects were not doing their job, and that they 'must be wholly "on the side of the law" or should not accept the office'.[28] He felt that an indication of this laxness was the prevalence of smoking, and he proclaimed fierce penalties: for a second offence the culprit would be expelled.[29] And everyone would be subject to the ruling that bedtimes were to be strictly enforced, and that even school prefects should be in bed with lights out by 11 p.m.[29] But even allowing that there were good prefects, how might they be equipped to perform their task better? Some prefects felt they ought to be allowed to 'slipper', as a half-way house between a trivial punishment and a beating by the house captain. That idea was discussed in 1961, and again in 1963, but no decision was taken.[30] Indeed events overtook that idea, as a feeling grew 'among the boys themselves' that corporal punishment should not be administered at all by boys.[31] In 1964 the HMC commissioned a survey of the public schools, and Cranleigh's answer to the question of beating was that only house captains could beat, and only after consultation with the housemaster.[32] In the next year, beating of boys by boys was abolished altogether, so that when the HMC survey was eventually published it was out of date. It showed that in the 98 boarding or mainly boarding schools surveyed, corporal punishment was administered by boys in 71 of them.[33] That figure should be 70, or less; it would be interesting to know how many schools had felt, as the masters at Cranleigh did, that this 'ultimate deterrent should be confined to operation by members of staff only'.[31] In the early seventies, caning was abandoned altogether at the school.

But if prefects were not allowed to beat, were they at least to continue to be privileged persons? The system certainly depended on their cooperation with members of staff, and privileges had always been part of the way in which they had been rewarded. Loveday in the thirties had drawn up a definitive list of twenty privileges ranging from having coats unbuttoned and being allowed 'hands in pockets' to being allowed to 'sleep on the fire escape with housemaster's permission'.[34] Emms found the prefects rather vague about their privileges when he raised the topic on several occasions.[30] He did in fact give them one: while he was tightening up dress regulations, house prefects were allowed to wear cardigan type pullovers, and school prefects cloth waistcoats, while 'the fancy clothes being worn by the juniors' were banned.[30] But the development of the debate on privileges runs parallel to that on beating; by 1965 the prefects themselves were petitioning that one of their long-standing privileges upon which all were agreed – having jacket buttons undone – should be cancelled. The housemasters concurred.[35] A similar fate overtook fagging. In 1964 some form of fagging existed in all but 34 of the 88 schools surveyed by Kalton.[36] The system had never been very refined at Cranleigh; Loveday explained in 1944 that 'the system of shouting "fag" and employing the last boy to come which was neither sensible nor economical of time is not employed, but we do not object to junior boys doing small jobs or running messages for prefects'.[37] Even so, the system was probably open to abuse and it came under criticism from housemasters in 1963.[38] Within a year it had been decided to abandon all personal fagging, except for the senior prefect. In September 1964 it was declared that 'personal fagging is now ended, as out of touch with modern times'.[38]

These developments in fagging and beating, and their eventual abolition, had a profound effect on the quality of the relationships between boy and boy. It was not that the whole authority structure crumbled; indeed the headmaster set the tone – which was bound to bolster the confidence of prefects in their disciplinary dealing – of firm government. John Rae identifies the effects of such changes and relates them in the long term to a decline in homosexual activity (though the development of co-education is another factor here), fewer bullying incidents and the role of prefects being 'closer to that of the friendly neighbourhood policeman than the platoon sergeant'.[39] In the long term they also had profound effects on the role of masters and on relations between masters and boys, but that was a development of the seventies. If, as we have seen, relationships between boy and boy changed at Cranleigh during the early sixties, so too did relations between boys and authority. While boys could be allowed to declare their interest in abandoning privilege or beating or fagging, it was rather more delicate when they opposed compulsory activities such as the Combined Cadet Force. In the mid-sixties, most boarding schools still had a compulsory CCF.[40] At Cranleigh, as at many schools, it had been founded during the Boer War, had become the 'OTC' in 1908, the 'JTC' from 1940–48, and since 1948 had been the CCF.[41] It was large enough to maintain a band, draw considerable support from the War Office, and reflect within its ranks something of the discipline structure of the school at large. During the sixties the feeling grew that it was an anachronism. The great events in the world at large – the nuclear threat, the Cuba Missile Crisis of 1962, the long, painful and fully-televized Vietnam War in the late sixties – had their effects on the young. Rather than steeling their resolve to defend their democratic way of life against totalitarianism they posed instead questions about the morality and practicality of large, and ultimately nuclear, defence establishments. Other factors played their part in this: Britain's withdrawal from empire raised questions about the country's role as a great power; the folk heroes of the young were men of the left – Che Guevara, Nelson Mandela, Ho Chi Mihn. In 1963 the play 'Oh What a Lovely War' appeared on the London stage, and perfectly encapsulated the cynicism and sense of futility that the thought of war evoked. These feelings percolated through to schools after the heyday of CND but even before the widespread anti-war demonstrations in the USA of the mid to late sixties. Already in 1960 the Commanding officer of the Corps had 'remarked on the criticism of the CCF which was common these days'.[42] That was in Jacob's last term. Emms, when he arrived, could feel that this lack of enthusiasm was merely a symptom of a more general malaise at Cranleigh. For several years the problem lay dormant; the headmaster acted only to try to stimulate enthusiasm generally and forbid the calling of masters by their military ranks (except on corps parade or during PT periods!) When passing this directive on to the prefects, he remarked on the 'rather amateurish CCF' in the school.[43] As with fagging and beating, it was to be the headmaster and outside forces which had as much to do with the changes that came about as any pressure from the boys. Other headmasters in the area voiced their concern in 1962 that government cuts would undermine their contingents.[44] And in 1966 it was a representative from the Ministry of Defence, Major-General J. A. d'Avigdor-Goldsmid, who was pressing for the introduction of voluntary corps.[45] In 1967 the headmaster was still defending the principle of compulsion, and noting the interest and support from parents: 'perhaps they regard it as a sort of buttress of discipline in the worrying world with which they are faced at the present time'.[46] To bolster morale within the CCF and help boys see it as an integral part of school life he instituted in that year housemaster visits on corps days; in fact these tended to have an opposite effect, and to make the officers in particular feel that they were being 'inspected'. But already things were changing: in June 1967 it was announced that the most recent intake of cadets would be given the option of leaving the corps once they had passed the Proficiency Test and had attended an annual camp or an arduous training session.[47] Ironically, all this happened in the wake of Cranleigh's foremost shooting success: in June 1967, the school team won the Ashburton shield at Bisley and were photographed proudly bearing their trophy – and wearing their CCF uniform.[48]

The 'lack of enthusiasm' which the headmaster had diagnosed in 1961 also affected other areas. Critical among these was the issue of compulsory chapel. Cranleigh had always been a Church of England school and there had never been any exceptions to the rule that all boys attended chapel regularly, on Sundays and weekdays. More than that, it was Christian values – in schools and in the nation at large – which had seemed to provide that moral consensus which is the vital underpinning in any community or society. These values, and with them the doctrinal and ritual structures represented by church or chapel, came under attack more significantly in the sixties than at any time since the founding of the school. Royston Lambert, who spent the years 1964–67 compiling information and comments from boarding school masters and pupils (including Cranleighans), lists some of these criticisms:[49]

> 'Many pupils resent the dogmatic, narrow and above all compulsory aspect of religion in an institution which, in so many other respects, sets out to inculcate criticism, discrimination, breadth of view, self-direction and freedom of choice. This contradiction causes anger . . . The final cause of the discontent with religion is the nature of the services. For large numbers of boys and girls the content is monotonous . . .'

There was much discussion of compulsory chapel and religion in schools at a session of the centenary conference, led by an OC, the Revd Harry Williams. He pointed out that what he called 'vulgarized Freud' and 'popular science' had played a large part in the current attack on the Faith by inculcating cynicism and simplistic notions of scientific 'proof'.[50] But in fact, again, the authorities at Cranleigh had moved before they were pushed. In 1962 the first voluntary service was introduced – a Sunday evening service of compline.[51] It was a modest beginning, but by the end of 1963, after a long debate in housemasters' committee, daily compulsory chapel was abolished.[52] In its place there were three compulsory morning chapels (one of which was congregational practice) and two voluntary ones. Despite occasional heartsearchings about the new order, it survived; with all the subsequent reshufflings and permutations, the principle has remained that only two acts of worship on weekdays are compulsory. House prayers in the evenings were unaffected and remain a matter for the house authorities. In a sense, it had been a preemptive strike by authority: Cranleigh suffered little of the latent or overt chapel troubles that plagued many schools in the late sixties and early seventies. It did mean, however, as the chaplain said in 1967, that Christianity had 'in a way to sell itself'.[48] The relaxation of the old disciplines, in chapel as in other areas of school life, threw more responsibility onto the masters, or the prefects; automatic discipline or acquiescence could not be taken for granted. In chapel, and in the classroom, masters had to compete in a world that was increasingly dominated by television, advertising, and the cult of the 'new' and the 'instant'.

The chapel building itself came under scrutiny. Like the services within its walls, it had changed little over previous decades. Seating was a problem as the school grew bigger. So too was the decor. To modern eyes the dull red brick inscribed with 'appropriate' texts, and the stained glass, made it 'a very dark and rather gloomy building'[53] Redecoration and new lighting were organized. The result was a brighter chapel, with white walls and a blue ceiling, brought into use on Whitsunday 1965. To the purist, especially with the revival of interest in Victoriana after the sixties, it was an act of vandalism. To the school authorities at the time it represented a determination to present the Faith in attractive surroundings; it was another preemptive strike.

The chapel at the Junior School also received attention. It was a wooden building, and rather shabby. The man behind the moves to remedy this was known as 'Ancient OC', which preserved his annonymity until his death in 1964. He was in fact the Revd J. F. Spink, who had already given £2,500 towards the tuck shop conversion when in 1960 he approached the Junior School authorities with the offer of money to build a chapel. In the end he paid £12,500, and while he did not entirely approve of the modern lines of the new building, it was a triumph for Cranleigh. It is an outstanding small building, on rather Scandinavian lines; its chief feature is the east wall which is all glass, giving the altar a back-drop of the ever-changing greens, browns and golds of the Surrey countryside. It was opened in 1962 and bore a suitable and well-researched inscription in Latin which the punctilious Spink had had vetted by some of the country's top classics.[54] The 'new look' at the Junior school which had begun in the mid-fifties was also enhanced in the sixties by the building of four new classrooms in 1962, and the acquisition of a new 4–5 acre playing field, two new classrooms and new washing facilities in 1964. In a decade, the appearance and capacity of the Junior School had been utterly transformed. Its first master, Mertens, had lived long enough to see the changes wrought by his successors, Moore and Blackshaw, and now – and these were the most significant advances – in the time of Michael Wheeler, who had taken over the Mastership in 1961 after the sudden death of Charles Blackshaw.

By the time of the centenary, just half way through Emms's headmastership, it was evident that a firm hand and an innovative mind had been at work. The headmaster had announced, perhaps prematurely in 1962, that 'the school was recovering the balance and happiness which, for a time, it had lost'.[55] But by 1965 that was true. Great changes had taken place, and smaller innovations were in train as well. The link with St Catherine's had been revived in 1960 when girls had come over to act in a school production for the first time since the pageant in 1926.[56] From 1961 there were regular meetings between sixth formers from the two schools, involving discussions, tea and sometimes dancing, 'thus adding to the many advantages of a Public School a more cosmopolitan and colourful atmosphere'.[57] Other small changes moved Cranleigh forward. In the summer of 1961 tennis achieved the status of a minor sport, with inter-school fixtures.[58] In the same term housemasters were informed that coloured boys might in future be admitted 'in moderation'.[59] In 1963 the housemasters' campaign to have doors fitted to the school lavatories finally succeeded.[60] It was a symbolic moment. So too were all the events of the Centenary. One thing was missing: the school did not manage to secure a member of the Royal Family for any of the events of 1965; it was a disappointment. But it was a busy and eventful year anyway:[61] there was a celebration concert with a performance of *Jabberwocky* especially composed by an OC, Derek Bourgeois; there was a Centenary Ball at the Dorchester Hotel; there was an Open Day at the school and the production of a school film;[62] there was the announcement that the Centenary Appeal Target of £200,000 had almost been reached. And there was a service in Guildford cathedral. Giving the sermon the Rt Revd George Reindorp, Bishop of Guildford and a member of the Council, told the congregation of over a thousand:[63]

'Do not look back on your hundredth birthday. Look ahead. "Behold, I make all things new" says our God'.

It was a good motto for the middle years of the decade and the school took his advice. It is interesting that 1965 was also the year when the quiet, smooth moves towards solving the public school 'problem' in the nation at large took a new turn.[27] The Department of Education's Circular 10/65 proclaimed the Labour Government's intention of moving towards a fully-comprehensive educational system. And the Newsome Commission began its deliberations on the future of the public schools. It was, it seemed, a time of growing threats to the independence of the public schools, which were to suffer from the wave of student unrest and activism that swept the country, and indeed the western world, in the late sixties. By 1968 the Public Schools Commission was reporting that 'the country's leading boarding schools' should be 'turned into State-supervized comprehensives' as one newspaper proclaimed,[64] or as another cried with zest, 'No more of those Eton suits – No more fagging – And . . . I say, chaps, Girls in the remove'.[65] Cranleigh could well feel rather complacent as far as that headline was concerned. In fact the school in the mid to late sixties was formulating its own response to the challenge of the times. As one reporter observed in 1968, it 'seems to be shooting in all directions with elan'.[66] *West Side Story* indicates how things were moving. In 1963 plans got under way for what was to be the most exciting and radical departure in drama at Cranleigh since Redgrave's activities of the early thirties. There had been much good drama in the school since then but *West Side Story* was different. It involved two girls' schools, a ballet school, three professionals and an augmented orchestra. It was long in the planning stage with much discussion on both the technicalities and the ethics of the production.[67] It was a huge success when performed in March 1964. And it initiated a run of musicals and plays directed or inspired by a director of drama who believed that 'the place for drama in the school curriculum is not just as an occasional happening but as an integral and co-ordinated part of the school's life' in which 'the human mind and body are uniquely exercised and developed'.[68] In subsequent years productions included *Othello* (1964), *Cavaleria Rusticana*, *Waiting for Godot* (1965), *The Insect Play* (1966), *Anthony & Cleopatra*, *Carmen* (1967), *Carmina Burana*, *Salad Days* (1968), *Boris Godunov*, *Trial by Jury* and *Twelfth Night* (1969). And it was a feature of these years that the music, art and drama departments all worked hand in hand, making Cranleigh again a 'place of culture'.

There was an evident explosion of other activities in these years as well: expeditions to Norway, Wales, the Rhine, Paris, and the Lake District gave Cranleighans, as never before, the opportunity to travel in school parties. This in part reflects not only the expansion of activities in the school but also the greater affluence of parents in these years. A new general studies course was initiated in 1969 and a master appointed especially to mastermind it: it broke new ground based as it was on large weekly sixth form 'conferences' on important issues, supplemented by regular 'cluster' or small group meetings as well. It was a project that attracted the attention of other schools. And all these changes and events were recorded in a school magazine which, as if to symbolize the way things were moving at Cranleigh, adopted in 1967 a different size and style breaking with a ninety-year old tradition.

In 1968 *The Times* criticized the Public School Commission's report: 'Until a better scheme is produced the public schools should be left to their own resources – to flourish if they can: to wither away if they must'.[69] Emms was determined that Cranleigh should flourish; this had already meant adaptation and innovation. The process could not stop now. In response to the Royal Commission's report he began to identify ways in which Cranleigh was developing and might develop in the future: more casual clothes, more contact with parents, a better general education, more contact with girls. And significantly he said, 'I think the school can develop a role as a neighbourhood boarding school'.[70] These were all pointers to the future, to the Cranleigh of the seventies and beyond. But meanwhile innovation could not preempt all the demands that arose in the late sixties. There were signs of strain within common room itself, the headmaster being particularly anxious that 'no apparent split between senior and junior' masters should become evident to the boys.[71] To the strain on masters caused by the greater work-load that had resulted from a general easing of the disciplines imposed on boys by boys and by the erosion of hierarchy, was added the further strain of a common room in which the younger masters often tended to feel sympathy with boy demands. It was a phenomenon that would grow as young masters were recruited who had themselves been part of the teenage revolution of the mid and late sixties, and who often came in straight from universities where student ferment was given much freer rein than in schools. If the 'moral consensus' looked threatened by changing attitudes to chapel, it looked even more shaky when masters themselves could not agree or could not retain some kind of united front. It threw into relief, though never very starkly or dramatically at Cranleigh, the problem which perhaps lay at the heart of the 'permissive society'. One commentator, though not dealing with schools in particular, notes the threat the new age posed to ideas of community. 'It is the common experience of the permissive society that its citizens do not belong',[72] he notes. Translated into action within a boarding community, the response to the permissive society meant, in the words of the headmaster, a belief that 'most boys . . . were helped by a framework of routine and of certain standards'.[71]

The problem was: what standards could be regarded as irreducible? Having made the innovations and changes which were at some other schools to become issues – about fagging, beating, chapel, CCF, privilege – where was the sticking point? One issue that looked as if it might loom very large was the question of dress; it was a 'good' issue for the young because it

was an outward symbol and seemed to say a lot about confor-
mity or individuality. Desultory warfare continued over this in
the second half of the sixties; headmaster's letters to parents
often specified the prohibitions: no boots or 'bootees', no
non-regulation overcoats, sober coloured socks only, turn-ups
required on all trousers. It was an issue that would continue on
into the seventies, mitigated somewhat by the gradual permission to wear casual clothing on more and more occasions. But
school uniform was never quite the *casus belli* that hair became.

> 'To the young, short hair was identified with the adult world,
> with the military and the police, with "squareness". To grow
> your hair long was to identify with other young people in their
> rebellion against convention. It was also seen, paradoxically, as
> a gesture of individuality . . . it was an expression of adolescent
> sexuality'.[39]

Beginning in 1964, the question of hair length featured regularly in headmagisterial edicts.[73] It was a battle that lasted for a
full decade, though it was only gathering force in 1964, and had
lost most of its vigour by 1974. It was a battle that engaged
parents and governors and old boys – most of whom had a
feeling that schools were being rather weak in not insisting
upon sterner standards. Schools pointed to the dictates of
fashion; Emms held that 'the length of boys' hair . . . bore no
relation to scholastic attainment', but still was aware that he
had to hold a line, and he 'had no intention of budging
whatsoever'.[71] He did budge, as did the country, and adults,
and the whole climate of the age; even the hair of elder
statesmen began to creep over the ears and to touch the collar.
And when the fashion changed, as it had done decisively by the
late seventies, only then did the issue of hair cease to be a
talking point and a symbol of rebellion in schools.

Hair length seemed to show how times were changing. At
Cranleigh in the sixties, times changed as people departed from
the scene and links with the past were broken. In 1964 J. F.
Spink died; he had been Allen's senior prefect in 1901, and had
become a generous and anonymous donor to the school; only in
1969 was it revealed that his benefactions had totalled

£25,481.[74] In 1967 Monty Aldridge died; he had begun teaching at Cranleigh in 1912, and although he often talked of moving because of poor health he had only finally retired in 1954.[47] In 1968 Mrs March died[75] and on Christmas Eve of that year so too did Canon J. S. Purvis.[76] In 1969 Arthur Germany retired; he had served at the school since 1916; he had been common room butler since the thirties; he stayed on part-time, and died finally in 1981 after only seven years of full retirement.[76] In 1970 Max Machin died; he had first arrived at Cranleigh to teach in 1922. And his dorm-mate from his own school-days at Lancing, Roland Hopewell, a nephew of Rhodes who had taught at Cranleigh for forty years, died a few months before Machin.[77] In the nature of things news of these events, these breaks with the past, would have meant little to the Cranleighans who read about them in their school magazine. One dramatic break would affect them: in July 1969 David Emms announced that he was accepting the headship of Sherborne and was leaving Cranleigh in 1970. There was much journalistic license in the comment of the reporter who said that Emms had found the school 'dozing away at dusty classics under the old regime, remote from the outside world'.[78] Certainly he had taken over the school at a bad time and it had pulled through. The world of school – any public school and not merely Cranleigh – in the 1950s seemed in many senses light years away from the world of the 1970s. History does not break into neat decades in quite the same way as the calendar does; but as the sixties were different from the fifties so too the seventies were to be very different from the sixties, and at Cranleigh there was to be a new hand on the tiller. In December 1969 the governors announced the appointment of Emms's successor. Marc van Hasselt was much the same age as Emms, and from much the same background: public school, university, war service. He had been a housemaster at Oundle during the troubled sixties. David Emms had been a tough man who was prepared to innovate. The new headmaster would perhaps need to be, in the climate of the seventies, the innovator who was prepared to be tough. And so it transpired.

CHAPTER ELEVEN

An Independent School Today

IN THE SUMMER OF 1973 the school magazine carried an article entitled 'The School as an Enterprise'.[1] It was a report of a conference for sixth formers at which a senior trainee specialist from British Leyland encouraged Cranleighans to look at their school as a business, with directors (governors), managers (masters and boys), customers (parents and boys) and a product (boys). This way of looking at independent education was commonplace by the end of the decade, when it was widely accepted that the schools were 'selling a commercial product'.[2] Indeed one of their early successes in salesmanship was the substitution of the term 'independent' instead of 'public': a deliberate move to shed the image of class exclusiveness and snobbery which the term 'public school' seemed to connote, and to use instead the term 'independent school' which seemed to suggest sturdy self reliance and enterprise.[3] They were going to need all the self reliance, enterprise and salesmanship they could muster as they experienced a period of inflation such as they had never faced before and as their very existence came under increasing threat from the political left.

In the nineteen sixties, despite unprecedented affluence, there had been 'gloom about the future'.[4] The conventional wisdom of the age seemed to regard public schools as outmoded. 'Pupil Power' had become 'a real force on the educational scene', which threatened their internal cohesion and stability.[5] The film *If*, released in 1968 and depicting in lurid if fantastic detail some of the worst aspects of traditional public school life, 'both mirrored and fuelled the unrest and disaffection in the schools'.[6] Even in the early seventies, with a Conservative government in power, it was a Tory who wrote of 'the public schools' fatal rigidity'.[7] And although Cranleigh had weathered the storms of the sixties well, a new threat now loomed: inflation. 'The outlook is bleak', was the message in 1972.[8] By 1975 however there were signs of hope: 'Private schools hold their own against inflation and a Labour government'.[9] This theme continued at the end of the decade. 'More pupils at public schools despite fee rises', ran a headline in 1979,[10] or, as another newspaper put it in the following year, 'Independent schools getting more pupils despite spiralling fees'.[11] It was the problem of fees rather than the incidence of student unrest which was central in the seventies. At the beginning of the decade Cranleigh's fees were on the low side; in ten years there was a rise of 350%, just ahead of rises in costs. An increase of 20.7% in 1971 put Cranleigh among the more expensive schools, and rises of 9.6% and 12.1% in the subsequent two years made the school fourth in the fees league table published by the *Sunday Times*.[12] The most expensive school (from September 1973) was Winchester at £1,092; second and third were Gordonstoun and Marlborough; Cranleigh came fourth at £1,030. Eton and Harrow fees stood at £897, Uppingham and Shrewsbury at £900, and Tonbridge at £897. But generally fee differentials were far smaller now than they had been in the pre-war years, and in fact comparisons became difficult as schools sometimes charged supplements or raised fees termly; and there was always the problem of knowing what other costs were involved though Cranleigh's fees remained, as they had traditionally been, all-inclusive. The greatest single fee rise came in 1975 in the wake of the Houghton report on teachers' salaries; large increases were recommended for the maintained sector, and these would be reflected in independent schools' salary scales. On average, boarding school fees went up by 35%; Cranleigh's leapt further with an increase in September 1975 of 46%. Increases in subsequent years were smaller, and indeed the 1977 rise of 6.5% was well below the level of inflation. But the policy widely adopted was a linkage of fees with projected rates of inflation; Cranleigh, unlike some schools, adopted a policy of one fee rise per year in September, pegging the level there and making the school seem very expensive at the beginning of the academic year but rather less so in the following two terms.

In spite of these huge fee increases, parents looked to Cranleigh in increasing numbers. In the period 1970–72, 498 parents saw round the school; in 1979–81 that figure had risen to 984. A parental visit was only a first stage of course; the next was registration and the numbers registering their sons (and they might not have made a preliminary visit to the school when they did so) rose from 702 in the earlier period to 1089 in the latter. This does not simply reflect a growing popularity. Parental habits were changing. The traditional practice of putting a child's name down at birth (or before) was becoming less common; parents tended to 'shop around' as they would for a commercial product. They began to see, rightly, that schools can change enormously in quite a short time-span; the closer was their decision to the actual starting time for their son, the more realistic would be their assessment of the school. There was another aspect too at Cranleigh. The development of the house system had at last reached the point where parents felt it necessary to make a choice of house for their son, and were encouraged to do so. It reflected the final demise of the 'hostel' system and said something too about the increased size of the school, and about the parents' desire for optimum choice. Other factors were at work as well. Emms had predicted that closer contact between home and school would be a feature of Cranleigh in the seventies. The new headmaster noted in 1971 that 'the geographical factor continues to be increasingly important'.[13] Both of these observations bear on the development in the early seventies of a system of what amounted to 'fortnightly boarding'.[14] The idea of the exeat system was that boys could go home on specific weekends (almost every other one) from Saturday teatime until Sunday bedtime. This helped to reduce the differences between dayboys and boarders, strengthened the links between school and home, and probably reduced – for boys and masters – the pressures of living in a small and intensive community. At the same time, the school maintained its 'pastoral umbrella' during exeats: boys can choose to remain at school and on average about 10% do, though the number rises before examinations. This exeat system, and the high cost of petrol, helped to make Cranleigh a more local school during the seventies; pupils living in England tended increasingly to come from homes within an hour's drive of the school, mainly in Surrey, London and Sussex. At the same time – and really for the first time – Cranleigh became an international school. This reflected a national trend, and indeed it was calculated that in 1976 Britain earned more than £17m in foreign currency from such a source, twice as much as the profits from book royalties from overseas, and nearly three times as much as the profits from selling films and TV material abroad.[15] In 1980 24% of the new entrants at Cranleigh lived overseas, either as foreign nationals or as expatriates. One reason was Cranleigh's geographical position, near to Heathrow and Gatwick. Another was probably that it was still overwhelmingly a boarding school. Even the exeat system has not militated against this trend. But the overseas market is subject to many variables. In the mid seventies, it could be said that American parents would find an English boarding school education, even with the travel involved, as cheap as or cheaper than an American equivalent; changes in the exchange rate altered the position entirely in the late seventies. Political as well as economic factors could have their effect. A housemasters' discussion in 1976 on 'Foreign boys at Cranleigh' was much concerned with the growing demand from Iran;[16] the fall of the Shah changed all that. The demand from the Far East continued unabated into the eighties, and the headmaster's tour of South East Asia in 1980 led to better means of assessing entrants from that area.[17]

Parental occupations followed in broad outline the trends already established earlier in the century. A breakdown from 1974 shows the major categories:[18]

32.0% business executives; company directors
15.5% banking; accountancy; brokerage
 9.2% engineering
 5.6% armed forces

There can be no definitive evidence about how these parents pay the fees, or about why their choice settles on Cranleigh. Factors must include academic standards, and the school's location in the populous and prosperous south east, its closeness to airports and motorways and its own distinctive style and ethos, difficult though that is to quantify. Other factors affect parental choice: the cost of travel, the level of school fees, the exeat system, the presence of girls in the sixth form. There may be national factors at work as well. As the policy of comprehensivization progressed, and then in the late seventies as the maintained sector experienced government cut-backs, the middle classes seem to have been attracted increasingly to the independent sector. A 1978 survey of people in social classes A and B showed that 22% were convinced that educational standards were very much worse than they had been, and a further 23% thought they were somewhat worse.[19] Education at an independent school might be the answer. On the other hand, rising fees have put many boarding schools beyond the pockets even of reasonably affluent people, especially if they have more than one or two children to educate. And the withdrawal of the direct grant has increased parental choice within the independent sector as many ex-grammar schools have chosen to go it alone, rather than be integrated with the comprehensive system: most of these schools cater only for day pupils and are a less expensive alternative. Indeed in the early seventies the headmaster had begun to think that there would be a trend at Cranleigh towards more demand for dayboy places and a shift away from boarding.[20] But it did not happen. In 1970 the boarding percentage of the school was 87.4; in the late seventies it was 86%, and in the early eighties over 87% again. These were minor fluctuations. The fee structure had meanwhile changed, lowering the differential between boarder and dayboy fees; similarly the exeat system had eroded the difference between boarders and dayboys, and indeed the latter tended to remain at school from after (or sometimes before) breakfast in the morning until almost bedtime. Cranleigh remained a boarding school.

While the dayboy percentage stayed fairly constant the size and shape of the school changed in other ways during the seventies. First, it got bigger. Senior school numbers rose by 21.5% in the decade, a much bigger growth rate than during the sixties (9.5%) but marginally smaller than the fifties (21.7%).[22] This put enormous pressure on accommodation, and determined priorities for much of the school's building and improvement programme for the decade. There were other important consequences: as well as providing a larger fee income (much of which would be spent on providing the extra accommodation needed) this growth also altered the shape of the school, and most significantly saw a rapid growth in the size of the sixth form.[23] During the sixties the fear had grown in boarding schools that boys would increasingly wish to leave after O levels; that they would seek the greater freedom of technical or sixth form colleges; that fee levels might induce parents to remove their sons at that stage; that the new sixth form colleges might pose an academic as well as a social threat to boarding school sixths. These fears were scarcely realized at Cranleigh. In 1970 the sixth form was 32.2% of the school; by 1975 it was 41.9% and in 1980 was 49.3%.[24] This meant increased intellectual and social demands on members of staff and increased pressure on accommodation as the school strove towards the ideal of a study for each individual sixth former. There were other pressures too. Boys and girls over sixteen may legally purchase cigarettes; at eighteen they may legally visit public houses and buy alcohol. These remained forbidden activities for Cranleighans, as they had always been. It could be argued that the problem had not changed much and that young people will always find ways of challenging authority and indulging in illicit pleasures. There were differences now, however. Not only was a much higher proportion of the school legally emancipated but also social pressures had changed. 'Attitudes have changed with the end of the "age of the nanny"', as the headmaster declared in 1974.[25] Parents were now more indulgent, levels of pocket money higher, advertising more persistent, and national trends (especially regarding consumption of alcohol) more insidious. The end of the decade saw much publicity in the press over two exemplary issues. One was the charge that as in the nation at large, there was a considerable problem of theft in public schools.[26] Another was the charge that public schoolboys were increasingly 'selfish', a characteristic which in a materialistic society was not confined to public schoolboys.[27] Cranleigh could only hope that it could counter such trends by its own internal organization and values, and by increasing links between school and home to encourage parents to uphold the standards set by the school.[28] The PHAB course for physically handicapped and able bodied young people which the school runs, or social service in general, could counter charges of selfishness. The school buttery where sixth formers might drink legally and under supervision could help answer the alcohol problem. But the problems would not be solved. They would continue to be exacerbated by the nature of society, a society with which Cranleighans came more frequently into contact as they belonged to a less and less monastic, isolated community.

The monastic nature of boarding schools has undergone considerable erosion since the sixties. Television has contributed as has the prevalence of more liberal exeat arrangements, the increasing numbers of married masters, and perhaps also the earlier arrival of physical (if not intellectual) maturity which seems to be a common feature of modern western nations. And the arrival of girls has played a major part. Girls also played their part in changing the shape and size of the school. It was a national trend: by 1979, 107 out of 208 HMC schools took girls, and 11 had gone completely co-educational.[29] At the end of the sixties, the Cranleigh governors had shown no inclination to take girls.[30] In November 1970, however, common room voted unanimously in favour of the idea.[31] In the following year there were three girls in the school; in 1974 the admissions policy began in earnest with the arrival of seventeen girls into the lower sixth. 'Penthouse for girls – but Cranleigh stays a boys' school', a local newspaper proclaimed.[32] The term 'penthouse' for the girls' accommodation (which happened at that stage to be at the top of the headmaster's house) was soon wisely phased out; but Cranleigh did remain a boys' school. In 1975 11.7% of the sixth form were girls; this increased to 14.3% in 1978 and to 20.7% in 1980. It seemed likely to stay around this figure, so that the school would not grow any larger, and because of accommodation problems. By the early eighties the girls were housed in seven 'flats', looked after by resident wardens. But each girl was also a full member of a boys' house, where she had her study. This integration proved widely popular with the boys and girls themselves, as well as with prospective parents. But the girls were not the only female presence in the school. Even before their arrival the headmaster had recognized that 'Cranleigh would be a very different place without the willing efforts of many of the wives of the community'.[33] Most masters were now married; indeed the school had a much smaller proportion of bachelors than many others. And whereas in the 1880s a boy's only female contact was with the school matron, his range of contacts was now much greater. There were girls of course; there were also wives of members of staff teaching cookery, or entertaining to meals, or serving as house matrons. Increasingly a boy would meet female members of staff in the classroom. It was all these influences, and not merely the arrival of girls in the sixth form, which meant 'rediscovering normality', as one headmaster put it.[34]

Many schools had realized that by taking girls they might off-set the boy drop-out after O levels; undoubtedly this calculation operated as potently as any idealistic or social reasons. At Cranleigh in the late sixties the drop-out rate had been nearly 30%, whether for academic, financial or social reasons. By the late seventies it was around 20% – and then usually for financial reasons, or because on academic grounds the boy was not suited to sixth form work. Social reasons were less evident. Girls helped to normalize sixth form life: they also helped to raise academic standards. Royston Lambert, in a not wholly sympathetic survey of boarding schools in the late sixties and early seventies, concluded that they had changed remarkably little in style and aims, but 'quite exceptionally uniform, however, was the amount of change stressing the academic side'.[35] It was clear in the early seventies that academic standards were going to be of crucial significance in public schools. There was increasing national pressure for university places and for jobs. And in a world of increasing attacks from the left, schools realized that 'academic excellence' was a weapon of defence that might prove as effective as any other. When the new headmaster arrived in 1970 he was looking for ways of focussing on academic standards. He looked critically and questioningly at the school farm, which for so long had had a somewhat anomalous existence within the school. He suggested that it should be turned into a sixth form centre.[36] There was something of a national trend towards such places in boarding schools – there were twenty by 1973.[35] But Cranleigh would get in early and could provide a set of buildings second to none. It was to be a residential unit for some twenty sixth formers, and a focus for other sixth form activities as well: 'an investment in our sixth form academic tradition and quality of life'.[37] The plan went forward and in September 1972 the new complex opened, imaginatively created out of former piggeries and farm buildings, with at its heart a seventeenth century tithe barn which was in the throes of being renovated as a theatre and meeting place. The new accommodation helped to take pressure off the houses; the occupants would be the Oxbridge sixth in each Michaelmas term, and other upper sixth formers in the two subsequent terms, chosen from among any upper sixth formers who chose to apply. It was a welcome 'feature' for the school; it was socially beneficial, and it helped to underline the school's academic commitment. Other new features of the school pointed in the same direction. In 1971 a school bookshop opened in the cloisters, a more appropriate function for a site so near the heart of the institution than the laundry which it displaced. In the same year, a distinctive tie for scholars was introduced. In 1972 a 'Dons' Dinner' was held, with sixty dons from the universities entertained to a meal in Hall, hosted by masters and boys. This became in subsequent years an annual 'Cranleigh Dinner' with representatives from the universities, industry, the professions and the armed forces. In 1973 (and again in 1980) the library and reading room were revived, modernized and extended and their budget substantially increased. In 1975 the school's pass mark at Common Entrance was raised from 55% to 60%, a proclamation to the outside world that academic standards were rising. Teaching facilities were modernized and extended: the language laboratory in 1971, the art school in 1973, the chemistry and biology departments in 1975 and 1979. In 1977 a new physics department building was opened by Viscount Watkinson, President of the CBI and chairman of the school Council. It cost £75,000, and he pointed out that 'not a penny of this money has been provided by the state'.[38] In the year which saw a Labour government withdraw the 'seal of approval' which the Inspectorate had hitherto awarded to all independent schools 'recognized as efficient',[39] it was perhaps appropriate that he should point out that the government studiously avoided recognizing any of the good which such schools did, or acknowledging any of their many contributions to the life of the nation. One such contribution made by Cranleigh is worth recording: a succession of fine musicians. So when in the mid-seventies the school received a legacy of some £30,000 it was appropriate that it should be devoted to the purchase of a new chapel organ, to replace the ailing Compton. Two OC organists of repute – Richard Seal of Salisbury and Christopher Dearnley of St Paul's – gave their advice, and the school decided to purchase a mechanical action instrument from the firm of Grant, Degens and Bradbeer.[40] Its installation on the west wall of the chapel in 1977 led to other major improvements there: the seating was reorganized, plans were drawn up for a major redecoration and rewiring of the building, and the old organ pipes were removed from behind the altar, so that for the first time in half a century the sanctuary was lit by the windows in the ambulatory.

The emphasis on academic standards (and even the new organ could be seen in this light, as it was a teaching instrument) may be said to have paid off. For one thing, the success rate at A level improved dramatically in the seventies. In 1966–70 it had averaged a 76% pass rate in all papers taken; in 1971–5 the average was 86%; by 1976–80 it was 91%. The performance of the girls helped: in 1981 their pass rate was 98.6%, as opposed to the boys' 91.6%; their grade A achievement level was 36.1% as opposed to the boys' 24.3%. In that same year, 52% of all papers taken were given an A or B grade: this was good. It was also vitally important in terms of university entrance. In that area, too, there was progress. In the twenties, a tiny number of Cranleighans had gone on to further education each year; almost all had gone straight into business. By 1967 the picture had changed, with 59% of leavers going on to some form of higher education. A decade later this figure had risen to 90%: 66% went to university, 14.6% to polytechnic, 7.8% to art or music college, and 1.9% to agricultural college. It marks a considerable development of the whole nature and style of the school, as does the increasing number returning each year after A levels to sit the Oxford and Cambridge entrance examinations. Here the success rate, in terms of scholarships won, again shows how things were progressing. In the period 1964–9 Cranleighans had taken nineteen awards; in the five years up to 1981 they took forty. The presence of such a large and successful Oxbridge sixth was not only good in itself; it also helped to raise the whole intellectual tone of the sixth form in general.

But this emphasis on academic standards did not detract from other aspects of school life. Games continued to flourish. Indeed the first teams in the three major sports – rugger, hockey and cricket – had their best seasons ever. In terms of decades, the seventies were the most successful to date, with those teams winning 50% of all matches played, as opposed to 46.6% in the twenties, 43.5% in the fifties, 42.6% in the sixties, 41% in the forties and 34.7% in the thirties. It was a fine record, especially since the fixture lists had grown ever longer, and the competition was fierce from schools much larger than Cranleigh.[41] It is significant too that the record should improve at a time when games worship had declined dramatically; this decline suggested to outside observers that games no longer mattered or that standards had slipped. Neither of these observations was true, and it was untrue even though boys now had far greater choice. Cricket experienced its most successful years ever in the seventies, at a time when boys no longer had to play it and could opt instead for athletics, golf, tennis, swimming, sailing or shooting. National trends were also reflected, as with the growing popularity of squash. The opening of two new squash courts in 1979 was further encouragement to a sport which could be played in all weathers, which was easily organized and which boys realized they could continue to play long after leaving school. Cranleigh's success in the Premiere Cup at the beginning of the eighties showed that the school was among the best in the country for this sport. Similar success attended hockey, which had its best decade ever; it was given extra stimulus by the building of a new all-weather pitch in 1979, close to the original 'redgra' which had opened in 1968.

In common with many independent schools in the seventies, Cranleigh emphasized academic work, while at the same time there was every increasing choice of activities outside the classroom; and despite high costs there was much major building development. Educational plant was invested in more heavily than ever before, which involved the arrival of audio-visual aids, computers, carpeted classrooms for better acoustics, and even the disappearance of the traditional blackboard which gave way first to the white board, and then to the stainless steel enamelled board. Nevertheless there were those who maintained that the independent schools were 'bastions of resistance to educational change'.[42] Just before the great inflation of the mid-seventies, which seemed to threaten public schools more effectively than politicians had ever done, the Labour front bencher Mr Roy Hattersley told the annual conference of the

Incorporated Association of Preparatory Schools that his party was firmly committed to the abolition of fee-paying schools.[43] By the end of the decade that commitment was, if anything, even stronger. The general secretary of the party, introducing Labour's latest document on the subject in 1980, wrote that[44]

> 'the existence of private schooling fragments society, enshrines privilege for the few at the expense of the majority, and seriously impedes the establishment of a national system of education that is genuinely fair to the talents, aspirations and needs of every child'.

By then, however, the Conservative party was in power and had launched an 'assisted places scheme', providing public funds for the maintenance of clever children at independent schools, costing up to £55m in a full year, and providing up to 15,000 places.[45] This rather unexpected 'hidden subsidy' to the independent sector was not universally popular even within the schools themselves: it was liable to be withdrawn peremptorily by a future Labour government, and might meanwhile create bad feeling in the maintained sector. And it did nothing to counteract the alarming habit among politicians of all parties of regarding (or seeming to regard) the education of the nation's children as an issue in political football rather than as a vital national priority. However, Cranleigh applied to become a registered school for assisted place candidates and took its first pupils via competitive examination into both the senior and preparatory schools in September 1981.

Whoever pays the fees, income from that source is Cranleigh's sole means of support: there are no endowments, and the rich acres of Surrey land upon which the school stands are something of a frozen asset. The only other sources of income are occasional bequests (the Weston paid for the organ, and the Pickup for the hockey pitch), and of course appeals. The idea began to form in 1977 that an appeal was necessary once more. Perhaps a scholarship fund should be set up as a result. In 1972 the school had abandoned the practice of awarding only nominal scholarships, making awards sufficiently worthwhile to attract clever boys some of whom might not otherwise get to a public school. In 1975 a full-fees scholarship was offered for the first time and other awards were up-graded and linked to fee levels. In 1976 a total of £20,400 worth of scholarships and music awards was made in that one year. By the end of the seventies well over £100,000 p.a. had to be set aside for the funding of all scholars in the school. It was an enormous commitment and one which deliberately underscored the school's determination to set high store by academic excellence. But while a scholarship fund had its attractions, the head-master saw the priorities differently. He began to argue the merits of an eighth house. The houses were again too big; the accommodation they offered was too cramped. More important, it was even more difficult now than it had been in the early sixties for a housemaster to cope with large numbers. The effect of the 'public school revolution' of the sixties, which eroded the old authority structures and removed much of the hierarchy and privilege attached to it, was to make the job of schoolmastering more difficult.[46] Prefects mattered less: we saw how their position changed at Cranleigh in the early sixties; besides they now took very seriously the job of getting good A levels, so however keen they might be to act effectively as prefects, this was a constraint on them and on the time available to them. It seemed right, as the seventies drew to a close, to tackle the task of creating smaller, more intimate house units. The school decided to build an up-to-date house for the eighties, departing at almost every point from the traditional house pattern of Cranleigh: the new building would be an out-house built around a quadrangle like a college; It would provide accommodation for a married housemaster, a married assistant, and a bachelor house tutor. It would set new standards of boy-accommodation: all boys (and sixth form girls) would have a study bedroom, except for the new boys. This would provide the privacy lacking in the older houses, which would be gradually updated by imaginative internal reconstruction. The new house soon acquired a name – Loveday.[47] By September 1980, even before the appeal had run its full course, the new house was ready for occupation, by a set of new boys entering at 13, and by other pupils recruited from the other houses. It was the most distinguished building the school had erected, certainly since 1929.[48] It was opened formally by one of the most distinguished visitors the school had had in recent times, the former prime minister, Lord Home of the Hirsel. His father-in-law, Cyril Alington, had by happy coincidence been David Loveday's headmaster at Shrewsbury. It was a vitally important new building. It highlighted the concern felt that the pastoral care of boys and girls should be a first priority in a boarding community. It emphasized, in its provision of study bedrooms, the growing awareness that privacy and quiet must be essential ingredients of boarding school life. It affirmed that Cranleigh intended to remain as a boarding school into the foreseeable future.

Well into its second century, Cranleigh is still, as it was in 1865, a boarding school for the middle classes of Surrey. Those middle classes have changed in their wealth and their occupations; the school has changed out of recognition in its size and shape; the world too has changed. What has not changed is the need for good schools, and their essential role as transmitters and conveyors of the riches of our culture and civilization from one generation to the next. Cranleigh remains, as it always has been, mainly a boys' school. It remains, in a confused world and in a pluralist society, a Christian school. The Headmaster ended his speech to parents in 1982 with an affirmation which springs from this fact, and which is more important than all the changes and chances that afflict the day to day and even the decade to decade development of a school:[49]

> '. . . that the permanence of Cranleigh in the future depends finally not on the status it confers, or the success, academic or otherwise, it brings, but on the permanence of the values it really believes in'.

Notes

INTRODUCTION

1. J. A. Froude, *Short Studies on Great Subjects*, vol. I, p. 1
2. G. Kitson Clark, *An Expanding Society: Britain 1830–1900*
3. For England in the 1860s see W. L. Burn, *The Age of Equipoise*
4. N. Sykes, *Man as Churchman*, p. 164
5. See 'Middle Class Education: Moral Training', *The Museum and English Journal of Education*, 15 June 1865
6. *The Times*, 24 Nov 1860; quoted in D. W. Sylvester, *Robert Lowe and Education*, p. 22
7. S. Rothblatt, *The Revolution of the Dons*, p. 180
8. Address to the students of St Andrews, 19 Mar. 1869, in *Short Studies on Great Subjects*, vol. ii, p. 468
9. *Speeches on Questions of Public Policy by Richard Cobden MP*, edited by J. Bright and J. E. Thorold Rogers, p. 609
10. D. W. Sylvester, *Robert Lowe and Education*, p. 41
11. P. T. Marsh, *The Victorian Church in Decline*, p. 67
12. Nigel Middleton, 'The Education Act of 1870 as the start of the modern concept of the child', *British Journal of Educational Studies*, vol. xviii, no. 2, June 1970, p. 16
13. Archbishop Tait, *Middle Class Education*, p. 4
14. F. V. Thornton, *The Education of the Middle Classes in England*, p. 5
15. D. R. Fearon in *Schools Inquiry Commission*, vol. vii, p. 237
16. H. C. Barnard, *A History of English Education from 1760*, p. 134
17. See T. W. Bamford, *The Rise of the Public Schools*, p. 18; and in general chapter 2 for 'The Growth of the System'
19. Woodard to Bishop Fraser, 13 June 1871; quoted in T. W. Bamford, *The Rise of the Public Schools*, p. 30
20. See B. Heeney, *Mission to the Middle Classes: The Woodard Schools 1848–1891*
21. Fortescue to Brereton, 26 Sept 1874, *Brereton MS* B8013
22. For Brereton and the county school movement see B. Heeney, *Mission to the Middle Classes*, J. Roach, *Public Examinations in England*, and especially J. R. Honey, *Tom Brown's Universe*
23. The site in Cambridge is now occupied by Homerton College: appropriately enough, a college of further education
24. J. R. Honey, *Tom Brown's Universe*, pp. 78–81

25. *The Times*, 10 May 1873; see also *Brereton MS*, B4701/15
26. Fortescue to Brereton, 3 Nov. 1862, *Brereton MS* B8012
27. Earl Fortescue, *Public Schools for the Middle Classes*, p. 2
28. O. Banks, *Parity and Prestige in English Secondary Education*, p. 1
29. *The Museum and English Journal of Education*, vol. I (ns), April 1864, p. 16

CHAPTER ONE

1. This area, and much besides, has been part of Greater London since 1889
2. James Caird in 1852, quoted in G. E. Mingay, *Rural Life in Victorian England*, p. 61
3. *Schools Inquiry Commission*, vol. iv, p. 484
4. S. Meacham, *Lord Bishop: The Life of Samuel Wilberforce 1805–1873*, p. 135
5. The sources for Sapte's life are limited; best is the special number of the *Cranleigh Parish Magazine*, 27 June 1906
6. 'Cranley' became 'Cranleigh' in 1867 to avoid postal confusion with Crawley; the Cranleigh spelling will be used throughout
7. W. Welch, 'Cranley in 1846', *Cranleigh Parish Magazine*, June 1897
8. There is a full discussion and description of the many duties and responsibilities of the mid-century parson in G. Kitson Clark, *Churchmen and the Condition of England Question 1832–1885*, chs 3–7.
9. See eg. *Cr*, May 1887
10. C. P. Snow, *A Coat of Varnish*, p. 8
11. Quotations are from the *Dictionary of National Biography*
12. Curiously, George Cubitt has no entry in the *DNB*
13. Undated fly-sheet in *CM*, probably October 1862
14. *CM*, 6 Nov 1862
15. *CM*, 19 Nov 1862; see also 23 Dec. 1862. The site cost £400; another 8 members of the committee promised £385 in all – or 13 boys' fees at 1865 fee levels; 13 boys' fees in 1982 would exceed £50,000
16. *CM*, 15 Jan. 1863 (for printed proof of the prospectus)
17. *CM*, 5 Aug 1863; the Victorian Society in London has copies of the plans
18. *CM*, 6 Oct 1863; see also *SR*, Christmas 1866
19. Unfortunately Benson's Diaries and Letters (MSS) in the Library of Trinity College, Cambridge, are very thin for the 1860s; but see *Diary*, 30 July 1884; see also Merriman's comments on Benson's influence, *OC Club Notes*, no. 39, Nov. 1896. For Benson's life see A. C. Benson, *The Life of Edward White Benson*
20. *Schools Inquiry Commission*, vol. iv, pp. 477–484; and printed 'Report of the Committee on the subject of Education' in *CM*, 19 Jan. 1864
21. *Report of the Committee on the Subject of Education*, p. 9
22. Printed handbill entitled *Appeal*; see *CM*, 26 Jan. 1864
23. See below, p. 33
24. On science in public schools during this period see B. Simon and I. Bradley, *The Victorian Public School*, passim; also T. W.

Bamford, *The Rise of the Public Schools*, ch. 5
25. The Revd O. Manning, *History & Antiquities of the County of Surrey*, vol. I, p. 534
26. See M. C. Morgan, *Cheltenham College: the First Hundred Years*, ch. 3
27. 21 Oct. 1865
28. Letters dated 14, 16, 18, 19 Feb. 1863; in *CM*
29. J. H. Sapte to T. Grissell (later a member of the Council), 7 Nov. 1862; in *CM*
30. *CM*, 6 Oct. 1863
31. J. Gathorne-Hardy, *The Public School Phenomenon*, p. 95
32. The best source is his obituary in that finest of college magazines, *The Eagle* (St John's College Magazine), vol. xxvi, June 1905, pp. 389–396
33. See J. A. Mangan, *Athleticism in the Victorian and Edwardian Public School*, p. 127, and S. Rothblatt, *The Revolution of the Dons*, p. 229
34. E. Miller, *Portrait of a College*, p. 85
35. He is not mentioned in A. F. Leach, *A History of Bradfield College* or in J. Blackie, *Bradfield 1850–1975*, but he is referred to as 'ex-second master' in the *Bradfield College Register* for 1871
36. H. F. Howard, *Finances of St John's College Cambridge*, pp. 195 & 207
37. *CM*, 19 Jan 1864; 9 Apr 1875
38. See A. K. Boyd, *Radley College 1847–1947*, pp. 155–6; 176. For

the living of Dorking see *Benson Letters*, Benson to G. Cubitt, 18 Apr. 1870
39. G. Best, *Mid-Victorian Britain 1851–75*, p. 90 and passim
40. J. R. Honey, *Tom Brown's Schooldays*, p. 325
41. Quoted in T. W. Bamford, *The Rise of the Public Schools*, p. 129.
42. Printed prospectus dated April 1865, in *CM*, 23 May 1865
43. B. Heeney, *Mission to the Middle Classes*, pp. 32–39
44. A. K. Boyd, *Radley College 1847–1947*, pp. 155–6
45. Fees according to the *Public & Preparatory Schools Yearbook*, 1979
46. For his life see F. Storr, *Life & Remains of Rev R. H. Quick*, which is virtually unobtainable; the only known copy in Britain is in the British Library.
47. See, for example, his *Essays on Educational Reformers* and *The Schoolmaster: Past and Future*
48. E. C. Mack, *Public Schools and British Opinion since 1860*, p. 168
49. *CM*, 7 June 1865
50. *CM*, 26 July 1865; his Christian name is not known, and he appears to have stayed only for a few terms
51. F. V. Thornton, *The Education of the Middle Classes in England*, p. 5
52. *The Museum and English Journal of Education*, Mar. 1865; a full column of the journal was given over to a description of the new school

CHAPTER TWO

1. *Cr*, Nov. 1879
2. J. Gathorne-Hardy, *The Public School Phenomenon*, p. 101
3. *Schools Inquiry Commission*, vol. xiii, p. 106
4. According to Quick; see F. Storr, *Life & Remains of Rev R. H. Quick*, p. 16
5. Probably now classrooms Q1 and Q2

6. *SR*, 1866
7. *The Guardian*, 18 Oct 1865: this was not, of course, the *Manchester Guardian*
8. See Appendix II
9. John Russell, quoted in F. Storr, *Life & Remains of Rev R. H. Quick*, p. 22
10. *SR*, 1869
11. According to Quick; see F. Storr, *Life & Remains of Revd R. H. Quick*, p. 16
12. *The Times*, 25 May 1866
13. *Cr*, July 1887 (an article on the history of the school)
14. See below, chapter 5
15. F. Storr, *Life & Remains of Rev. R. H. Quick*, pp. 19–20
16. *The Guardian*, 30 Jan 1867
17. See B. Heeney, *Mission to the Middle Classes*, p. 93
18. *The Guardian*, 20 Feb. 1867
19. *Schools Inquiry Commission*, vol. iv, pp. 480–481
20. *The Guardian*, 18 Oct. 1865
21. *Debating Society Minutes*, 10 Feb. 1866
22. *ibid*, 24 Mar. 1866
23. J. Merriman, *Secular Education as Severed from Religious*, p. 29
24. Lord Midleton at Speech Day; *Cr*, Nov. 1893
25. *Masters Meeting Minutes*, 13 Feb. 1885; *Register of Chapel Services*, 1906–26: entries for Ash Wednesday 1912 and 1913
26. As remembered by Peter Green; in H. E. Sheen, *Canon Peter Green*, p. 16
27. D. Newsome, *Godliness and Good Learning*, p. 1
28. Speech quoted in full in *Cr*, July 1887
29. Quoted in G. Watson, *The English Ideology*, p. 191 (Speech of April 1872)
30. Peek to Brodrick, 1 Dec. 1868; *Brodrick MS* 1248/23/91

31. And a newly-built mansion and estate near Lyme Regis which cost him more than £250,000
32. Tait, something of a liberal, had abstained in the disestablishment vote, much to the chagrin of the Irish bishops.
33. *Cr*, Nov. 1887
34. T. W. Steele, *Musings of an Old Schoolmaster*, p. 20
35. F. Storr, *Life & Remains of Rev. R. H. Quick*, p. 17
36. *The Globe*, 21 Oct. 1875
37. *Masters Meeting Minutes*, 3 Feb. 1888
38. *Debating Society Minutes*, 1 Oct. 1886
39. *Masters Meeting Minutes*, 28 May 1880
40. *Cr*, July 1880
41. *Cr*, Dec. 1879
42. T. W. Steele, *Musings of an Old Schoolmaster*, p. 25
43. G. Tautz (2 N 1915–20) to author; his father was at Cranleigh under Merriman
44. A. J. R. Whiteway (1 N 1917–20) to author
45. W. Welch, 'Cranleigh in the 1860s', *Cr*, Oct. 1925
46. *Cr*, July 1944; D. H. Tudor records meeting an OC named de Kantzow (the name is misspelled as De Kreutzow) who recounted this story to him
47. *Moss of Shrewsbury*, by his wife, p. 35
48. B. H. Garnons Williams, *History of Berkhamsted School*, p. 186
49. See below, chapter 3
50. T. W. Steele, *Musings of an Old Schoolmaster*, p. 35
51. *ibid*, p. 153
52. F. Fletcher, *After Many Days*, p. 14
53. G. Orwell, 'Such such were the

joys' in *Collected Essays*, vol. IV, pp. 346–8. Information on food at Cranleigh from L. Northover (E 1906–10) whose father was at Cranleigh under Merriman; also E. A. Barton (3 S 1875–70) to Headmaster, 17 Nov. 1947. Barton had been baptized by John Keble at Hursley – an interesting if irrelevant fact!

54. M. C. Morgan, *Cheltenham College*, p. 99
55. *FMC*, 10 Feb. 1891
56. *Masters Meeting Minutes*, 23 Nov. 1877
57. *ibid.*, 19 Oct 1888 (a directive from the headmaster)
58. *SR*, 1866; *Surrey Times & Weekly Press*, 15 Feb. 1958
59. Quoted in W. D. Smith, *Stretching their Bodies*, p. 35
60. *Cr*, June 1888
61. *Cr*, Oct. 1888
62. A. O. Temple Clarke, *A Tangled Skein of Reminiscence*, pp. 56–7
63. A. C. Benson, *The Life of Edward White Benson*, vol. I, p. 163
64. J. R. Honey, *Tom Brown's Universe*, p. 127
65. For diagram of the age structure of the school in 1885, 1925, 1955, 1981, see Appendix IV
66. *CM*, 18 Feb. 1880
67. J. R. Honey, *Tom Brown's Universe*, p. 67
68. J. R. Cornah (master 1891–2) in *Cr*, Mar 1941
69. F. Storr, *Life & Remains of Rev. R. H. Quick*, p. 252
70. *Schools Inquiry Commission*, vol. iv, p. 477
71. *Cr*, Dec. 1888
72. The corona has vanished completely; but the substantial iron hook from which it was suspended is still embedded in the chancel archway
73. Quoted in *SR*, 1891
74. *Cr*, Mar. 1889
75. See J. Roach, *Public Examinations in England 1850–1900*; chapter 2 is useful generally on middle class education
76. See H. C. Barnard, *A History of English Education from 1760*
77. *Masters Meeting Minutes*, 28 June 1888
78. The Headmaster's speech at Speech Day, *SR*, 1878
79. *SR*, 1876
80. *ibid*; see also *Vincent Warren Low: A Memoir* by M. L. and others: Merriman put university expenses at £400 p.a., but they could be less – see Revd W. Emery, 'Expenses of University Education at Cambridge', *Journal of the Statistical Society*, vol. xxvi, 3, Sept. 1863
81. *Cr*, Oct. 1872; the school celebrated with a half holiday
82. *Cr*, Dec. 1882
83. Lord Coggan, *These were his gifts* p. 9
84. *Cr*, Oct 1897
85. H. M. Wilmshurst, *The Life and Work of W. L. Wilmshurst*, p. 20
86. *Cr*, Mar. 1935.
87. *The Times*, 11 Apr. 1946
88. J. Gathorne-Hardy, *The Public School Phenomenon*, p. 440; but see the whole vast literature on Eton especially, which beguiles friends and critics of the public schools into supposing that Eton is somehow representative; it is not.
89. P. Bailey, *Leisure and Class in Victorian England*, p. 74

90. For a table of occupations of parents, see Appendix III

91. C. Smyth, *Cyril Foster Garbett, Archbishop of York*, pp. 25–7

92. *Cr*, July 1925 (by Rowlatt Jones, 1 N 1872–76)

93. There is a file on Kofi Nti in the School Archives, A 251

94. A. A. Deck to Bursar, 10 Feb. 1939 (CSA)

95. Quoted in T. W. Bamford, *The Rise of the Public Schools* p. 21

96. *Cr*, Oct. 1879

97. T. W. Steele, *Musings of an Old Schoolmaster*, p. 12

98. *Cr*, Mar. 1894

99. *Cr*, Apr. 1901

100. For the absence of fagging see *Masters Meeting Minutes*, 4 Mar. 1910

101. J. R. Honey, *Tom Brown's Universe*, p. 123

102. For attempts to change the names, see below p. 149

103. C. Dilke, *Dr Moberly's Mint-Mark*, ch. viii; 'tunding' was a beating with a long, whippy ash stick

104. H. W. Moss was headmaster of Shrewsbury from 1866–1908; see J. R. Honey, *Tom Brown's Universe*, pp. 197 & 318

105. J. Gathorne-Hardy, *The Public School Phenomenon*, p. 110

106. *Masters Meeting Minutes*, 22 Sept. 1876

107. *Cr*, Apr. 1882; Mar 1896

108. *Prefects Book*, 1865–93

109. *CM*, 8 Oct. 1866

110. *Vincent Warren Low* by M. L. and others, p. 8

111. This is Gathorne-Hardy's term for the regimented late Victorian public school

112. *Cr*, Dec. 1871

113. *Masters Meeting Minutes*, 24 Oct. 1879

114. R. J. Evans, *History & Register of Aldenham School*, p. 128

115. E. D. Laborde, *Harrow School Yesterday and Today*, pp. 212–3

116. Now Abingdon School

117. See A. C. Percival, *Very Superior Men: Some Early Public School Headmasters and their Achievements*; also her chapter 'Some Victorian Headmasters' in *The Victorian Public School*, edited by B. Simon and I. Bradley, pp. 72–94

118. Merriman to Midleton, 14 Oct. 1891, *Brodrick MS*, 1248/24/173

119. *Cr*, Mar. 1941

120. *CM*, 3 Mar 1892

CHAPTER THREE

1. *The Public Schools and the General Education System*, p. 29

2. On the 'pressures of the market-place' see below, chapter 4

3. J. Gathorne-Hardy, *The Public School Phenomenon*, p. 285

4. *Cr*, Mar. 1899

5. D. Leinster-Mackay, 'Victorian Quasi-Public Schools', *British Journal of Educational Studies*, vol. xxix, no 1, Feb. 1981

6. See *St Catherine's Minute Book*, 6 Mar 1894; Benson was impressed with the girls and the buildings: *Diary*, 6 Mar. 1894

7. D. Newsome, *A History of Wellington College*, p. 221

8. *CM*, 19 Feb. 1892

9. D. Newsome, *Godliness and Good Learning*, p. 81

10. J. A. Mangan, *Athleticism in the Victorian and Edwardian Public School*, p. 68

11. D. Newsome, *Godliness and Good Learning*, p. 223
12. *The Times*, 16 Jan. 1928
13. *Cr*, Mar. 1929
14. There is a full record of results 1887–1913 in *Cr*, July 1913
15. J. R. Honey, *Tom Brown's Universe*, ch. 4
16. *Cr*, Oct. 1895
17. *Cr*, Oct. 1899
18. *Cr*, Dec. 1895; also Dec. 1894
19. *Cr*, June 1896
20. *Cr*, Dec. 1897
21. *Cr*, Oct. 1896
22. *FMC*, 19 Feb. 1903
23. Words in *Cr*, 1898; words and music in *Cr*, Dec. 1900
24. There is a collection of such songs (but not including any from Cranleigh): G. Ewart, *Forty Years On: An Anthology of School Songs*
25. A. F. Greenwood (2 N 1890–96) writing in *Cr*, Dec. 1965
26. *Cr*, Apr 1897
27. *Cr*, Mar. 1907.
28. M. Bragg, *Speak for England*, p. 306
29. E. C. Mack, *Public Schools and British Opinion since 1860*, p. 199
30. This was at football, *Cr*, Oct. 1898; for details of OC Society see *SR*, 1891; *OC Society Register*, 1924; *OC Club Notes*, 1890–98
31. *Cr*, Apr. 1903
32. *Cr*, Feb. 1904.
4. *Cr*, Mar. 1899
33. William was a great benefactor and was fascinated by health problems; see chapter 4
34. *Cr*, Apr. 1897
35. A. J. R. Whiteway (1 N 1917–20) to author
36. E. A. Barton (2 & 3 S 1875–79) to Headmaster, 17 Nov. 1947 (CSA)
37. F. S. Brereton, *King of Ranleigh*, p. 126
38. L. Northover (E 1906–10) to author
21. *Cr*, Oct. 1896
39. C. P. Snow, *Variety of Men*, p. 28
40. T. J. Ward, Fellow of St John's, Cambridge; Mathematical Report in *SR*, 1890
41. *Cr*, July 1890
42. Interview with the author, Nov. 1980
21. *Cr*, Oct 1896
43. *Cr*, Oct 1897
44. *Debating Society Minutes*, 17 Feb. 1906
45. *Secondary Education Commission*, vol. xxxv, p. 26
46. L. Northover (E 1906–10) to author
47. E. C. Mack, *Public Schools and British Opinion since 1860*, pp. 209–216
48. The title of a useful chapter on science teaching in *The Victorian Public School*, edited by Brian Simon and Ian Bradley
49. Quoted in J. R. Honey, *Tom Brown's Universe*, p. 128; and generally see chapter 3, part 4
50. *Cr*, Mar. 1894
51. *Cr*, July 1897
52. See J. Roach, *Public Examinations in England*, p. 238
53. J. Roach, *Public Examinations in England*, p. 239
54. *OC Club Notes*, no. 9, Nov. 1891
55. In E. M. Jameson, *Charterhouse*, p. 137; the Charterhouse mission began in 1883/4
56. (The Revd A. Mearns), *The Bitter Cry of Outcast London*, p. 1
57. E. R. Norman, *Church and Society in England 1770–1970*, p. 164
58. *Cr*, Dec. 1894
59. Report on Speech Day, *Cr*, Oct. 1898
60. *ibid*; photographs in the school magazine were rare, the first being of the gym competition

champions Nai Vin and F.
Taverner in June 1892
17. *Cr*, Oct. 1899
61. Listed and dated in *Mission Fund
Subscribers Address Book,
1894–1927*
62. *Cr*, Dec. 1907
63. C. W. Previte Orton to Hon.
Sec. of the School Mission
Fund, 16 June 1917 (CSA)
64. See below pp. 104 and 118
65. C. B. Otley, 'Militarism and
Militarization in the public
schools 1900–72', *British Journal
of Sociology*, vol. 29, no. 3, Sept.
1978, p. 330
66. Letter from 'Rustic' to *Surrey
Advertiser*, quoted in *Cr*, July
1886
67. Letters to the Editor, *Cr*, July
1897 and Oct. 1897
68. R. Wilkinson, *The Prefects*, p. 15
69. G. Best, 'Militarism and the
Victorian Public School', ch. 8
of *The Victorian Public School*,
edited by B. Simon and I.
Bradley, p. 136
70. There are two pictures of the
Corps in *SR*, 1900; Godfrey
Taylor (see above p. 52) is
recognizable in one of them
71. *Cr*, Apr. 1900
72. *Cr*, June 1900
73. See *Cr*, June 1900, Oct. 1900,
Apr. 1901

74. See above
75. *Cr*, Mar 1902
76. Major-General L. C.
Dunsterville, *Stalkey's
Reminiscences*, p. 23
77. G. C. Beresford, *Schooldays with
Kipling*, p. 47
78. *Cr*, Nov. 1914
79. R. Kipling, *Stalky and Co* was
published in 1899 (and televised
in 1982)
80. I am indebted for this information to Mr R. A. Maidment
of Bristol (Letter to the author,
18 Sept. 1979)
81. *Secondary Education Commission*,
vol. xxxv, p. 26
82. *CM*, 25 Feb. 1897
83. From 1893 onwards
84. *Charter*, IV, 5 (p. 9)
85. *Cr*, Mar. 1899
86. See below, chapter 9
87. *Report of the Committee of the
Corporation appointed to examine the
working arrangements of the
Council, September 1959*, p. 3
(CSA)
88. J. R. Honey, *Tom Brown's
Universe*, p. 285; see also p. 264
89. The *Public (and Preparatory)
Schools Year Book* made the first
of its annual appearances in the
following year

CHAPTER FOUR

1. T. McKeown, *An Introduction to
Social Medicine*, p. 3
2. W. Benham (editor), *Catherine
and Crauford Tait, a Memoir*, pp.
272–391; I am indebted for this
reference to J. R. Honey, *Tom
Brown's Universe*, p. 375.
3. F. Musgrove, 'Middle-class
Families and Schools 1780–
1880: Interaction and Exchange
of Functions between Insti-

tutions', in *Sociology, History and
Education*, edited by F. W.
Musgrave, p. 125
4. J. Honey, *Tom Brown's Universe*,
p. 164
5. Lady Diana Cooper, *The
Rainbow Comes and Goes*, pp.
27–37
6. Letter in *The Scotsman*, 21 Aug.
1877, quoted in D. Rubinstein,
Victorian Homes, p. 88

7. In the 1870 'Transactions of the National Association for the Promotion of Social Science', quoted in D. Rubinstein, *Victorian Homes*, p. 88
8. A. Moscow, *The Rockefellers*, p. 433
9. *FMC*, 6 Nov. 1900
10. *Housemasters Meeting Minutes*, 15 Dec. 1963
11. *SR*, 1875
12. For the whole business of death and Victorian funerals see J. Morley, *Death, Heaven and the Victorians*
13. This seems to have been the favourite hymn on these occasions
14. *Cr*, May 1875
11. *SR*, 1875
15. *Cr*, Apr. 1876
16. Strictly speaking England's first 'village hospital' not 'cottage hospital'; see R. M. S. McConaghey, 'The Evolution of the Cottage Hospital' in *Medical History*, vol. xi, Apr. 1967, pp. 128–140; there are some useful comments here on Sapte and Napper, as well as on the village hospital – which still flourishes
17. *British Medical Journal*, 1894, 2, p. 1211; see also *ibid*, p. 706 for a description of a new ventilation system invented and recorded by Napper just before his death
18. *CM*, 28 June 1876
19. A. P. Stewart and S. Jenkins, *The Medical and Legal Aspects of Sanitary Reform*, p. 95
20. *CM*, 13 Mar. 1877
21. For A. A. Napper see *Cr*, Oct. 1928 (obituary)
22. T. McKeown, *Medicine in Modern Society*, p. 51; also J. Honey, *Tom Brown's Universe*, p. 165

23. *CM*, 1 Mar. 1881
24. *CM*, 18 Feb. 1880
25. *SR*, 1880
26. W. M. Fraser, *A History of English Public Health 1834–39*, p. 163; he suggests, at the time of writing (1950) that this was 'the common opinion, which has lasted up to the present day'
27. *CM*, 8 Feb 1893
28. T. McKeown and C. R. Lowe, *An Introduction to Social Medicine*, pp. 80, 85–6
29. *CM*, 5 June, 26 July 1893
30. A. P. Stewart and S. Jenks, *The Medical and Legal Aspects of Sanitary Reform*, p. 31
31. *Cr*, Oct. 1894
32. *FMC*, 21 Feb 1896
33. *Cr*, Oct. 1897
34. See D. Winterbottom, *Doctor Fry*, p. 22
35. *FMC*, 25 Mar. 1914
36. *Cranleigh Parish Magazine*, Nov. 1925 (reminiscences of J. Walder OC)
37. *Cr*, July 1887
38. *Cr*, Mar. 1941 (letter to the editor)
39. *FMC*, 20 Feb. 1885
40. *CM*, 3 Mar. 1885
41. *FMC*, 4 Feb. 1886
42. *Masters Meeting Minutes*, 11 Mar. 1887
43. *Master of the Week Report Book*, 18–25 July 1908
44. L. Northover (E 1906–10) to author
45. *Cr*, Oct. 1907
46. *Master of the Week Report Book*, 18–25 July 1908
47. G. Tautz (2 N 1915–20) to author
48. *Master of the Week Report Book*, 15–22 May 1914
49. *Cr*, May 1947 (obituary of J. W. Williams)
50. *Cr*, July 1907

51. See F. Harrisson, *An Essay on Physical Education*, which was awarded the Athletics Society gold medal in 1864

52. F. S. Brereton, *King of Ranleigh*, p. 92

CHAPTER FIVE

1. *FMC*, 7 Oct. 1908
2. *Cr*, Oct. 1908
3. E. C. Mack, *Public Schools and British Opinion since 1860*, p. 263; and chs VII and VIII
4. For indexes of prices and costs of living, B. R. Mitchell and P. Deane, *Abstract of British Historical Statistics*, pp. 471–478
5. See below, ch. 6
6. T. W. Bamford, *The Rise of the Public Schools*, p. 273
7. E. Halevy, *Imperialism and the Rise of Labour*, p. 205
8. *Public Opinion*, 13 Sept. 1912
9. J. A. Mangan, *Athleticism and the Victorian and Edwardian Public School*, p. 211
10. A. C. Percival, *The Origins of the Headmasters' Conference*, p. 76
11. See D. Leinster-Mackay, 'Victorian Quasi-Public Schools', *British Journal of Educational Studies*, vol. xxxix, no. 1, Feb. 1981, pp. 54–69
12. V. Ogilvie, *The English Public School*, p. 196
13. K. M. J. Ousey, *McClure of Mill Hill*, p. 118; R. R. Oakley, *A History of Oswestry School*, p. 185; H. J. Channon, *Queen's College, Taunton*, pp. 92–4; A. K. Boyd, *Radley College 1847–1947*, p. 375; R. D. Hill, *A History of St Edward's School*, p. 120; J. B. Oldham, *A History of Shrewsbury School*, p. 311; D. C. Somervell, *History of Tonbridge School*, p. 146; *Uppingham School Roll 1888–1960*

14. A. K. Boyd, *Radley College 1847–1947*, p. 375
15. J. Blackie, *Bradfield 1850–1975*, p. 115
16. R. Blumenau, *A History of Malvern College 1865–1965*, p. 71
17. R. D. Hill, *A History of St Edward's School*, p. 120; this school, and Malvern, were exactly the same age as Cranleigh
18. J. Gathorne-Hardy, *The Public School Phenomenon*, p. 297; but then not only the text, but also his bibliography, would lead one to suppose that his source material is drawn almost exclusively from the grander schools
19. *Victoria County History of Surrey*, vol. iv, p. 447
20. *ibid.*, vol. ii, p. 224
21. *FMC*, 15 Jul. 1899
22. *FMC*, 27 Apr. 1900 and 10 July 1900
23. See Appendix III for geographical distribution of Cranleighans
24. Speech Day, 28 July; *Cr*, Oct. 1908
25. *CM*, 23 Oct. 1908
26. *CM*, 1 Dec. 1908
27. *Cr*, Mar. 1909
28. *FMC*, 4 Dec. 1908, 23 Dec. 1908
29. *CM*, 23 Apr. 1909; Headmaster's Report to the governors
30. *FMC*, 5 May 1909
31. *FMC*, 15 Nov. 1909; Finance Committee Report

32. *CM*, 15 Nov. 1909
33. *Cr*, Dec. 1909, Mar. 1910
34. Letter to the OCs, 21 Apr. 1910; in *Cr*, May 1910
35. L. Northover (E 1906–10) to author
36. *Cr*, Mar. 1901
37. *CM*, 8 June 1910
38. Examiners Reports, Dec. 1910; A712
39. *FMC*, 13 Oct 1909
40. See *FMC*, 9 Dec. 1909; *Cr*, Apr. 1911
41. Recorded in the school magazine for 1909 and 1910
42. J. P. Carter (1 & 4 S 1908–12) to author
43. *Masters Meeting Minute Book*, 15 Nov. 1910
44. Diary entry by Lord Stanley, 21 Jan. 1862; in *Disraeli, Derby and the Conservative Party*, edited by J. R. Vincent, p. 182
45. The whole subject is dealt with well in T. J. Honey, *Tom Brown's Universe*, and rather more luridly in J. Gathorne-Hardy, *The Public School Phenomenon*
46. An OC (E 1909) to author
47. *Master of the Week Report Book*, 14–21 May 1909
48. *ibid.*, 7–14 Oct. 1910
49. C. Dukes, *Health at School*, p. 88
35. L. Northover (E 1906–10) to author
50. *The Gresham*, 18 Oct. 1930; I am grateful to Mr P. G. Corran, housemaster at Gresham's School, Holt, for having this information ferreted out for me
51. 'Rules etc. for Prefects', 1910; A1153
52. *Master of the Week Report Book*, 1–8 July 1910
53. *Masters Meeting Minute Book*, 4 Mar. 1909, 14 May 1909, 8 July 1910
54. *ibid.*, 24 June 1910
35. L. Northover (E 1906–10) to author
55. Numbers during each of Tyler's terms were: 1909^1 168 1909^2 157 1909^3 159 1910^1 164 1910^2 154 1910^3 157 1911^1 160 1911^2 168
56. But see *FMC*, 21 Sept. 1910; *CM*, 19 Dec. 1919, 1 May 1911
57. *CM*, 19 Dec. 1910
58. *CM*, 1 May 1911
59. *CM*, 15 May 1911
60. *Cr*, July 1911
61. *The Gresham*, 19 Oct. 1912; 18 Oct 1930; 11 Apr. 1945

CHAPTER SIX

1. *CM*, 3 July 1911
2. R. Perry, *Ardingly 1858–1946*, p. 33
3. E. W. Swanton, *Sort of a Cricket Person*, p. 33
4. R. Perry, *Ardingly 1858–1946*, p. 164
5. *CM*, 3 July 1911: the matter was referred to the Finance Committee and there is no record of the result
6. As Rhodes told Charles Crowhurst, a young Ardingly master who joined Rhodes at Cranleigh and later became second master; see *Cr*, May 1956
7. *FMC*, 18 Dec. 1911
8. L. Northover (E 1906–10) to author
9. *Cr*, Oct 1912: report on speech day and on opening of the new building
10. *CM*, 25 Nov. 1912
11. *CM*, 5 May 1913
12. *Cr*, Nov. 1913; also Oct. 1925

13. He was succeeded by F. H. Moore who arrived at Cranleigh in the term the new 'House' opened, and was Master of the school from 1934 to 1946
14. C. Stephenson, *Merrily on High*, pp. 43–4; Father Eustace later 'went over' to Rome
15. A. N. A. Paul (2 & 3 S 1926–32) and others to author
16. Heath Robinson, whose sons attended the prep. school, donated 6 specially executed drawings in his usual style, which are still in the Prep. school
17. *CM*, 4 May 1914
18. *FMC*, 31 Mar. 1915
19. P. Green, *Teaching for Lads*, p. 5
20. *Cr*, Mar. 1914
21. *Cr*, July 1914
22. G. C. Bateman (2 N 1914–19) to author
23. E. Raymond, *Good Morning Good People*, pp. 45–6
24. The sketch book is in the school archives, A238
25. *Master of the Week Report Book*, 31 Oct. – 5 Nov. 1915
26. *FMC*, 6 June 1917
27. *FMC*, 24 Aug. and 31 Oct. 1917
28. J. P. Carter (1 & 4 S 1908–12) to author
29. *Cr*, Nov. 1914; Editorial
30. Details are recorded in *The School and The War 1914–1918*
31. See W. S. Churchill, *The World Crisis*, vol. 2, pp. 948–9; for less flattering comments on Townshend see N. Dixon, *On the Psychology of Military Incompetence*
32. J. Rae in *Times Literary Supplement*, 7 Dec. 1979, reviewing Alan Wilkinson's *The Church of England and the First World War*
33. *Cr*, Oct 1921; the commemorative pillar was removed in 1951: *FMC*, 1 Dec. 1951
34. *Cr*, Apr. 1916
35. *Cr*, Dec. 1896
36. See obituary, *Cr*, March 1949; Fawcus was joint headmaster of Bilton Grange, a Preparatory School, from 1921–35
37. He is so described on the outdoor benches given to the school by the OCs
38. J. Gathorne-Hardy, *The Public School Phenomenon*, p. 151
39. *Cr*, Nov. 1963
40. Information from an OC (2 & 3 S 1926–32)
41. Memorandum by Rhodes, 24 Feb. 1931 (CSA)
42. J. P. Everett (2 N 1923–31), and others, to author
43. E. W. Swanton, *Sort of a Cricket Person*, pp. 36–7
44. *Daily Telegraph*, 29 Jan. 1958
45. *Cr*, Mar. 1922
46. *Cr*, Oct. 1926
47. *The Tatler*, 12 Mar. 1952
48. E. Dunning & K. Sheard, *Barbarians, Gentlemen and Players*, p. 236–238
49. *Cr*, Jan. 1930
50. *Cr*, Mar. 1912, at the OC Dinner
51. *Cr*, Dec. 1926
52. S. Glynn & J. Oxborrow, *Interwar Britain: A Social & Economic History*, p. 49–50
53. See below, chapter 7
54. *FMC*, 24 Mar. 1924
55. *CM*, 4 May 1925
56. An architect's drawing and a description first appeared in *Cr*, Mar., 1926
57. A whole range of photographs of this and the other new buildings were taken at various stages of the work and are in the School Archives, and in *Cr*, 1926–30

58. *Cr*, Dec. 1912
59. *Cr*, Nov. 1875
60. *Cr*, July 1896
61. Headmaster to Headmaster of
    Shrewsbury, 2 Jan. 1933 (CSA)
62. *FMC*, 31 Mar. 1926
62. *Cr*, Mar. 1931
63. *CM*, 5 May 1930
64. *FMC*, 3 Apr. 1929
65. *CM*, 21 Nov. 1928 and 6 Feb.
    1931
66. I. Nairn and N. Pevsner, *The
    Buildings of England: Surrey*,
    p. 174
67. *Cr*, Oct. 1925 and Oct. 1929
68. *Cr*, Oct. 1929; Midleton was
    now chairman of the council
69. J. Connell, *The End of Tradition*,
    p. 45
70. *FMC*, 10 Dec. 1930

CHAPTER SEVEN

1. R. F. Delderfield, *To Serve them
   All my Days*, p. 557
2. George Orwell, 'Boys'
   Weeklies', in *Collected Essays*,
   vol. I, p. 473
3. I have eschewed footnotes
   throughout this chapter almost
   entirely; the information is
   drawn from the pages of the
   school magazine, from house
   log books, and from information
   supplied by 57 OCs who were
   schoolboys in the twenties. I
   have not documented slight
   variations from house to house,
   or changes that took place from
   time to time as these do not
   affect the overall picture
4. This room later became the
   tuck shop, and is now the
   electronics laboratory (R9)
5. C. Stephenson, *Merrily on High*,
   p. 46
6. For information on Purvis see
   The Times, 28 Sept. 1963, 1 Jan
   1963, also *Cr*, May 1969; there
   is much material by and about
   him in the School Archive
7. 'Doc' Simpson was still
   teaching, and still being
   outrageous, at Portora in the
   mid-sixties; the author has vivid
   recollection of sitting in
   Simpson's lab overlooking
   Lough Erne, drinking whisky
   from a chemical beaker. At that
   stage the author had no
   connection with Cranleigh, and
   knew nothing of Simpson's
8. See Appendix IV

CHAPTER EIGHT

1. Created Baron May in 1931; see
   obituary in *The Times*, 11 Apr.
   1946
2. *Cm*, 6 Feb. 1931
3. See *The Burning Bow: T. F. Coade
   of Bryanston*, an anthology
4. D. Newsome, *On the Edge of
   Paradise*, p. 330
5. *Benson Diary*, 156/26 (Oct.
   1915)
6. *ibid.*, 156/52 (Dec. 1915)
7. *Benson Diary*, 168/6 (Aug. 1922);
   Benson died in 1925
8. *ibid.*, 172/32 (Jun. 1923)
9. B. G. Sullivan to Headmaster,
   17 Jul. 1982 (HMF)
10. B. A. Timbs (2 & 3 S, 1931–36)
    to author
11. H. A. Williams, *Some Day I'll
    Find You*, p. 83

12. Loveday to N. Hobson, 17 June
    1935 (CSA)
13. *Cr*, Oct. 1931
14. *FMC*, 15 July 1932, 28 Mar.
    1933; a loan of £10,000 was
    raised from the Commercial
    Union Assurance Co.
15. *CM*, 2 May 1932
16. *Cr*, Feb. 1934
17. *Cr*, July 1931
18. *FMC*, 4 Nov. 1931; *CM*, 2 May
    1932
19. *Housemasters Meeting Minutes*,
    1 May 1931
20. *Masters Meeting Minutes*, 20 Jan.
    1932
21. *Cr*, July 1934
22. *Masters Meeting Minutes*, 2 May
    1931
23. see e.g. B. G. Sullivan (2 & 3
    1938–43) to author; Head-
    master to Major Hawkins, 19
    May 1944 (CSA)
24. *Cr*, Dec. 1935; Letter to the
    editor
25. *Report of Inspection 1935*, pp. 6–7
26. R. Findlater, *Michael Redgrave:
    Actor*, p. 18–19
27. *Cr*, Mar. 1939; private in-
    formation from A. N. A. Paul
    2 & 3 S 1926–32) and others
28. Production copies, notes and
    drawings by Purvis are in the
    school archives
29. *Cr*, July 1933
30. *Cr*, Feb. 1934
31. C. Stephenson, *Merrily on High*,
    pp. 45–47
32. *Games Committee Minute Book*, 27
    Sept. 1933
33. *Cr*, Mar. 1923
34. *Punch*, 24 May 1911
35. For cricket on the Common see
    (G. H. Brewer), *A Century of
    Cranleigh Cricket 1856–1956*, and
    F. Swinnerton, *Reflections from a
    Village*
36. *The Times*, 28 Mar. 1931

37. *Masters Common Room Minutes*, 20
    March 1936
38. *Housemasters Meeting Minutes*, 30
    Mar. 1933
39. *Masters Common Room Minutes*, 1
    Oct. 1928; *Cr*, July 1936, Dec.
    1936; Appeal Letter, 11 Feb.
    1936 (CSA)
40. *The Times*, 13 June 1940
41. C. L. Potts, *Gordon and Michael*,
    p. 9
42. *ibid.*; also A. N. A. Paul (2 & 3 S
    1926–32) to author; cf. similar
    developments at Charterhouse
    in the 30s; E. M. Jameson,
    Charterhouse, p. 91
43. Loveday to Governors of King's
    School, Peterborough, 10 May
    1939 (CSA)
44. *Daily Mail*, 30 July 1934; other
    contributions to the debate in
    ibid., 23, 28 July 1934
45. *Cr*, Nov. 1960
46. R. F. Tomlinson (E 1931–37) to
    author
47. *Cr*, July 1950
48. *Housemasters Meeting Minutes*, 31
    July 1933
49. *Daily Mail*, 15 Mar. 1938
50. So-called from their colour;
    currently nicknamed 'razzers'
51. *Cr*, Dec. 1937
52. *Inge Diary*, 27 May 1934; other
    entries show Inge had a soft
    spot for Loveday
53. There is an obituary tribute in
    Cr, Mar. 1960
54. Expelled by the Nazis, and with
    Salem closed down, Hahn came
    to Britain and founded
    Gordonstoun on the same
    principles
55. *Housemasters Meeting Minutes*, 20
    Sept. 1938
56. *ibid.*, 20 Jan. 1939
57. *ibid.*, 30 Mar. 1939, the best
    source for Cranleigh 1939–45 is
    Ex Cultu Robur: The School at

War, published in July 1947 as a supplement to the *Cranleighan*

58. *Cr*, Dec. 1939
59. Churchill, with his usual panache and feel for language, changed the name from Local Defence Volunteers to Home Guard
60. B. G. Sullivan (2 & 3 S 1938–43) to author
61. *Housemasters Meeting Minutes*, 22 Sept. 1942
62. *Ex Cultu Robur: The School at War*; I have been unable to verify this statement
63. Headmaster to Mrs Hayes, 18 June 1940 (CSA)
64. *FMC*, 3 July 1942
65. In 1959 a new (open-air) swimming pool was opened as a further memorial, given by the old boys
66. *Cr*, Mar. 1942
67. *Cr*, July 1945
68. *Cr*, July 1946

CHAPTER NINE

1. Viscount Chandos, *The Memoirs of Lord Chandos*, p. 329
2. *Manchester Guardian*, 27 July 1945 (editorial)
3. *The Public Schools and the General Educational System* (The Fleming Report) 1944
4. J. Gathorne-Hardy, *The Public School Phenomenon*, pp. 369–370
5. *FMC*, 28 July 1945; Queen Anne's Bounty was part of the Church of England's financial system, soon to be incorporated with the Church Commissioners
6. *Cr*, July 1946
7. *Cr*, Dec. 1946; the editorial began with the words, 'School wit is on the decline.'
8. *Cr*, May 1946
9. *Cr*, Dec. 1947
10. *Cr*, July 1948
11. *Cr*, Dec. 1948
12. In comparing numbers and fee rises I have taken the following schools to compare with Cranleigh: Aldenham, Ardingly, Berkhamsted, Blundells, Brighton, Charterhouse, Eastbourne, Epsom, Haileybury, Lancing, Mill Hill, Radley, St John's (Leatherhead), Tonbridge, Wellington and Worksop
13. See A. H. Halsey (editor), *Trends in British Society since 1900*, p. 170
14. *Report of Inspection 1952*, pp. 7, 22
15. *Cr*, July 1964
16. Now the Sixth Form Centre
17. *FMC*, 25 Nov. 1946; 10 May 1964
18. *FMC*, 5 Dec. 1947
19. *CM*, 28 Feb. 1947
20. *Cr*, July 1947
21. *Cr*, Mar. 1949
22. The rest of the sixth form was sub-divided into specialist groups relating to the subjects taken by a boy, and identified by a code letter – a practice continued until the early 1970s
23. *Cr*, 13 May 1949
24. B. E. Cracknell, *Portrait of Surrey*, p. 223
25. *FMC*, 13 May 1949
26. W. H. G. Armytage, *Four Hundred Years of English Education*, p. 243
27. *FMC*, 11 Dec. 1948
28. *FMC*, 21 Mar. 1953
29. Headmaster to Mrs Gartside, 3 June 1941 (CSA) gives a good picture of and defence of the

wartime diet at Cranleigh
30. *Housemasters Meeting Minutes*,
    24 July 1946
31. See T. McKeown and C. R.
    Lowe, *An Introduction to Social
    Medicine*, esp. pp. 122–3
32. *Housemasters Meeting Minutes*,
    1 May 1951
33. *ibid.*, 20 Jan. 1953
34. *FMC*, 20 June 1955; Letter to
    HM and Sir Francis Floud, 22
    Jan. 1956 (CSA)
35. *Games Committee Minute Book*,
    8 May 1949
36. *ibid.*, 29 July 1951; also *Cr*, Oct.
    1954 (letter to the editor)
37. L. H. Garrett to Headmaster, 9
    March 1948 (CSA)
38. *CM*, 28 Nov. 1953
39. *FMC*, 14 May 1955
40. See Appendix IV for the shape
    of the school; in 1955 17% of the
    school was aged 17 or more; in
    1981 the percentage was 25
41. *Cr*, Mar. 1956
42. *Housemasters Meeting Minutes*, 15
    Dec. 1955
43. Headmaster to Gabbitas
    Thring, 5 Dec. 1931 (CSA)
44. For difficulties over art at
    another school see *Marlborough
    (An Anthology)* p. 47
45. *Cr*, May 1955
46. For the statistically minded: the
    pool is 110′ × 42′; depth 3′6″ to
    12′6″; capacity 200,000 gallons;
    provision was made for heating
    it, and the machinery came into
    operation in 1973
47. *Cr*, Oct. 1955; see also *Cr*, Mar.

1956 (editorials)
48. Speech Day, 15 Oct. 1955; *Cr*,
    Mar. 1956
49. Chairman of the Council to
    Bursar, 12 June 1956 (CSA)
50. *FMC*, 23 Nov. 1957; the boards
    were subsequently removed
51. *FMC*, 22 Nov. 1958
52. *Daily Telegraph*, 30 Sept. 1937
53. Full details of the 'affair' are in
    a file in the school archives
54. *Cr*, Mar. 1959
55. The Association of Governing
    Bodies of Public Schools; Birley
    was now Headmaster of Eton
56. *Masters Meeting Minutes*,
    25 March 1959
57. *CM*, 12 Dec. 1959
58. Eg: *The Times*, 16 Apr., 28 Apr.
    1959; *Daily Telegraph*, 17 Apr.
    1959; *Daily Mail*, 16 Apr. 1959
    (headline: 'Now Head quits
    after atheist row'), 30 June 1959
59. *CM*, 24 Oct., 12 Dec. 1959;
    27 Feb., 19 June 1960
60. *Surrey Times and Weekly Advertiser*,
    24 Oct. 1959
61. *FMC*, 21 Nov. 1959; report to
    the governors by acting
    headmaster
62. It is tempting to see in the
    departure of the headmaster
    from Berkhamsted in 1953 a
    parallel with events at
    Cranleigh; unfortunately the
    school's history does not
    provide sufficient detail: see
    B. H. Garnons Williams, *A
    History of Berkhamsted School
    1541–1972*, pp. 295–6

CHAPTER TEN

1. *Times Educational Supplement*,
   23 June 1972
2. *The Pendulum Years* was the title
   of Bernard Levin's book on the
   sixties, published in 1970
3. See J. Rae, *The Public School
   Revolution*, chapters 1 and 2
4. Letter from the Ministry,
   29 June 1960 (CSA)
5. Letter from IFASES, 14 Jan.

1960 (CSA); *CM*, 27 Feb. 1960;
on IFASES see I. Weinberg,
The English Public Schools,
pp. 71–2

6. *Cr*, Mar. 1961
7. *GBM*, 25 Nov. 1961
8. *Report of Inspection 1961*, p. 5
9. *Housemasters Meeting Minutes*,
12 July 1962
10. *ibid.*, 31 Mar. 1963
11. *Scimitar*, Easter 1962
12. J. Gathorne-Hardy, *The Public
School Phenomenon*, ch. 16
13. *ibid.*; also R. Lambert, *The
Hothouse Society*
14. *Housemasters Meeting Minutes*,
15 May, 5 June 1962
15. *Guardian*, 10 Nov. 1980
16. *Housemasters Meeting Minutes*,
8 July, 24 July, 2 Dec. 1964
17. *ibid.*, 30 July 1962
18. *Masters Meeting Minutes*, 15 Dec.
1960
19. 'Major Projects 1962–70', draft
plan, 14 Nov. 1962 (CSA)
20. Emms to Windle, 14 May 1963
(CSA)
21. Plans and specifications in *Cr*,
Nov. 1964
22. *Housemasters Meeting Minutes*,
2 Dec. 1964; see also *Cr*, 1923
(letter to editor)
23. Improvements listed in *Cr*, June
1964; and generally see *Cr*,
1961–64
24. *GBM*, 19 Nov. 1960
25. '. . . that strange shape of shoe,
projecting like some antenna,
reaching out to bridge the gap
between beatnik and
Sputnik . . .' *Cr*, Mar. 1961
(Emms at Speech Day)
26. *Housemasters Meeting Minutes*,
12 Oct. 1960
27. J. C. Dancy, *The Public Schools
and the Future*, pp. 76, 174
28. *Housemasters Meeting Minutes*,
31 July 1961

29. *ibid.*, 2 May 1961
30. *School Prefects Minute Book*,
29 May 1961; 18 Feb. 1963;
31 Mar. 1962
31. *Housemasters Meeting Minutes*,
1 May 1965
32. *ibid.*, 3 June 1964
33. G. Kalton, *The Public Schools:
A Factual Survey*, p. 125
34. *Privileges of a School Prefect* (no
date, but mid-thirties), A 711
35. *Housemasters Meeting Minutes*,
23 Mar. 1965
36. G. Kalton, *The Public Schools: A
Factual Survey*, p. 124
37. Loveday to Major Scoble
Hodgins, 19 May 1944
(CSA)
38. *Housemasters Meeting Minutes*,
9 and 24 July, 22 Sept., 30 Oct.
1964
39. J. Rae, *The Public School
Revolution*, pp. 96–7, 125
40. G. Kalton, *The Public Schools: A
Factual Survey*, p. 119; 88 of the
94 boarding or mainly boarding
independent schools had CCFs.
In at least two thirds of these it
was compulsory
41. C. B. Otley, 'Militarism and
Militarizations in the public
schools, 1900–72', *British Journal
of Sociology*, vol. 29, no. 3, Sept.
1978, pp. 330–334
42. *Masters Meeting Minutes*, 25 July
1960
43. *School Prefects Minute Book*,
22 June 1961
44. *HMC Eastern Division Minutes*,
23/24 May 1962 (CSA)
45. *Inter-Service Cadet Committee
Minutes*, 20 Dec. 1966 (CSA)
46. Emms to Headmaster of
Canford, 24 Feb. 1967 (CSA)
47. *Cr*, Jun. 1967
48. *Cr*, Summer 1967
49. R. Lambert, *The Hothouse Society*,
pp. 102–3

50. *Proceedings of the Centenary Conference*, pp. 49–50
51. *Housemasters Meeting Minutes*, 5 June 1962
52. *ibid.*, 2 Dec. 1963 and 15 Dec. 1963; this was long before a great press discussion on the subject; *The Times*, 15–22 Dec. 1970 (letters); 22 Dec. 1970 (editorial)
53. Emms to N. H. Martin, 25 May 1963 (CSA)
54. *Cr*, Nov. 1964; there is a file of correspondence on the building in CSA
55. Headmaster's speech to the OCs; *Cr*, Mar. 1963
56. *Cr*, Nov. 1960
57. *Cr*, May 1961
58. *School Prefects Minute Book*, 29 May 1961
59. *Housemasters Meeting Minutes*, 22 June 1961
60. *ibid.*, 15 Dec. 1963, and see also 17 Sept. 1963
61. *Centenary Year*, (Headmaster's Letter), January 1965 (CSA)
62. Oddly, all copies of this film have completely disappeared
63. *Surrey Advertiser and County Times*, 26 June 1965
64. *Daily Mail*, 23 July 1968
65. *Daily Mirror*, 23 July 1968
66. *Guardian*, 18 Nov. 1968
67. *Housemasters Meeting Minutes*, 22 May 1963, 14 Jan. 1964
68. D. Noel-Paton, 'To the very life – some thoughts on school drama', *Conference*, vol. 3, no. 3, Dec. 1966
69. *The Times*, 23 July 1968
70. *Guardian*, 18 Nov. 1968; already in 1962 Emms had reported to the OCs the introduction of regular parent-master meetings: *Cr*, Mar. 1963
71. *Masters Meeting Minutes*, 3 Apr. 1965; it should be noted that in the midst of the turmoil of the late sixties Cranleigh became one of the first schools to run its own PHAB course for physically handicapped and able bodied young people; see 'Opportunity, not pity', by W. J. Booth, *Conference*, vol. 8, no. 1, Feb. 1971, pp. 33–35
73. J. S. Gummer, *The Permissive Society*, p. 168; also p. 30
73. *Headmaster's Letter to Parents*, July 1964, July 1965, Mar. 1968, Mar. 1969, Dec. 1969, July 1970
74. *Cr*, Nov. 1964, May 1969
75. *Cr*, May 1968
76. *Cr*, Feb. 1969; July 1981
77. *Cr*, May 1970
78. *Guildford and Godalming Times*, 10 June 1967

CHAPTER ELEVEN

1. *Cr*, June 1971
2. *Times Educational Supplement*, 22 Jan. 1982,
3. J. Rae, *The Public School Revolution*, p. 15; *Sunday Times*, 22 Nov. 1981
4. *Sunday Times*, 2 Oct. 1966 (reporting on the Headmasters' Conference)
5. *Illustrated London News*, 1 Nov. 1969
6. J. Rae, *The Public School Revolution*, p. 109
7. *Spectator*, 1 Sept. 1973; the author, Richard Ryder, was a former chairman of the Cambridge University Conservative Association, and lecturer at Swinton Conservative College.
8. *The Times*, 21 June 1972
9. *ibid.*, 24 Jan. 1975
10. *Daily Telegraph*, 6 June 1979

11. *The Times*, 4 Sept. 1980
12. *Sunday Times*, 22 Aug. 1973
13. *HMR*, 11 Dec. 1971
14. See the article on 'Fortnightly Boarding' by John Vallins (Housemaster at Cranleigh 1967–74) in *Conference*, vol. 7, no. 2, June 1970, pp. 11–13
15. *The Times*, 17 Apr. 1978
16. *HMR*, 13 Mar. 1976; Appendix 1
17. *HMR*, 15 Mar. 1980
18. *HMR*, 16 Mar. 1974; as has been the case throughout the century, the category 'agriculture' was small −4.2%
19. *The Times*, 28 Oct. 1978
20. *HMR*, 10 July 1971
21. The Preparatory School increase was even more dramatic: the decade saw a 27.5% increase, though the proportion of boarders fell somewhat from 56.5% to 50.3%; it was of course a very much better school now than it had been in the late 50s: see the fairly severe criticisms of it: Minutes of a meeting between HMIs and Governors, 14 Oct. 1961 (CSA)
23. See Appendix IV, for the shape of the school
24. Figures for the Michaelmas Term which could be said to be atypical because of the Oxbridge sixth; nevertheless figures for the other two terms (when Oxbridge candidates have gone) tell the same story: 1971, 30.1%; 1976, 36%; 1981, 44.7%
25. *West Sussex County Times*, 31 May 1974
26. *The Times*, 17 & 18 Oct. 1980; *Daily Telegraph*, 25 Sept. 1980; *Observer*, 31 Jan. 1982
27. *Daily Telegraph*, 26, 28 Feb. 1979; 1 Mar. 1979 (editorial), 2 Mar. 1979
28. It has been argued that the opposite problem obtained in many state schools, where the staff were more permissive and progressive than parents: Edward Norman, 'Fodder for the theorists', *Listener*, 18 Nov. 1976
29. *HMR*, 31 Mar. 1979; one school, Downside, renegued in 1980
30. 'Report of the Corporation's Committee on Co-Education', 6 Dec. 1969 (CSA)
31. *HMR*, 4 Nov. 1970
32. *West Sussex County Times*, 21 July 1973
33. *HMR*, 1 July 1972
34. Richard Bull (headmaster of Oakham, which is fully co-educational) in *Sunday Times*, 22 Nov. 1981
35. R. Lambert, *The Chance of a Lifetime?*, p. 299, p. 297
36. *HMR*, 18 Nov. 1970, 5 Dec. 1970
37. *Headmaster's Termly Letter to Parents*, Dec. 1970
38. *Daily Telegraph*, 5 Mar. 1977
39. *The Times*, 17 June 1977; the subsequent Conservative government failed to keep its promise to restore recognition, on grounds of cost: *Daily Telegraph*, 19 July 1979
40. *Places where they sing* (Report of the sub-committee appointed by the Headmaster on the new organ), Appendix 4 of *HMR*, 13 Mar. 1976; see also G. M. Donald's detailed description and specification of new organ in *Cr*, June 1977
41. The first teams played 360 matches in the seventies, and 272 in the sixties

42. A comprehensive school headmaster in *The Times*, 11 Sept. 1973

43. Speech of 7 Sept. 1973, printed in full by the Independent Schools Information Service, *ISIS Newsletter*, no. 3 (Sept. 1973); see also *Economist*, 15 Sept. 1973 and 17 Aug. 1974; *ISIS Newsletter*, no. 4 (Nov. 1973); *Spectator*, 22 Sept. 1973

44. Ron Hayward in preface to *Private Schools: A Labour Party national executive discussion document*: see *The Times*, 31 July 1980; also 27 June 1980

45. *Guardian*, 25 Jan. 1980; *The Times*, 7 Jan., 11 Jan., 6 Feb., 7 Oct. 1980

46. An interesting discussion on the pressures on the boarding school masters in seventies appeared in the Bloxham Project *Newsletters* of 1979

47. *HMR*, 6 Dec. 1975, 4 Dec. 1976, 10 Dec. 1977; the bursar drew up the specifications for the new house, 5 May 1978 (CSA)

48. See the article on the new house by its first housemaster, *Conference*, vol. 17, no. 3 (pp. 17–20)

49. Headmaster's Report, Speech Day, 29 May 1982

APPENDIX I

Succession Lists

HEADMASTERS

Sept. 1865   THE REVD JOSEPH MERRIMAN

b. 1836 educ.: St John's College, Cambridge & St Mark's College, Chelsea BA (5th Wrangler) 1860 MA 1863 BD 1881 DD 1882 Fellow of St John's 1861–8 Deacon 1862 Priest 1863 HM of Cranleigh 1865–91 Rector of Freshwater (IoW) 1891–1905 d. 1905

Apr. 1892   THE REVD GEORGE CANTRELL ALLEN

b. 1855 educ.: Wellington & St John's College, Cambridge BA 1878 MA 1881 BD 1904 DD 1906 Deacon 1881 Priest 1882 Assistant Master at Wellington 1878–81 and at Dulwich 1881–92 HM of Cranleigh 1892–1908 Vicar of Send (Kent) 1908–12 Vicar of Higham 1912–21 d. 1921

Jan. 1909   CHARLES HENRY TYLER

b. 1867 educ.: Charterhouse & Pembroke College, Cambridge BA 1889 MA 1909 Assistant Master at Matfield Grange School 1890–1 Librarian at Charterhouse 1892–4 Assistant Master at Rossall 1894–1908 (Housemaster 1907–8) HM of Cranleigh 1909–11 Assistant Master & Librarian at Gresham's (Holt) 1912–30 d. 1945

Sept. 1911   THE REVD HERBERT ALEXANDER RHODES

b. 1869 educ.: Shrewsbury & Christ Church, Oxford BA 1892 MA 1895 Deacon 1898 Priest 1899 Assistant Master at Yarlet Preparatory School (N. Staffs) 1892–4, at Felsted 1894–6, at Giggleswick 1896–9 Curate of Brewood (Staffs) 1899–1900 Chaplain & Assistant Master Bilton Grange Preparatory School 1900–02 Master of Christ's Hospital Preparatory School 1902–4 HM of Ardingly 1904–11 HM of Cranleigh 1911–31 Vicar of Iford with Kingston-near-Lewes 1932–45 d. 1956

Apr. 1931   THE REVD DAVID GOODWIN LOVEDAY

b. 1896 educ.: Shrewsbury & Magdalene College, Cambridge War service with Oxfordshire Regt 1915–17 BA 1922 MA 1926 Deacon 1923 Priest 1924 Assistant Master at Malvern 1917–19 Assistant Master and Chaplain at Aldenham 1922–5, & Clifton 1915–31 HM Cranleigh 1931–54 Archdeacon of Dorking 1954–7 Bishop of Dorchester 1957–71

Apr. 1954   HENRY ARTHUR MARCH

b. 1905 educ.: Leighton Park & St John's, Oxford BA 1927 MA 1931 Assistant Master at Merchant Taylor's 1929–39 Head of Modern Languages at Charterhouse 1940–54 (Housemaster 1945–54) HM of Cranleigh 1954–59 Assistant Master at Marlborough 1959–61 and at Charterhouse 1961–65 (Acting Headmaster 1964)

Sept. 1959   H. P. JACOB

b. 1902 educ.: Cranleigh & Hertford College, Oxford; Assistant Master at Cranleigh 1930–54 (Housemaster 1937–53) & Second Master 1954–59 Acting HM of Cranleigh 1959–60

Sept. 1960   DAVID ACFIELD EMMS

b. 1925 educ.: Tonbridge & Brasenose, Oxford BA 1950 MA 1954 War service with Royal Artillery 1943–47 Assistant Master at Uppingham 1951–60 HM of Cranleigh 1960–70 HM of Sherborne 1970–74 & of Dulwich 1975–

Sept. 1970   MARC VAN HASSELT

b. 1924 educ.: Sherborne & Selwyn, Cambridge BA 1949 MA 1953 War Service with Royal Horse Artillery 1944–46 Lecturer at RMA Sandhurst 1950–58 Assistant Master at Oundle 1959–70 (Housemaster 1963–70) HM of Cranleigh 1970–

SECOND MASTERS

1865 The Revd R. H. Quick (Trinity College, Cambridge; d. 1891)
1866 The Revd W. H. Brayshaw (St John's College, Cambridge; d. 1920)
1869 The Revd A. W. Watson (St John's College, Cambridge; d. 1917)
1873 W. Welch (Exeter College, Oxford; d. 1922)
1877 The Revd E. W. Ford (Trinity College, Cambridge; d. 1897)
1878 The Revd W. E. Inchbald (Clare College, Cambridge; d. 1926)
1883 The Revd C. G. Duffield (Queens' College, Cambridge; d. 1923)
1886 The Revd T. Layng (Jesus College, Cambridge; d. 1930)
1893 The Revd E. T. Clarke (St John's College, Cambridge; d. 1937) 1905–1936 No second master
1936 The Revd C. Crowhurst (University of London; d. 1958)
1942 M. Aldridge (St Catherine's College, Oxford; d. 1967)
1954 H. P. Jacob (Hertford College, Oxford)
1959 O. F. Tucker (Jesus College, Cambridge)
1964 G. P. Maguire (King's College, Cambridge)
1974 K. S. G. Wills (Exeter College, Oxford)

BURSARS*

1892	I. Hardy	1952	H. J. Linnell
1901	The Revd H. Crawford	1956	Capt. D. S. Wareham
1910	R. C. Winsloe	1968	Capt. N. S. Grant
1942	F. Winsloe	1976	Capt. K. A. Crawley

* The first headmaster acted as his own bursar, but on retirement recommended the establishment of a separate post

MASTERS OF THE PREPARATORY SCHOOL*

1880 I. Hardy
1901 The Revd H. Crawford

1910 The Revd F. N. Bird
1912 The Revd R. H. C. Mertens
1934 F. H. Moore
1946 C. B. Blackshaw
1961 M. A. C. Wheeler
1978 A. W. Wyatt

* The school has undergone some changes of name: 1880–1916 'The House'; 1916–31 'Preparatory House'; 1931–68 'The Junior School'; 1968– 'Cranleigh Preparatory School'

CHAIRMEN OF THE COUNCIL (of the Corporation of Cranleigh & Bramley Schools)

Until the Incorporation by Royal Charter in 1898, meetings of the Council were chaired by various members, in no apparent order of rotation or precedence

1898 G. Cubitt MP (from 1892, Lord Ashcombe)
1916 Sir Charles Chadwyck-Healey
1919 Viscount Midleton (St John Brodrick MP until 1907; Earl of Midleton 1920–)
1938 Lt General Sir Alfred Bingley
1942 Sir Francis Floud
1957 C. G. Windle
1960 Sir Arthur fforde
1963 Sir Edwin Herbert (Lord Tangley of Blackheath 1964–)
1973 Admiral the Hon. Guy Russell
1974 Viscount Watkinson

CHAIRMEN OF THE CRANLEIGH GOVERNING BODY

From at least 1878 until 1913 there was a Finance Committee which met more frequently than the Council to deal with the affairs of the school (and there was also one for St Catherine's after its founding in 1887). From 1899 there was a Committee of Management as well. These were amalgamated in 1913 to form the Finance and Management Committee which in 1959 became the Governing Body of Cranleigh School (with a parallel development at St Catherine's, Bramley)

Chairmen of the Finance Committee

1878   The Revd J. H. Sapte

1906   J. F. C. Ramsden

1909   Sir Charles Chadwyck-Healey

Chairmen of the Committee of Management

1899   Lord Ashcombe

1912   Sir Charles Chadwyck-Healey

Chairmen of the Finance and Management Committee

1913   Sir Charles Chadwyck-Healey

1919   Earl of Midleton

1930   Lt General Sir Alfred Bingley

1942   Sir Francis Floud

1954   C. G. Windle

Chairmen of the Governing Body

1959   C. G. Windle

1966   T. A. Roberts

1972   Sir Richard Way

1978   J. S. Ferrier

1980   Sir Hugh Cubitt

HOUSEMASTERS

Until the first world war 'dormitory masters' were not very significant, often had tenure for brief periods, and sometimes moved from one dormitory to another. Each list therefore begins with the incumbent at the end of the war, when 'houses' began to develop, though they retained the original names of the dormitories which were originally arranged around the quad (hence the geographical designations) Names in parenthesis are temporary wartime appointments.

2 & 3 South		*West*	
	R. Harris		F. A. Brett
1924	Revd T. W. Thomas	1924	A. F. J. Hopewell
1928	E. R. Hopewell	1928	E. R. Hopewell
1949	A W. Young		R. W. Bowyer
1967	D. R. J. Bird	1935	M. Aldridge
1972	K. J. Bain	1937	H. P. Jacob
1980	L. D. Adam	1953	R. Bellwood
1982	J. Leigh	1968	H. D. Gregson
		1978	C. A. Clark

1 & 4 South

	F. Winsloe
1939	J. S. Upcher
(1940	Revd N. E. Wilkinson)
1946	J. S. Upcher
1952	Revd L. E. Tanner
1965	A. J. West
1979	C. J. Allen

1 North (Out-house from 1965)

	J. S. Purvis
1937	L. H. Garrett
(1939	M. L. Goodeve-Docker)
(1941	J. Collinson)
(1945	D. D. Lees)
1946	L. H. Garrett
1959	K. S. G. Wills
1974	Revd A. J. Megahey

2 North

	C. Crowhurst
1936	S. M. Allen
1937	O. F. Tucker
(1941	Revd C. Crowhurst)
(1942	M. I. Machin)
1945	O. F. Tucker
1958	J. M. F. Steede
1967	J. Vallins
1974	A. J. Corran

East (1 & 2 East until 1922)

	R. C. J. Hayter
1921	B. L. Read
1935	C. B. Blackshaw
1946	G. P. Maguire
1963	I. P. Campbell
1968	C. N. Richardson
1973	B. D. Gowen

Cubitt (Out-house, opened 1961)

1961	L. Marshall
1976	J. Polglase

Loveday (Out-house, opened 1980)

1980	K. J. Bain

The Size of the School

FIVE-YEAR AVERAGES

(note: the Preparatory School became a separate entity in 1913, so the boys there are included in the total for the quinquennium 1910–14, but shown separately thereafter)

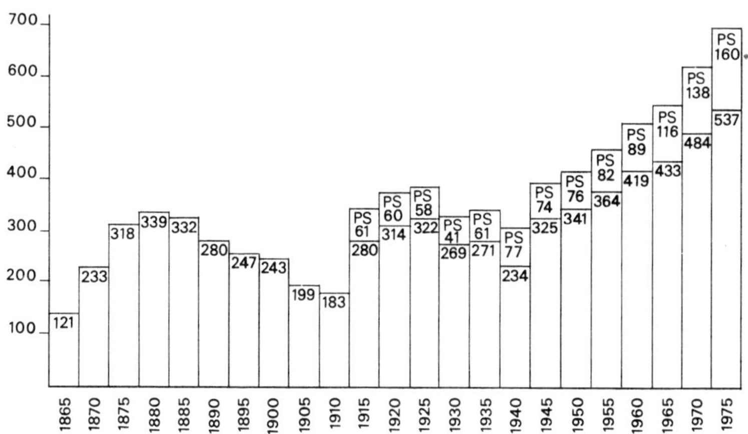

CHART ILLUSTRATING NUMBERS IN THE SCHOOL

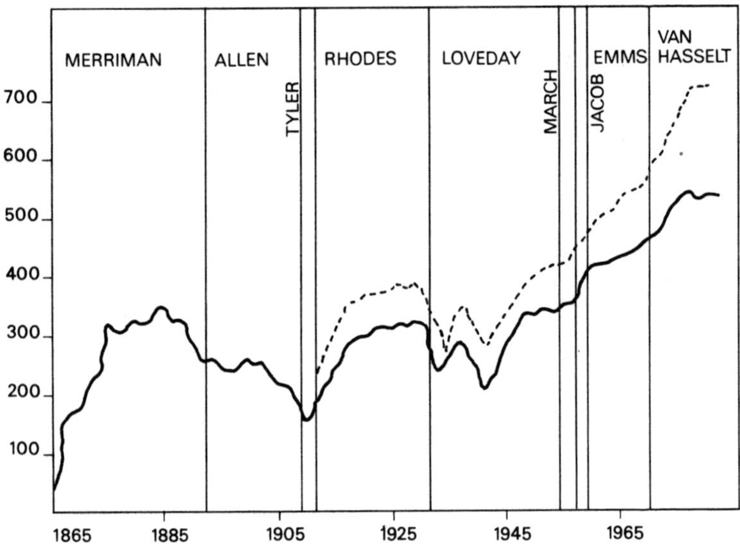

Note: From 1912 Preparatory School numbers are not included; thereafter Prep + Senior School total illustrated by dotted line

APPENDIX III

Parents

OCCUPATION OF PARENTS (some selected categories)

	1865	1895	1925	1955	1980
Agriculture (farmers, hop & fruit growers, land agents)	24%	22%	6%	1%	2%
Wine Trade	11%	8%	2%	–	–
Merchants & shopkeepers	14%	20%	4%	7%	–
Managers, secretaries, solicitors, directors	4%	14%	40%	44%	56%
Armed forces, clergy, doctors, surgeons	4%	4%	6%	10%	10%

LOCATION AND OCCUPATION OF TWO GROUPS OF PARENTS:

First term of the school: Sept.–Dec. 1865
All boys on the roll for that term

1.	Railway Agent	Farnham, Surrey
2.	Shopkeeper	Cranleigh, Surrey
3.	Hop Planter	Farnham, Surrey
4.	Clergyman	Usk, Wales
5.	Cordwainer	Cranleigh, Surrey
6.	Farmer	Compton, Surrey
7.	Farmer	Caterham, Surrey
8.	Farmer	Worplesdon, Surrey
9.	Builder	Croydon, Surrey
10.	Innkeeper	Alfold, Surrey
11.	Farmer	Cranleigh, Surrey
12.	Oilman	Guildford, Surrey
13.	Yeoman	Alresford, Hampshire
14.	Farmer	Petersfield, Hampshire
15.		

16.	Civil Magistrate	Calcutta, India
17.		
18.	Agent to Sir A. Bellingham	Castle Bellingham, Ireland
19.	Widow	Rudgwick, Sussex

First 19 boys admitted in Michaelmas Term 1980

1. Commodity Broker — Woking, Surrey
2. Marketing Director — Weybridge, Surrey
3. Company Director — Kenya
4. Chartered Secretary — Cranleigh, Surrey
5. Market Researcher — Dorking, Surrey
6. Stockbroker — U.S.A.
7. Sales Manager — Wincanton, Somerset
8. Businessman — nr Henley, Oxfordshire
9. RAF officer — West Clandon, Surrey
10. Business Executive — Guildford, Surrey
11. Army Officer — B.A.O.R.
12. Businessman — Cranleigh, Surrey
13. Company Director — Godalming, Surrey
14. Engineering Executive — Tadworth, Surrey
15. Builder — East Grinstead, Sussex
16. Civil Engineer — Purley, Surrey
17. Manager — Swindon, Wiltshire
18. Company Manager — Hong Kong
19. Doctor — Sutton, Surrey

GEOGRAPHICAL DISTRIBUTION

	1870	1880	1890	1900	1910	1920	1930	1940	1950	1960	1970	1980
Total entrants in given year	66	120	78	108	45	88	88	78	99	122	126	162
% from:												
Surrey	30	21	23	19	24	26	41	52	60	49	65	53
London	23	30	24	31	31	32	19	22	9	12	4	3
Sussex	6	7	8	0	7	6	8	11	5	8	7	8

GEOGRAPHICAL DISTRIBUTION (*contd*)

	1870	1880	1890	1900	1910	1920	1930	1940	1950	1960	1970	1980
Total entrants in given year	66	120	78	108	45	88	88	78	99	122	126	162
Kent	6	7	8	8	4	6	2	2	5	6	5	1
Hants; IoW	4	9	13	6	9	6	6	3	7	2	4	4
Bucks; Berks; Wilts; Oxon; Glos	11	3	5	12	9	5	1	3	1	5	1	4
Dorset; Devon; Soms; Cornwall	0	2	0	16	0	2	1	0	0	1	1	2
Essex; Herts	1	3	6	1	9	3	7	1	3	5	1	0
Norfolk; Suffolk; Beds; Leics; Cambs	6	5	4	1	0	4	2	0	1	2	1	0
Rest of England; Channel Is	11	2	8	1	0	2	2	1	1	0	1	1
Ireland; Wales; Scotland	0	1	0	2	2	2	0	0	2	1	1	0
Rest of Europe	0	1	0	0	2	0	2	0	4	3	1	4
Americas	0	0	0	0	0	3	6	0	1	2	1	4
Africa	0	0	0	0	0	0	0	0	0	2	1	4
Asia; Australasia	0	0	0	0	0	1	1	0	0	1	5	12
Unknown	3	8	1	2	2	1	1	0	0	0	0	0

SIZE & AGE STRUCTURE OF SCHOOL IN SELECTED YEARS

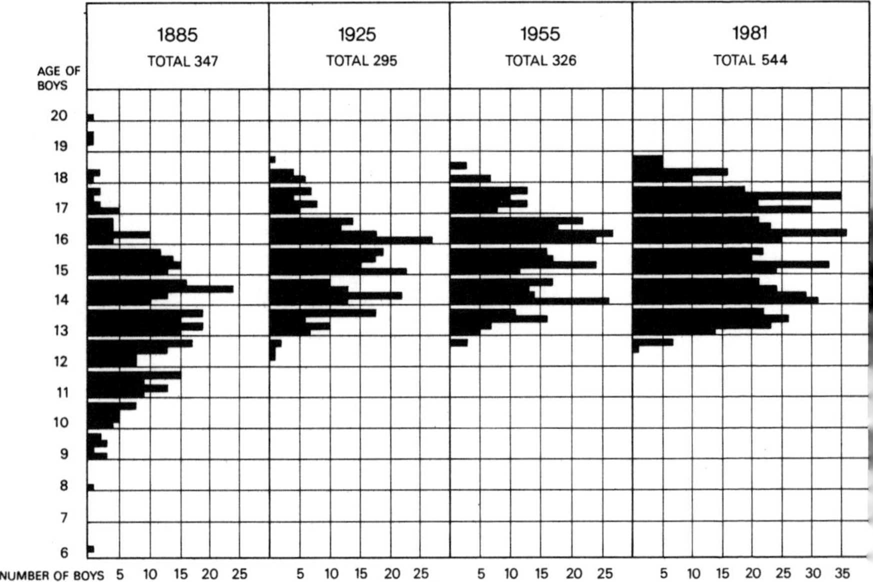

Notes:

(a) Mean ages: 1885: 13 years 7 months   1925: 15 years 4 months 1955: 15 years 6 months   1981: 15 years 7 months.

(b) The enormous age range in 1885 (from 6.2 to 20.2) is typical of the Victorian public school; a separate and semi-autonomous preparatory school really only existed from 1913. Obviously the prep school has been left off the patterns for 1925, 1955 and 1981.

(c) The figures for 1981 include girls, who are members of the sixth form only.

(d) The average length of time at Cranleigh for a boy has increased: in the 1920s it was 3½ years; it is now 5. Girls stay for 2 years.

(e) The number of 18 year olds in the 1981 figures is indicative of the existence of a 'Third Year Sixth' working for the Michaelmas Term only for entry to Oxford or Cambridge. In previous years this was confined to a few boys, and there was no third year sixth form until 1966.

(f) The ages are given for the first, second, third and fourth quarters of each year.

School argot or slang

IN CURRENT USE

BONE   (verb) to book or claim (a seat e.g.); (verb & noun) to punish; a punishment

COMPACTUM   The heavy wooden locker beside each boy's bed

FLANNEL PARADE   The lost property hunt, and general sort out of belongings, at the end of each term; formerly an inspection of kit

HRA   literally 'House Room Afterwards'; the name for the house meeting which takes place after lunch each day

JIM   the domestic servant in the dining hall (faintly offensive)

LISTS   The final orders at the end of each term, published on the notice boards; the names of the best boys are read out at the 'Final Assembly and Lists' at the end of each term; formerly 'lists' were published fortnightly

MOAB   The small kitchens provided in each house; see Psalm 108, v. 9

RAZZER   Formerly razzo; the raspberry coloured blankets on the beds in the dorms; rapidly giving way to duvets

TOYE   The desk/cupboard occupied by a junior boy in the 'toyes room'; of Winchester origin (where the spelling is toy)

VILL   Cranleigh village; in use certainly as early as the 1890s

OBSOLESCENT

BRA   literally 'Boot Room Afterwards', where nasty things might happen (see ch. 7)

BEAKIE   a domestic servant in hall

BIMMING   caning

FODGE   paper

MERT   (verb) to fool about (noun) a village lad, or a dirty person

SCRUB   a boy of 12 or under (so called because washed by the maids at bathtime)

SWIPES   beer provided at mealtimes

TOKE   bread

The above is not an exhaustive list, but includes all words in common use in the past or at present. Significantly, Cranleigh's slang was never very extensive.

Bibliography

(I) CRANLEIGH SCHOOL ARCHIVES

MANUSCRIPT SOURCES

Individual items in the archives (letters, documents, photographs etc.) carry a number prefixed by the letter 'A'. Items not yet catalogued, or those which are still in use and are in the Headmaster's files, are given the designation 'CSA'.

The following registers and minute books are also in the School Archives, and were particularly useful:

Council Minute Books:
Nov. 1862–Nov. 1889; Feb. 1890–Mar. 1898 (this minute book also contains Finance & Management Committee Minutes May 1899– Oct. 1929); June 1898–May 1933; May 1934–Aug. 1956; June 1957–June 1959; Oct. 1959–Nov. 1962

Finance (& Management) Committee Minute Books:
Feb. 1878–Mar. 1911 (entitled 'Audit Book'); Apr. 1930–Feb. 1956; Nov. 1956–May 1959

Games Record Book:
Oct. 1916–July 1951

Games Committee Minute Book:
May 1931–Dec. 1954

Governing Body Minute Books:
Nov. 1959–May 1961; Nov. 1961–Nov. 1962; Mar. 1963–Dec. 1964; 1965– (loose-leaf)

Headmaster's Reports to the Governing Body:
1970–1982

House Notes
(1 & 4 South): Sept. 1946–July 1967

House Report Books
(1 North): Jan. 1928–Mar. 1932; Sept. 1965–Mar 1968

House Record Book
(1 North): Sept. 1939–Dec. 1965

Literary, Scientific & Debating Society Minute Books:
1865–68; 1877–79; 1881–86; 1886–90; 1890–94; 1895–1914

Masters Meeting Minute Books:
Jan. 1876–Mar. 1894; Feb. 1909–June 1965 (includes Housemasters'
  Minutes, 1931–65)
Masters Common Room Minute Books:
Sept. 1920–Nov. 1937; Jan. 1940–Feb. 1945
Master of the Week Report Book:
May 1904–Dec. 1915
Mission Fund Letter Book:
Sept. 1894–Dec. 1894
Mission Fund Subscribers Address Books:
1894–1927; 1909–1913
Mission Fund Minute Book:
Jan. 1901–Sept. 1916
Registers of New Boy Entries:
1865–85 (nos 1–1921); 1865–90 (nos 1–2459); 1890–1939 (nos 2460
  –6435); 1931–56 (unnumbered); 1939– (nos 6436–)
Register of Chapel Services:
Jan. 1906–July 1926
School Prefects Minute Book:
Jan. 1961–Sept. 1963

SCHOOL PUBLICATIONS

School Roll   1873–1939 (termly; incomplete)
Call Over Book   1940– (termly)
Calendar   1934– (termly; combined with *Call Over Book* 1940–68)
Surrey County School Register   1867–1892 (yearly; incomplete)
Cranleigh School Register   1893–1907 (yearly; incomplete)
Cranleigh School Chronicle   Nov. 1871–Apr. 1878
Cranleigh School Magazine July 1878–Dec. 1899
The Cranleighan   Apr. 1900–
The School and The War 1914–1918 (1919)
Ex Cultu Robur: The School at War 1939–1945 (1947)
The Headmaster's Termly Letter to Parents 1964–
Compass (a sixth form magazine) 1955–62
Scimitar (Cubitt House magazine) 1961–1968
Proceedings of the Centenary Conference (1965)
O.C. Club Notes Sept. 1890–Mar. 1898
O.C. Society Register 1914 1924 1953 1960 1966 1975

(II) OTHER

MANUSCRIPT SOURCES

Benson Diaries: Diaries of A. C. Benson, Pepys Library, Magdalene College, Cambridge
Benson Diaries and Letters: Diaries and letters of Archbishop E. W. Benson, Wren Library, Trinity College, Cambridge
Brereton Papers: Letters and Papers of the Revd J. L. Brereton, Homerton College Library, Cambridge
Brodrick Papers: Letters and Papers of St John Brodrick, 1st Earl Midleton, Surrey County Record Office, Guildford
Inge Diaries: Diaries of W. R. Inge, Dean of St Paul's, The Old Library, Magdalene College, Cambridge

OFFICIAL PUBLICATIONS

Reports of Royal Commissions:
    Schools Inquiry (Taunton) Commission, 1868
    Secondary Education (Bryce) Commission, 1895
    Public Schools and the General Education System (Fleming Report), 1944
    Public Schools (Newsom) Commission, 1968
Board of Education:
    Reports of Inspection of Cranleigh School, 1921, 1935
Ministry of Education:
    Reports of Inspection of Cranleigh School, 1952, 1961

REFERENCE

Carey, G. V., *The War List of the University of Cambridge 1914–18* (Cambridge, 1921)
Crockford's Clerical Directory
Dictionary of National Biography
Foster, J., *Alumni Oxonienses 1715–1886* (4 vols, Oxford, 1888)
Public and Preparatory Schools Year Book
Rouse Ball, W. W. and Venn, J. A., *Admissions to Trinity College Cambridge* (5 vols, 1911–)
Venn, J. A., *Alumni Cantabrigienses Part II 1752–1902* (6 vols, Cambridge, 1940–)
Who's Who
Who Was Who

NEWSPAPERS, JOURNALS, MAGAZINES

British Journal of Educational Studies
British Journal of Sociology
British Medical Journal
Conference (magazine of the HMC)
Cranleigh Parish Magazine
Daily Express
Daily Graphic
Daily Mail
Daily Mirror
Daily Telegraph
The Eagle (magazine of St John's College, Cambridge)
Economist
Globe
Gownsman
The Gresham (magazine of Gresham's School, Holt)
Guardian
Guildford and Godalming Times
Illustrated London News
ISIS Newsletter (Independent Schools Information Service magazine)
Journal of the Statistical Society
Listener
(Manchester) Guardian
Medical History
Museum and English Journal of Education (continued as *Journal of Education*)
Observer
Public Opinion
Public School Magazine
Punch
Sphere
Sunday Times
Surrey Advertiser and County Times
Surrey Times and Weekly Press
Surrey Times and Weekly Advertiser
The Times
Times Educational Supplement
Times Literary Supplement
West Sussex County Times

BOOKS (published in London, except where stated; pb = paperback)

Anthology, *Marlborough: an open examination written by the boys* (1963)
——, *The Burning Bow: Coade of Bryanston: A selection of his papers* (1966)

Armytage, W. H. C., *Four Hundred Years of English Education* (pb, Cambridge, 1964)

Arnold, M., *A French Eton: or middle class education and the state* (1864)

Bailey, P., *Leisure and Class in Victorian England: rational recreation and the contest for control 1830–1885* (1978)

Baker, D., *Partnership in Excellence: a Mid-Victorian Educational Venture: The Ley's School, Cambridge 1875–1975* (privately published, 1975)

Bamford, T. W., *The Rise of the Public Schools* (1967)

Banks, O., *Parity and Prestige in English Secondary Education: a study in educational sociology* (1970 reprint)

Barnard, H. C., *A History of English Education from 1760* (2nd edn 5th imp. 1968)

Benham, W., *Catherine and Crauford Tait* (1979)

Benson, A. C., *The Life of Edward White Benson* (2 vols, 1900)

Beresford, G. C., *Schooldays with Kipling* (1936)

Best, G., *Mid-Victorian Britain 1851–75* (pb, 1971)

Bishop, T. J. H. and Wilkinson, R., *Winchester and the Public School Elite: a statistical analysis* (1967)

Blackie, J., *Bradfield 1850–1975* (privately published, 1976)

Blumenau, R., *A History of Malvern College 1865–1965* (1965)

Boyd, A. K., *Radley College 1847–1947* (Oxford, 1948)

Bradfield College Register 1871

Bragg, M., *Speak for England: An Essay on England 1900–1975* (1976)

Brereton, F. S., *King of Ranleigh* (1913)

Brett-James, N. G., *Mill Hill* (1938)

(Brewer, G. H.), *A Century at Cranleigh 1856–1956: A History of Cranleigh Cricket Club* (Privately published, 1956)

Burn, W. L., *The Age of Equipoise: A Study of the Mid-Victorian Generation* (1964)

Chandos, Viscount (Oliver Lyttelton), *The Memoirs of Lord Chandos* (1962)

Channon, H. J., *History of Queen's College, Taunton* (privately published, 1956?)

Churchill, W. S., *The World Crisis* (2 vols, 1938)

Clark, G. Kitson, *An Expanding Society: Britain 1830–1900* (Cambridge, 1967)

——, *Churchmen and the Condition of England 1832–1885; a study in the development of social ideas and practice from the old regime to the modern state* (1973)

Coggan, Archbishop Lord, *These were his gifts* (Exeter, 1974)

Connell, J., *The End of Tradition: Country Life in Central Surrey* (1978)

Cooper, Lady Diana, *The Rainbow Comes and Goes* (1958)

Cracknell, B. E., *Portrait of Surrey* (1970)

Dale, R. R., *Mixed or Single-Sex School? a research study about pupil-teacher relationships* (1969)

Dancy, J., *The Public Schools and the Future* (2nd edn, 1966)

Delderfield, R. F., *To Serve Them All My Days* (1972)

Dilke, C. W., *Dr Moberly's Mint Mark: A Study of Winchester College* (1965)

Dixon, N. F., *On the Psychology of Military Incompetence* (pb, 1979)

Dukes, C., *Health at School* (4th edn, 1905; first published in 1883)

Dunning, E., and Sheard, K., *Barbarians, Gentlemen and Players: a sociological study of the development of rugby football* (Oxford, 1979)

Dunsterville, L. C., *Stalky's Reminiscences* (1928)

Evans, R. J., *History and Register of Aldenham School* (8th edn, privately published 1948)

Ewart, G., *Forty Years On: an anthology of school songs* (1969)

Findlater, R., *Michael Redgrave: Actor* (1956)

Fletcher, F., *After Many Days: a schoolmaster's memories* (1937)

Fortescue, Earl, *Public Schools for the Middle Classes* (1864)

Fraser, M., *Surrey* (1975)

Frazer, W. M., *A History of English Public Health 1834–1939* (1950)

Froude, J. A., *Short Studies on Great Subjects* (4 vols, new impression, 1898)

Garnons Williams, B. H., *A History of Berkhamsted School 1541–1972* (privately published, 1980)

Gathorne-Hardy, J., *The Public School Phenomenon 597–1977* (1977)

Glynn, S., and Oxborrow, J., *Interwar Britain: a social and economic history* (1976)

Green, P., *Teaching for Lads* (1914)

Gummer, J. S., *The Permissive Society: Fact or Fantasy?* (1971)

Halevy, E., *Imperialism and the Rise of Labour 1895–1905* (pb, 1961)

Halsey, A. A., *Trends in British Society since 1900: a guide to the changing social structure of Britain* (1972)

Harrisson, J., *An Essay on Physical Education* (1865)

Heeney, B., *Mission to the Middle Classes: The Woodard Schools 1848–1891* (1969)

Hill, R. D., *A History of St Edward's School 1863–1963* (privately published, 1962)

Honey, J. R. de S., *Tom Brown's Universe: the development of the public school in the nineteenth century* (1977)

Hope Simpson, J. D., *Rugby since Arnold* (1967)

Howard, H. F., *Finances of St John's College Cambridge* (Cambridge, 1935)

Jameson, E. M., *Charterhouse* (1937)

Kalton, G., *The Public Schools: a factual survey* (pb, 1966)

Laborde, E. D., *Harrow School Yesterday and Today* (1948)
Lambert, R., *The Hothouse Society* (1968)
Lambert, R. (with R. Bullock & S. Millham), *The Chance of a Lifetime?: a study of boys' and co-educational boarding schools in England and Wales* (1975)
Leach, A. F., *History of Bradfield College* (Oxford, 1900)
Levin, B., *The Pendulum Years* (pb, 1970)

Mack, E. C., *Public Schools and British Opinion since 1860: the relationship between contemporary ideas and the evolution of an English institution* (New York, 1941)
Mangan, J. A., *Athleticism in the Victorian and Edwardian Public School* (Cambridge, 1981)
Manning, O., *The History and Antiquities of the County of Surrey* (2 vols, 1804)
Marsh, P. T., *The Victorian Church in Decline: Archbishop Tait and the Church of England 1868–1882* (1969)
Meacham, S., *Lord Bishop: The Life of Samuel Wilberforce 1805–1873* (Cambridge, Mass, 1970)
Mearns, A., *The Bitter Cry of Outcast London* (1883)
Merriman, J., *Secular Education as severed from religious* (privately published, 1881)
Miller, E., *Portrait of a College: a history of the College of St John the Evangelist in Cambridge* (Cambridge, 1961)
Minchin, J. G. C., *Old Harrow Days* (2nd edn, 1898)
Mingay, G. E., *Rural Life in Victorian England*
Mitchell, B. R. and Deane, P., *Abstract of British Historical Statistics* (Cambridge, 1962)
M. L. and others, *Vincent Warren Low: a memoir* (privately published, 1945)
Morgan, M. C., *Cheltenham College: the first hundred years* (privately published, 1968)
Morley, J., *Death, Heaven and the Victorians* (1971)
Moscow, A., *The Rockefellers* (New York, 1977)
Moss, Mrs H. W., *Moss of Shrewsbury: a memoir 1841–1917* (privately published, 1932)
Musgrave, P. W. (editor), *Sociology, History and Education: a reader* (pb, 1970)
McKeown, T., *Medicine and Modern Society* (1965)
McKeown, T. and Lowe, C. R., *An Introduction to Social Medicine* (Oxford, 1966)

McNeile, R. F., *A History of Dean Close School* (privately published, 1966)

Nairn, I. and Pevsner, N., *The Buildings of England: Surrey* (Harmondsworth, 2nd edn, 1971)
Newsome, D., *A History of Wellington College 1859–1959* (1959)
——, *Godliness and Good Learning: four studies on a Victorian ideal* (1961)
——, *On the Edge of Paradise: A. C. Benson, Diarist* (1980)
Norman, E. R., *Church and Society in England 1770–1970: a historical study* (1976)

Oakley, R. R., *A History of Oswestry School* (privately published, 1957)
Ogilvie, V., *The English Public School* (1957)
Oldham, J. B., *A History of Shrewsbury School 1552–1952* (Oxford, 1952)
Orwell, S. & Angus, I., (eds) *The Collected Essays, Journals & Letters of George Orwell* (4 vols, 1968)
Osborne, G. S., *Scottish and English Schools: a comparative survey of the past forty years* (Pittsburg, 1967)
Ousey, K. M. J., *McClure of Mill Hill: a memoir by his daughter* (1927)

Percival, A. C. *The Origins of the Headmasters' Conference*
Perry, R., *Ardingly 1858–1946: a history of the school* (privately published, 1951)
Potts, C. L., *Gordon and Michael* (privately published, 1940)

Quick, R. H., *Essays on Educational Reformers* (1868)
——, *The Schoolmaster, Past and Future* (Cambridge, 1879)

Rae, J., *The Public School Revolution: Britain's Independent Schools 1864–1979* (1981)
Raymond, E., *Good Morning Good People: an autobiography past and present* (1970)
Roach, J., *Public Examinations in England 1850–1900* (Cambridge, 1971)
Rothblatt, S., *The Revolution of the Dons: Cambridge and Society in Victorian England* (1968)
Rubinstein, D., *Victorian Homes* (1974)

Seaborne, M., *The English School: its architecture and organization 1370–1870* (1971)
Sheen, H. E., *Canon Peter Green: a biography of a great parish priest* (1965)
Simon, B. and Bradley, I. (editors), *The Victorian Public School: studies in the development of an educational institution* (Dublin, 1975)
Smith, W. D., *Stretching their Bodies: the history of physical education* (1974)
Snow, C. P., *Variety of Men* (Harmondsworth, pb, 1969)
——, *A Coat of Varnish* (1979)
Somervell, D. C., *A History of Tonbridge School* (1947)
Steele, T., *Musings of an Old Schoolmaster* (1932)

Stephenson, C., *Merrily on High* (1972)
Stewart, A. P. and Jenks, S., *The Medical and Legal Aspects of Sanitary Reform* (1867)
Storr, F. (editor), *Life and Remains of Rev. R. H. Quick* (Cambridge, 1899)
Swanton, E. W., *Sort of a Cricket Person* (pb, 2nd imp, 1976)
Swinnerton, F., *Reflections from a Village* (1969)
Sykes, N., *Man as Churchman* (Cambridge, 1960)
Sylvester, D. W., *Robert Lowe and Education* (1974)

Tait, A. C., *Middle Class Education: A Speech delivered at the Devon County School, West Buckland* (1865)
Tarver, M. A. J., *Trent College 1868–1927* (1929)
Temple Clarke, A. O., *A Tangled Skein of Reminiscence* (privately published, 1955)
Thomson, T. R. (editor), *Epsom College Register 1855–1954* (privately published, 1955)
Thornton, F. V., *The Education of the Middle Classes in England* (1862)

Uppingham School Roll 1888–1960 (8th edn, 1962)

Victoria County History of Surrey (4 vols, 1902, 1905, 1911, 1912)
Vincent, J. R. (editor), *Derby, Disraeli and the Conservative Party: The Political Journals of Lord Stanley 1849–69* (Hassocks, 1978)

Watson, G., *The English Ideology: Studies in the language of Victorian Politics* (1973)
Weinberg, I., *The English Public Schools: the sociology of an elite* (pb, New York, 1967)
Wilkinson, R., *The Prefects: British Leadership and the Public School Tradition* (1964)
Williams, H. A., *Some Day I'll Find You* (1982)
Wilmshurst, H. M., *The Life and Work of W. L. Wilmshurst* (privately published, 1954)
Winterbottom, D., *Doctor Fry* (privately published, pb, 1977)